day trips® from portland, oregon

help us keep this guide up to date

We would love to hear from you concerning your experiences with this guide and how you feel it could be improved and kept up to date. Please send your comments and suggestions to:

editorial@GlobePequot.com

Thanks for your input, and happy travels!

day trips® series

day trips® from portland, oregon

second edition

getaway ideas for the local traveler

kim cooper findling

Globe
Pequot

Guilford, Connecticut

All the information in this guidebook is subject to change. We recommend that you call ahead to obtain current information before traveling.

Globe Pequot

An imprint of Rowman & Littlefield

Day Trips is a registered trademark of Rowman & Littlefield

Distributed by NATIONAL BOOK NETWORK

Copyright © 2015 by Rowman & Littlefield
Text design: Linda R. Loiewski
Maps: Design Maps Inc. © Rowman & Littlefield

British Library Cataloguing in Publication Information Available

Library of Congress Cataloging-in-Publication Data Available

ISBN 978-1-4930-1274-9 (paperback)
ISBN 978-1-4930-1787-4 (e-book)

∞™ The paper used in this publication meets the minimum requirements of American National Standard for Information Sciences—Permanence of Paper for Printed Library Materials, ANSI/NISO Z39.48-1992.

contents

about the author

Nationally published writer Kim Cooper Findling grew up on the Oregon Coast, spent several years in the Willamette Valley, and has lived in Central Oregon for two decades. She is the editor of *Cascade Journal* and the author of *Chance of Sun: An Oregon Memoir,* and her work has appeared in many publications including *Travel Oregon, The Oregonian, Horizon Air, Oregon Quarterly, Alaska Air, Sky West, The Best Places to Kiss NW,* and *High Desert Journal.* See kimcooperfindling.com.

acknowledgments

This book would not have come to fruition without the support and assistance of many others. First to thank in a cosmic shout-out is the Pacific Northwest, for existing as such a diverse, fascinating, and richly beautiful place. I am unbelievably fortunate to reside and write here. I extend appreciation to Kevin Sirois, of Globe Pequot, who first signed me to this task, and to Tracee Williams, who guided me through the second edition. I owe thank yous to dozens of Oregon and Washington tourism and travel professionals who contributed to these pages—too many to name here, but you are all awesome! Personal thanks to my friends and family, for support, companionship, and travel destination ideas. Finally, many hugs and big thanks to my children, Libby and Maris, who are the best road-trip sidekicks on the planet. I am so very lucky.

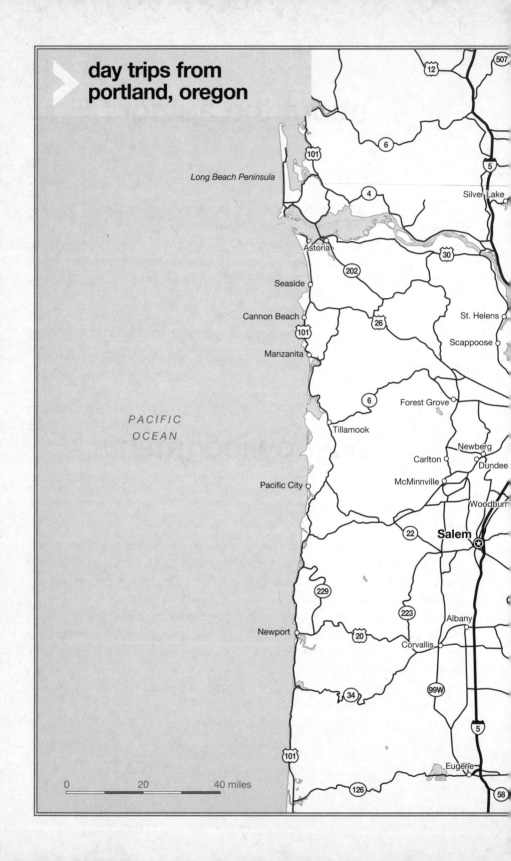

day trips from
portland, oregon

Long Beach Peninsula

PACIFIC
OCEAN

Astoria

Seaside

Cannon Beach

Manzanita

Tillamook

Pacific City

Newport

Silver Lake

St. Helens

Scappoose

Forest Grove

Newberg

Carlton

Dundee

McMinnville

Woodburn

Salem

Albany

Corvallis

Eugene

0   20   40 miles

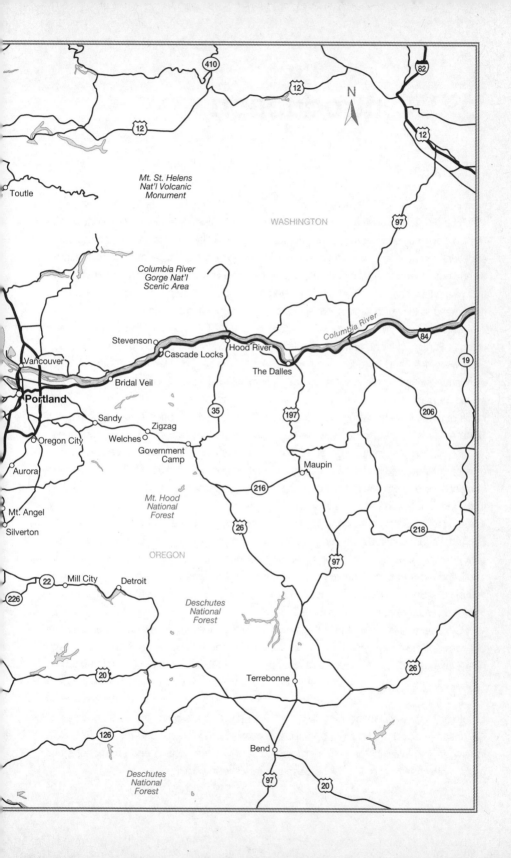

introduction

Portland, Oregon, is currently experiencing its own 15 minutes of fame. The city on the Columbia River that so many of us have loved for decades is suddenly a verifiable destination, loved by many others, far and wide. That love is revealed in new opportunities appearing nearly every other day. Portland offers the very best in terms of culture, dining, entertainment, and the outdoors. Yet, Portland still doesn't take itself too seriously. It's a city that wears fleece, sips coffee from funky ceramic mugs, and stops to smell the roses. You never need to leave Portland because it's so comfortable and amazing.

But leave we do. After all, we are descendents of the pioneers. Even the expansive acres of Forest Park and antiques shops in Multnomah Village can't substitute for the veritable wilderness and historical small towns that lie just beyond Portland's borders. When wanderlust strikes, Portland reveals its other primary advantage. We're so close to so many awesome places! The beach—an hour away. The mountains—an hour away. The fertile farms of the Willamette Valley—an hour away. The end of the Oregon Trail—an hour away. North America's most famous volcano—an hour away. Wine country—yes, an hour away.

In fact, there's so much beyond the city limits, you may not know where to start. The greater Portland area is rich with beauty, culture, and possible exploration. That's where this book comes in. Here you'll find more than 20 day trip ideas, each under a three-hour drive from Portland. Some visit one action-packed town and help you narrow down what to see there. Other trips cover two to four smaller towns, some more action-packed than others. Each trip is just a little bit different; each destination offers its own unique flavor. We suggest attractions, restaurants, shops, and outdoor destinations that might tickle your fancy. You'll find more options than you could possibly cover in one day, so pick and choose as you please. Should you find you want more of a certain city, check out the lodgings section—each trip has one, if appropriate.

Our intention is that in these pages you'll find nearly everything you need to blast out of town for a day-long adventure. A few words of wisdom to the savvy traveler, however. First—take a map. Even if your car is equipped with a GPS system or your smart phone is loaded with maps, these systems aren't foolproof and don't always include smaller or newer roads. In these cases, a paper map is an invaluable tool. If you have time, it's also a good idea to highlight the places you really want to see in your chosen day trip ahead of time and call ahead to check on hours of operation, necessary reservations, and the like. Especially in Oregon and Washington's smaller towns, hours vary seasonally, and small shops and restaurants change and even close permanently without warning.

With that in mind—get out of town! Take a hike, drink some wine, gaze upon the bucolic countryside, pick a pumpkin, buy an antique chiffarobe, eat some ice cream, walk the beach, eat some huckleberries, go windsurfing, hug a tree, hit the surf. Whatever you do, have a great time day trippin'! Then return to the most comfortable city in the US, kick back, and plan your next adventure.

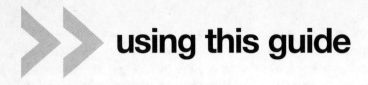

using this guide

Day Trips from Portland, Oregon is organized by general direction from Portland: north, northeast, east, southeast, south, southwest, west, and northwest. Listings in the Where to Go, Where to Shop, Where to Eat, and Where to Stay sections are arranged in alphabetical order, unless otherwise specified. If several places in a given town offer similar opportunities, listing titles highlight broad categories (e.g., "wineries") rather than the names of specific businesses or locations. Each stop on every day trip includes a Where to Go listing, but Where to Shop, Where to Eat, and Where to Stay are only included when there are appropriate listings worth visiting.

scheduling your day trip

Half the fun of day tripping is planning. Many a workday can be endured by imagining what fun you'll have come the weekend and an unencumbered day—just you and the open road, maybe a pal or two along for the ride, nowhere to go and all day to get there. As you fantasize about your next day trip, keep these things in mind. Saturday is often a better choice than Sunday to day trip in the Pacific Northwest, as, especially in smaller towns, many shops, destinations, and restaurants close up shop on Sunday or are open for limited hours. If your heart is set on a certain destination, call in advance to check on hours and plan your trip accordingly. If you have the luxury of day tripping mid-week, doing so can be a fabulous option. The crowds are thinner during the week, yet most services are open. That said, be aware that many tourist-dependent businesses in smaller towns choose to close shop mid-week, often on Monday or Tuesday, to accommodate the majority of travelers and yet still have a break themselves. A little foresight can help you to choose the best day to hit most of your selected destinations.

hours of operation

Many businesses change their hours frequently or seasonally. Hours of operation are frequently included in these pages, but be aware that this information may change without notice. Phone numbers and, when possible, websites for each listing are included here so that you can access current information on your own. Also, small businesses can be known to change location or phone number at whim. If a phone number turns out to be out of service, call information or try a web search. Keep in mind, too, that many businesses close on major holidays, even though that information may not be indicated in these pages.

pricing key

The price codes for accommodations and restaurants are represented as a scale of one to three dollar signs ($).

Most businesses take credit cards these days, but you can't always be guaranteed of this convenience. Should a business require cash only, in most cases they can direct you to a nearby ATM to access cash, which will sometimes assess a small banking fee. You will only pay sales tax in Washington (the percentage varies by area), not Oregon, and some Washington attractions may have already factored sales tax into their pricing schema.

restaurants

The price code used here is based on the average price of dinner entrees for two, excluding drinks, appetizers, dessert, tax, and tip. (Oregon has no sales tax; Washington does and it varies by county and city.) You can typically expect to pay a little less for lunch and/or breakfast, where applicable. If the business only serves lunch and/or breakfast, the code has been applied to those meals.

$ Less than $20

$$ $20 to $35

$$$ More than $35

accommodations

This book is intended primarily for those who wish to venture out of the city for just a day or half-day. However, overnight accommodations are included in many sections for those who wish to explore an area further. You wouldn't be the first to find yourself at the beach or in the mountains and not ready to leave yet. Accommodations included here are almost all local hotels and bed-and-breakfasts. Large national chains are typically not included, though many of the larger cities in this book do have chain hotels. Other cities in this book are too small for a chain—some are too small for any other lodging. In that case the Where to Stay section has been omitted. Each day trip does not include accommodation listings for every stop, though typically at least one stop per day trip includes a suggested overnight lodging. With few exceptions, most towns in each trip aren't more than 40 minutes apart, and many are much closer.

The following price code is used for accommodations throughout this book. It is based on the average price of a one-night stay in a standard, double-occupancy room, before taxes. This price does not include state and city hotel taxes, which vary but are typically around 8 percent. City taxes vary, and are typically lower in smaller towns. Keep in mind that lodging prices often change seasonally or between the weekend and mid-week. Summer pricing is almost always higher, and weekends are very frequently more expensive, as well.

$ Less than $100

$$ $100 to $200

$$$ More than $200

driving tips

In general, Oregon and Washington have good signage, and navigation between towns should be fairly straightforward. That said, especially in more rural areas, signage is more intermittent, and roads are narrower, more winding, and not as well lit. Drive cautiously and keep your eyes open for road changes and directional signage.

In the winter, many of the destinations included in this book can be subject to stormy weather. The beach can be windy and incredibly rainy; the mountains snowed in. Occasionally some of the roads in this book are closed due to weather conditions. Always travel with caution in the winter, and plan ahead. For road closures and weather information, call the **Oregon Department of Transportation Trip Check** at (800) 977-ODOT or check it online at tripcheck.com. Always stay on marked, plowed roads. If you aren't sure where you are or which way to go, ask for directions. It doesn't hurt to carry water, blankets, and food when traveling in the Pacific Northwest in the winter. A cellular phone is always handy—charge it up before you leave!

There are many differences of which day trippers should be aware between travel in Oregon and travel in Washington. Oregon is one of the last states in the nation in which travelers are not allowed to pump their own gas. Wait for an attendant and ask him or her for the gas type and quantity you desire. In Washington, gas is pump-your-own. Oregonians might find this an uncomfortable practice—ask for help if you aren't sure how to operate a gas pump.

Maximum highway speeds vary by state, too. Oregon's I-5 tops out at 65 mph, while Washington's I-5 allows speeds up to 70 mph. State highway top speeds vary, too. In Oregon you won't see any allowed speeds over 55 mph on rural highways; Washington may allow higher speeds. The best practice is to stay alert, pay attention, and obey the posted signs.

Keep in mind that speed limits can change abruptly from one town or stretch of highway to the next. While it's important to heed speed limits at all times when driving, be particularly cautious when passing through construction zones, where speeding ticket fines can be double the normal (already high) fine. Many smaller highways in these trips pass directly through small towns, necessitating a speed limit change on either end. Respect the residents of these towns, and slow down appropriately to avoid getting pulled over by a police officer.

Mileage is calculated, in most chapters, from the **Portland City Center.** Depending on from which specific part of Portland you begin your day trip, mileage and directions will vary. Use a good city or state map, or electronic navigation system, to determine how to best merge onto major arterials out of town from your exact starting point.

Another thing to keep in mind is that car travel isn't your only option for many of these day trips. Portland's Tri-Met bus system services many of the communities included in this book. See trimet.org. Another option is your bicycle. Many of the smaller more rural roads and destinations in this book are simply perfect for road biking. Be safe and wear a helmet, please.

highway designations

For consistency's sake, this book typically refers to state highways with "OR," "WA," or "SR" followed by the highway number (e.g., OR 20). In many cases, that number will be followed by a cardinal designation (e.g., OR 20 E). In some situations, multiple highways run along the same path. In other cases, the same highway may have more than one name. OR 26 W, for example, is also known as the Sunset Highway. The road in Washington State that leads to Mt. St. Helens is known as WA 504/Mt. St. Helens Way NE/Spirit Lake Highway. A good map, GPS, or mapping service like Google Maps or Mapquest can help you sort things out.

area codes

The northwest corner of Oregon uses the area code 503. This area extends south to Salem, southwest to Pacific City, east to Mt. Hood, and southeast to Detroit. Beyond those parameters, in Oregon, the 541 area code is the most prevalent, though you will also see the area code 458. In Washington, the areas covered in this book almost all use 564, though some north of Longview may use 509 or 360. Cell phone prefixes, obviously, vary widely.

where to get more information

Day Trips from Portland, Oregon attempts to cover a variety of interests and destinations, but those looking for additional travel information can contact the following agencies by phone, mail, or the web. Keep in mind that online reviews can be contradictory, as everyone experiences places differently. Call directly or stick with advice from respected travel organizations.

for general travel information:

Oregon Department of Transportation
Intelligent Transportation Systems
800 Airport Rd. SE, Room 81, Salem, OR 97301
(800) 977-ODOT
tripcheck.com (for hotels, food, attractions, and road condition information)

Oregon State Tourism
Travel Oregon and MEDIAmerica
715 SW Morrison, Suite 800, Portland, OR 97201
(800) 547-7842
traveloregon.com
Request a copy of the *Travel Oregon Visitor Guide.*

Washington State Tourism
tourism@cted.wa.gov
(800) 544-1800
experiencewa.com

AAA Oregon
600 SW Market St., Portland, OR 97201
(503) 222-6767 or (800) 452-1643
aaaorid.com

AAA Washington
4301 E Fourth Plain Blvd., Vancouver, WA 98661
(360) 696-4081
aaawa.com

for camping & recreation information:

Oregon Parks and Recreation Department, State Parks
725 Summer St. NE, Suite C, Salem, OR 97301
Main: (503) 986-0707
Reservations: (800) 452-5687
Information: (800) 551-6949
oregon.gov/OPRD
park.info@state.or.us

Washington State Parks and Recreation Commission
1111 Israel Rd. SW, Olympia, WA 98504-2650
(360) 902-8844
(888) CAMP-OUT
parks.wa.go

for information on farms & wineries:

Pick Your Own
pickyourown.org
This website features a listing of pick-your-own farms near you.

Oregon Farmer's Market Association
P.O. Box 13272, Portland, OR 97213
(503) 525-1035
oregonfarmersmarkets.org

Washington State Farmers Market Association
93 Pike Street, Suite 316, Seattle, WA 98101
(206) 706-5198
wafarmersmarkets.com

Oregon Wine Center
1200 NW Naito Pkwy., Suite 400, Portland, OR 97209
(503) 228-8336
oregonwine.org

Oregon Wine Country
Willamette Valley Visitors Association
(866) 548-5018
oregonwinecountry.org

Wines Northwest
P.O. Box 87575, Vancouver, WA 98687
(360) 604-1205
winesnw.com

north

day trip 01

north

the city to the north:
vancouver, wa

vancouver

When it comes to West Coast cities, Vancouver often gets overlooked. With a population of 165,000, Vancouver is smaller and less metropolitan than Portland and Seattle. And on an international scale, Vancouver, British Columbia, is the better known of the two Pacific Coast Vancouvers.

But when it comes to history, Vancouver, Washington, has all three other cities beat. Vancouver was established in 1857, a few years after Portland but long before Vancouver, B.C., or Seattle. And at that point, Vancouver had already been long inhabited by white settlers at the historic Fort Vancouver trading post.

In modern times, Vancouver is recognized for its culinary scene, including one of the Northwest's oldest farmers' markets, highly acclaimed restaurants, and an emerging wine region and microbrewery scene. Vancouver is also a budding hub for fashion design and boutique shopping. The downtown area continues to undergo a revitalization effort that has transformed it into a very popular and attractive destination.

Still, Vancouver's primary draws are its history and natural surroundings. Ft. Vancouver National Historic Site is one of the most visited historical destinations in the West. Much of the city fronts the massive, impressive Columbia River, and to the north is rich farmland, forests, old railroads, and wildlife. Vancouver was Washington's first city and remains its fourth largest today. As a day tripper, you'll find much to like about this city to the north.

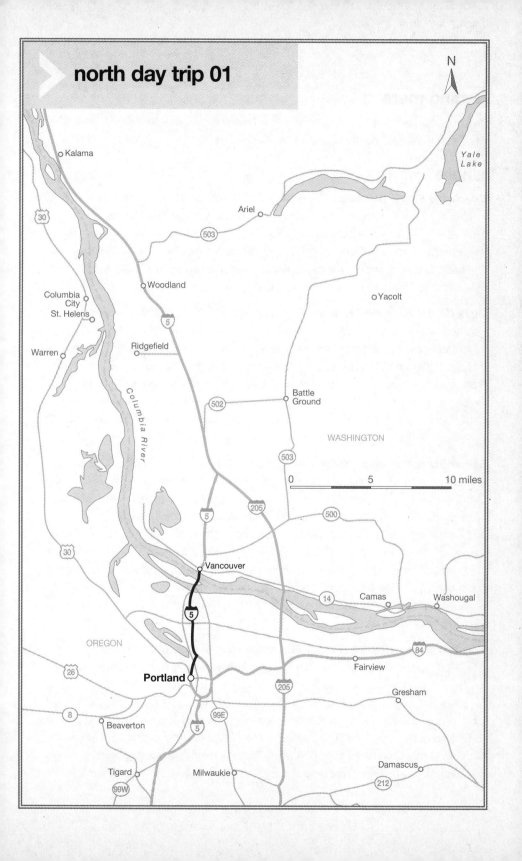

N

Yale Lake

Kalama

Ariel

503

Woodland

5

Columbia City
St. Helens

Yacolt

Warren

Ridgefield

Columbia River

502

Battle Ground

WASHINGTON

503

0   5   10 miles

30

205

5

500

Vancouver

30

14   Camas   Washougal

5

OREGON

84

26

Fairview

Portland

205

Gresham

8

99E

Beaverton

5

Tigard

Milwaukie

Damascus

99W

212

getting there

Vancouver is directly north of Portland, just over the state line into Washington. Vancouver city center is 10 miles north of Portland City Center on I-5.

where to go

Chelatchie Prairie Railroad. NE Railroad Avenue, Yacolt; (360) 686-3559; bycx.com. In logging boom days, this railroad line transported logs to Columbia River ports. Pulled by a 1929 ALCO 2-8-2T steam locomotive, the train today transports sightseeing passengers through scenic northern Clark County from Yacolt to Mouton Falls and Chelatchie Prairie and back. Special events include casino nights, murder mysteries, staged hold-ups, Christmas tree trips, leaf peeper trips, and barbeque trips.

Clark County Historical Museum. 1511 Main St.; (360) 993-5679; cchmuseum.org. The history of Clark County is on display at this Vancouver museum housed in a former Carnegie Library, built in 1909 and listed on the National Register of Historic Sites. Exhibits include a Native American gallery, railroad display, American military memorabilia, an old country store, country kitchen, and doctor's office. This museum is also the place to pick up a map for Tour through Time, a walking tour of Vancouver's historic properties. Open Tues through Sat 11 a.m. to 4 p.m. Admission to the museum is free on the evening of the first Thurs of each month from 5 to 9 p.m. during the museum's after-hours program.

Esther Short Park and Glockenspiel. 6th and Columbia Streets; cityofvancouver.us. In a corner of this 5-acre downtown park you'll find a hidden treasure—the Salmon Run Bell Tower and Glockenspiel. The bells for this magnificent public artwork were cast in the Netherlands and shipped in. There are four 5-foot-long bronze jumping salmon on the tower and several jets that spray water down the column. A Chinook Indian story is inscribed in the basalt column around the base of the tower and a fully animated three-scene glockenspiel depicts the Chinook Indian legend daily just after the bells ring at noon, then every 2 hours until 8 p.m. The entire park is a gem worth exploring—with so much to discover, it's no wonder it was named one of the top 10 public spaces in the nation by the American Planning Association.

Fort Vancouver National Historic Site and Visitor Center. 615 E Reserve St.; (360) 816-6200; nps.gov/fova. When the Lewis and Clark Expedition came through this region in 1805, Meriwether Lewis wrote that the Vancouver area was "the only desired situation for settlement west of the Rocky Mountains." But the first permanent European settlement did not occur until 1824, when Fort Vancouver was established as a fur trading post of the Hudson's Bay Company. This bustling fort became the center of political, cultural, and commercial activities in the Pacific Northwest. Today, interpreters in period clothing reenact mid-19th century daily life at the reconstructed fort. Open daily. The Visitor Center is free to

walk it off

With more than 40 miles of urban walking trails, it's no wonder Vancouver's Clark County received the Walkable Community Award from Walking *magazine. These two trails are the most popular and actually can be walked as one if you are feeling ambitious.*

- **Discovery Loop Trail.** *The 2.3-mile loop begins on East Evergreen Street and winds through Ft. Vancouver National Historic Site, Officers Row, and downtown Vancouver, joining the Waterfront Renaissance Trail at Vancouver Landing. Sights along the way include Ft. Vancouver, Pearson Air Museum, Providence Academy, and Esther Short Park.*

- **Waterfront Renaissance Trail.** *From downtown, head south on Columbia Avenue to pick up the trail at the waterfront. This 4-mile, 14-foot-wide shared-use trail connects downtown to the retail shops and restaurants along the Columbia River waterfront. The trail passes the plaza and a 7-foot tall statue dedicated to Ilchee, a Chinook Indian chief's daughter. There are many parks and picnic areas along the way.*

enter; Fort Vancouver admission is $5 for a family, $3 for adults, and free for youth under the age of 15.

Officers Row. 750 Anderson St.; (360) 992-1800; fortvan.org. Where else in the Northwest can you stroll past 22 preserved Victorian homes all listed on the National Historic Register? Built in the mid- to late 1800s, these beautifully restored homes were constructed to house US Army officers stationed with their families at Vancouver Barracks. The O. O. Howard House is home to the Visitor Information Center and is open to the public. The Grant House features a restaurant by the same name. The Marshall House offers tours and an exhibit on General George C. Marshall, its most famous resident. Group tours available. No admission fee.

Pearson Air Museum. 1115 E 5th St.; (360) 694-7026; nps.gov/fova/historyculture/pearson. Aviation history is on display at Pearson Air Museum, located at the oldest continually operating airfield in the US. Exhibition areas offer a collection of vintage airplanes, interpretive displays, an interactive children's center, theater presentations, and a gift shop. Open 10 a.m. to 5 p.m. Wed through Sat. Admission is free.

Pendleton Woolen Mills. 2 17th St., Washougal; (360) 835-1118; pendleton-usa.com. The Pendleton tradition of making quality woolen blankets in Native American motifs extends back to 1909. Visitors to this mill today can tour the facilities and see firsthand 100 percent virgin wool go through the state-of-the-art dye house, spinning and weaving, and finishing process. After the tour, shop the Mill Outlet Store and select from Pendleton's array of quality menswear, womenswear, distinctive Indian blankets, and fabrics. Group tours available.

Pomeroy Living History Farm. 20902 NE Lucia Falls Rd., Yacolt; (360) 686-3537; pomeroyfarm.org. Period-dressed interpreters help visitors experience 1920s farm life with activities like washing clothes, feeding livestock, grinding grain, and making rope at this farmstead registered on the National Register of Historic Places. Take a tour through the 6-bedroom log home. Open for special event weekends such as Pumpkin Lane, holiday-themed teas, and the herb fair. The farm also serves as home to the newly opened Pomeroy Cellars winery and tasting room, featuring wine the Pomeroy family has been making for generations and now shares with visitors to the farm.

Ridgefield National Wildlife Refuge and Cathlapotle Plankhouse. 1071 S Hillhurst Rd., Ridgefield; (360) 887-4106; ridgefieldfriends.org. The Ridgefield National Wildlife Refuge consists of more than 5,000 acres of vital migration and wintering habitat for spring and fall migrating birds. The mild winter climate and wetlands along the Columbia River create ideal resting and feeding areas for 180 species of birds such as Canada geese, sandhill cranes, great blue herons, swans, shore and song birds, and a variety of waterfowl. Visitors can see these and other wildlife while driving the 4-mile auto tour or hiking along the 2-mile Oaks to Wetlands Wildlife Trail. On site at the location of Cathlapotle, one of the largest Chinookan villages in the area, you will also find a full-scale replica of a Chinookan-style cedar plankhouse. This Lewis and Clark historical site is where the Corps of Discovery camped in November 1805 and again in March 1806. Visitors to the plankhouse learn about the culture and habitat of this area's original inhabitants. Refuge and trails open year-round. The plankhouse is open from noon to 4 p.m. on Sat and Sun from mid-Apr to Oct, and by special arrangement.

Wineries and Breweries. Lucky you—there are so many wineries and breweries in the Pacific Northwest, a good number of them in the Vancouver region. We've chosen just a few to name here, but there are many more. See visitvancouverusa.com/things-to-do/wineries-breweries for a complete listing.

    Bethany Vineyards. 4115 NE 259th St.; (360) 887-3525; bethanyvineyardand winery.com. Bethany Vineyard and Winery combines the best traditions of wine-making with the nearly perfect growing climate of southwest Washington to produce a wine with distinct flavor and character. Visit the winery and tasting room, bring a picnic lunch or have the folks at Bethany Vineyards prepare one for you, then take a stroll through the beautiful lakeside vineyard. Open Sat from 11 a.m. to 6 p.m., Sun noon to 5 p.m., and by appointment.

English Estate Winery. 17908 SE 1st St.; (360) 772-5141; englishestatewinery
.com. English Estate Winery makes a wide variety of award-winning wines from
its own pinot noir and cabernet sauvignon vineyards. Winemaker Carl English
takes great pride in the arts of wine grape growing and wine-making. The quaint
European-style buildings, towering trees, and seasonal flowers at this winery
make a perfect setting for tasting wine. Open tasting hours are Apr through Dec,
Fri, Sat, and Sun, noon to 6 p.m.

Loowit Brewing. 507 Columbia St.; (360) 566-2323; loowitbrewing.com. Loowit
Brewing was among the first breweries to join the recently reinvigorated craft brew
scene after the decades-old closure of Vancouver's iconic Lucky Lager Brewery.
The tasting room has a comfortable feel and great wood bar made of cedar
and fir. Loowit's large lineup of brews is distributed commercially throughout
the Northwest and has garnered multiple awards. In addition, bar snacks, retro
arcades games, live music events, and the hosting of the Mt. St. Helens Institute's
Volcano Views & Brews lecture series make Loowit a location with much more on
tap than just its brews.

Dirty Hands Brewing. 114 E Evergreen Blvd.; (360) 258-0413; dirtyhandsbrewing
.com. Downtown Vancouver's newest brewery, Dirty Hands, boasts a story as
rich as its selection of beers. Located in the historic *Columbian* newspaper building, Dirty Hands was founded by two chemists-turned-brewers who relocated
from the Midwest to join the Northwest's burgeoning craft brew scene. Beers
rotate seasonally, but are complemented by unique pub fare like the barbeque
meatloaf panini and six styles of hot dogs with the works.

where to shop

Agave Premium Denim and Apparel. 6210 S 11th St., Ridgefield; (360) 887-5400;
agavedenimoutlet.com. A favorite among stars such as Mark Wahlberg, Zooey Deschanel,
and Courteney Cox, Agave Denim opened an outlet store, design studio, and warehouse
in Ridgefield in 2010. This stylish shop is definitely a stand-out in the local shopping scene.

Downtown Camas. downtowncamas.com. The downtown area of Camas, just east of
Vancouver, is truly a treasure to be found. The quaint, tree-lined street running through the
heart of the city boasts a variety of shops, eateries, and the fully restored Liberty Theater
(circa 1927), all within walking distance of one another. The eclectic boutique shops here
offer antiques, ladies' fashions, accessories, jewelry, and home decor.

Uptown Village. 1701 Broadway; uptownvillage.com. The upper Main Street area of Vancouver offers a mixture of antique stores, gift shops, restaurants, and boutiques. Seasonal
activities and festivals are scheduled throughout the year here. From downtown Vancouver,
head north on Main Street.

Vancouver Farmers' Market. Esther Short Park, 6th and Columbia Streets; (360) 737-8298; vancouverfarmersmarket.com. From Apr through Oct each year, the street adjacent to Esther Short Park comes alive with more than 150 vendors offering local produce, plants, arts, and crafts. Food booths offering local and international specialties keep the crowd well fed while entertainers provide live music. This is the place to pick up local produce, arts, and culture.

where to eat

Beaches. 1919 SE Columbia River Dr.; (360) 699-1592; beachesrestaurantandbar.com. Beaches is a casual and fun dining establishment located on the banks of the Columbia River offering great views, especially in the summer. Chicken, steak, seafood, rice bowls, pizza, sandwiches, and a full and happening bar in a tropical-themed space transform a night out into a mini-vacation. $–$$$.

The Grant House. 1101 Officers Row; (360) 906-1101; thegranthouse.us. This place has been called "Vancouver's Best Kept Secret," but that might not last for long if the Grant House keeps getting the press it deserves. Set on the scenic Officers Row, this restaurant offers lunch and dinner as well as an extensive collection of single malt scotches, whiskies, bourbons, and more than 200 wines. Large windows overlook lovely grounds; in the summer, enjoy the outdoor patio or veranda. $$–$$$.

Joe Brown's Cafe. 817 Main St.; (360) 693-6375; joebrownscafe.com. My mother swears by this place, which was established in 1932 and claims to be the oldest restaurant in town. Casual breakfast and lunch are served with a twist of history; check out the old photos on the wall. Open 7 a.m. to 3 p.m., 7 days a week. $

La Bottega. 1905 Main St.; (360) 571-5010; labottegafoods.com. La Bottega, located in the Uptown Village section of downtown Vancouver, is a local's favorite. Wine lovers and foodies gather here to enjoy monthly special wine dinners with menus that change seasonally. La Bottega is also a deli. Stop in for a large variety of quality meats, imported cheeses, oils, vinegars, sauces, pasta, soups, entrees, and more, as well as retail beer and wine. Open Mon through Sat for lunch and dinner. Closed Sun. $$–$$$.

Lapellah. 2520 Columbia House Blvd.; (360) 828-7911; lapellah.com. The name Lapellah comes from the trade language used in the area in the 1800s and means "to cook or roast over an open fire." Similar to a language made up of words from many cultures, Lapellah's menu is a melting pot of foods. The restaurant features a full bar, an open kitchen, and a wood-fired grill. Dishes range from grilled Carlton Farms rib eye steak to New Orleans BBQ shrimp, but each is great. From the creation of dishes to the handmade interior, Lapellah takes a sustainable approach to dining. Open Mon through Thurs 11 a.m. to 10 p.m., Fri and Sat 11 a.m. to 11 p.m., and Sun 10 a.m. to 10 p.m. (brunch 10 a.m. to 2:30 p.m.). $$$.

Roots. 19215 SE 34th St.; (360) 260-3001; rootsrestaurantandbar.com. Brad Root's flagship restaurant Roots was voted by *Bon Appétit* magazine as "one of the best spots around the country for a romantic winter dinner." Dishes like seared duck breast with pumpkin risotto, cattail creek lamb shank with goat cheese polenta, and fish and chips with mac n' jacks beer batter keep guests coming back. Open for lunch and dinner 7 days a week. $$–$$$.

Tommy O's Pacific Rim Grill. Downtown Bistro: 801 Washington St.; (360) 694-5107; tommyosaloha.com. At Tommy O's, the vibrant, rich flavors of the cultures that compose the Pacific Rim serve as the inspiration for fresh and flavorful food. With influences from Honolulu to Hong Kong, Chef Tommy Owens designs specials featuring innovative and locally sourced organic ingredients. The downtown location is open for breakfast, lunch, and dinner 7 days a week. The eastside location is open for lunch and dinner every day. Call for details. $$–$$$.

where to stay

The Heathman Lodge. 7801 NE Greenwood Dr.; (360) 254-3100; heathmanlodge.com. This relaxing, rustic getaway in a mountain-like setting delivers a tranquil retreat brimming with Northwest ambience. The Heathman Lodge is a very big hotel, popular with conferences and weddings. There is a pool, spa, and health and fitness center on site. Hudson's Bar and Grill serves delicious foods of the Pacific Northwest and bakes all of its pastries and breads in their own kitchen. $$.

Hilton Vancouver. 301 W 6th St.; (360) 993-4500; hilton.com. It's true that this is a chain hotel, but the Hilton Vancouver is a relatively new facility, part of downtown Vancouver's renaissance efforts, across the street from Esther Short Park and truly one of the best places to stay in town. The boutique-style Hilton Vancouver offers 226 guest rooms and 10 suites that are exceptionally furnished. Built with recycled steel and brick, with 75 percent of the construction waste recycled, and rainwater collected for use in the hotel gardens, it was recently named by NW Meetings + Events as the best green venue in the state of Washington. The hotel's parking garage has charging stations for electric cars and complimentary parking is available for hybrid vehicle owners. $–$$.

day trip 02

north

the mighty columbia:
scappoose, st. helens

scappoose

The name Scappoose comes from the Chinook Indian language and means "gravelly plains." This region of Oregon, which fronts the southern shore of the Columbia River as it approaches the Pacific Ocean, once served as prime Indian hunting grounds. The rich riverfront soil, plains of wild grass, wetlands, and waters of the Columbia nurtured herds of elk and deer, spawning salmon, and flocks of upland birds. The bounty of wildlife astounded Lewis and Clark during their 1804 to 1806 travels, and later captured the attention of migratory fur traders, who came here to trap the beaver that lived in the rivers.

The fur trade died out long ago, but dairies, farming, and logging thrived as commercial endeavors in this region through the middle of the 20th century. Today, Scappoose is largely a bedroom community for Portland, as well as a popular weekend getaway.

Visitors still come to see the rich biodiversity and wildlife. Perhaps the biggest attraction to the Scappoose area is Sauvie Island—the largest island in the Columbia River. Because of its size and rich ecosystem, the island is the perfect destination for so many activities—biking, hiking, bird watching, hunting, boating, and kayaking. Sauvie Island's Columbia River beaches are the best riverfront sandy beaches in the greater Portland area, and fill up with families seeking a dip in the Columbia when the weather turns hot. Sauvie Island is also home to small farms, pumpkin patches, roadside produce vendors, and farmers' markets.

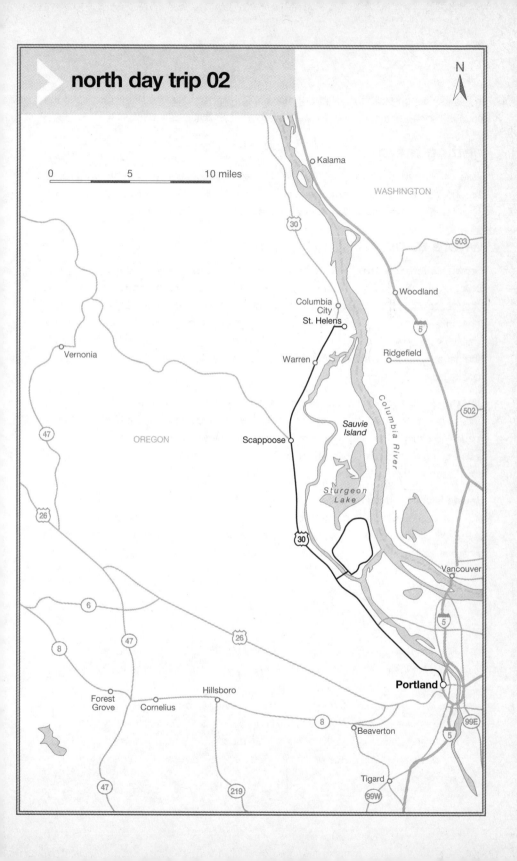

north day trip 02

0   5   10 miles

N

WASHINGTON

Kalama

30

503

Woodland

Columbia
City
St. Helens

5

Warren

Ridgefield

502

Vernonia

47

OREGON

Sauvie
Island

Columbia River

Scappoose

Sturgeon
Lake

26

30

Vancouver

5

6

47

26

8

Portland

99E

Forest
Grove

Cornelius

Hillsboro

5

8

Beaverton

47

219

Tigard

99W

In the summer and fall especially, thousands of Portlanders drive the short distance to this bucolic, beach-fronted, Pacific Northwest version of an island paradise.

getting there

Take I-405 north to the exit for US 30 W/St. Helens. Follow US 30 north out of Portland, through the industrial area and railroad switchyards that line the Columbia River. Soon, US 30 will become more rural. Scappoose is 20 miles north of Portland on US 30.

where to go

Crown Zellerbach Trail. The trailhead is located approximately 2 miles off US 30 on Scappoose-Vernonia Road. Part of the Rails to Trails program, this scenic trail connects Scappoose with Vernonia, where it connects to another popular and well-developed trail, the Banks-Vernonia Trail. Great for walking, jogging, bicycling, and horseback riding, the CZ Trail, as it is known, is a point of community pride and a great way to see the countryside and get some exercise at the same time. It's also mostly flat terrain, making it a great place to take kids.

Joy Creek Nursery. 20300 NW Watson Rd.; (503) 543-7474; joycreek.com. This 7-acre nursery has hundreds of plants for sale, offers classes, and can even dispatch a landscape gardening design team to your home to create the garden of your dreams. Open 7 days a week, 9 a.m. to 5 p.m., Mar through Oct, or by appointment. Please call 24 hours in advance to arrange to visit the nursery during the winter.

Sauvie Island. Sauvie Island lies approximately 10 miles northwest of downtown Portland and is accessed by a sole bridge from US 30. The island's unique character as a wildlife area, agricultural community, and recreational destination so close to the Portland metro area makes it a highly prized destination for visitors. The island is situated between the

movin' and groovin'

In the summer, this little port town comes alive. The outdoor amphitheater at Columbia View Park, right on the Columbia River near Olde Towne St. Helens, hosts outdoor concerts Thursday nights beginning in June. This "13 Nights on the River" series also includes an open air market with dinner options from local restaurants as well as a variety of merchandise vendors. Summer evenings are balmy and gorgeous here, and this is a great opportunity to take a little sunset escape from the bustle of the city. See travelcolumbiacounty.com for more information.

Columbia River to the east, the Multnomah Channel to the west, and the Willamette River to the south. At 26,000 acres, it is the largest island along the Columbia River—an island so large it has its own rivers, lakes, islands, and sloughs, and even a small school and a volunteer fire department.

Sauvie Island is also simply very beautiful. As visitors cross the bridge, a serene vista of fields, trees, and the Cascade Range spreads out before them. If the day is clear, folks spot Mt. Rainier, Mt. St. Helens, Mt. Adams, Mt. Hood, and Mt. Jefferson. Fruit (mostly berries), vegetables, flowers, and pumpkins are all available on the island for you-pick. If you are in a hurry or don't wish to pick your own produce, roadside farm stands sell just about everything grown on the island.

In the fall and winter, the island hosts over 150,000 migratory ducks and geese. The wildlife area is open to the public mid-Apr through Sept and closed to hunting permit only over the wintering months. Sun-and-sand seekers migrate to Walton Beach, accessed via Reeder Road and about 9 miles from the Sauvie Island Bridge. The beach is a mile long—be aware that beyond that is the area called Collins Beach, which in grand Pacific Northwest tradition has been considered clothing-optional since the 1970s. Also be advised that all beach parking is subject to Sauvie Island Wildlife Area parking permits, which are available at all the stores on the island and cost just a few dollars. Vehicles without a permit are subject to a ticket costing around $75.

Destinations on Sauvie Island actually use Portland addresses. The northernmost tip of the island reaches nearly to St. Helens, but there is no connecting road to the mainland on that end of the island. Services are limited on the island, as you might expect, but there are a few stores and small businesses, mostly at the southern tip of the island near the bridge. Here is a sampling:

Bella Organic Farm. 16205 NW Gillihan Rd.; (503) 621-9545; bellaorganic .com. Bella Organic is a certified organic farm on 100 acres of organic ground. This farm's goal is to promote responsible farming practices. Over 70 varieties of organic fruits and vegetables are grown here, including strawberries, heirloom tomatoes, beefsteak tomatoes, blueberries, blackberries, zucchini, green beans, carrots, garlic, sweet corn, cucumbers, and asparagus, available you-pick and already picked. Bella is also the site of a seasonal pumpkin patch as well as Sauvie Island's first winery, which makes fruit wines from grapes grown onsite. Open June through Nov.

Columbia Farms. 21024 NW Gillihan Rd.; (503) 621-3909; columbiafarmsu-pick .com. This large farm has been on the island for ages and offers 15 different types of berries on more than 80 acres, all available for you-pick. Visitors also find flowers, tomatoes, pumpkins, and all types of fall decor items. Open June, July, Sept, and Oct.

Sauvie Island Lavender Farms. 20230 NW Sauvie Island Rd.; (503) 577-6565; sauvieislandlavenderfarm.com. This beautiful farm pays homage to a Victorian garden with lovely paths leading to a flower-filled arbor where visitors can view four snow-capped mountain peaks and hundreds of acres of nursery and farmland. Purchase lavender bouquets, sachets, essential oils, and more. The farm is only open seasonally, but you can shop online all year.

Scappoose Bay Kayaking. 57420 Old Portland Rd., Warren; (503) 397-2161; scappoose baykayaking.com. Itching to get out on the water? This shop is your source for water access to the beautiful Scappoose Bay, offering kayak sales, tours, and rentals. Guided journeys include a wetland tour, slough tour, and lighthouse tour. Rentals include recreational kayaks in single, tandem, or pedal-powered styles, each popular with first-timers for their safe, flat bottom designs. Touring kayaks are also available in both single and tandems for more advanced paddlers. Try a canoe or a stand-up paddle board.

where to stay

Scappoose Creek Inn. 53758 W Lane Rd.; (503) 543-2740; scappoosecreekinn.com. Two beautifully restored farmhouses sit on this early 1900s-era dairy farm, where they've been transformed into a lovely bed-and-breakfast. The adjacent barn, once the site of one of the largest Prohibition-era busts in the region for housing a massive still and producing bootleg liquor, is now an event hall that can host up to 150 people. A tree-lined drive leads to this peaceful retreat for a romantic or personal getaway, where rooms are decorated with country charm and farm-inspired knick-knacks. $–$$.

st. helens

Most travelers don't find many reasons to drive US 30 unless they are en route to Astoria, putting the small town of St. Helens solidly off the beaten path. But this little city makes for a great close-at-hand escape from the big city and is the perfect day trip for those seeking the quirkiness and comforts of a visit to an old-fashioned small town.

Don't be fooled, though—St. Helens is more than antiquated. This is one cool hamlet. In fact, it might be your kids who drag you here. Why? Because St. Helens has appeared in many films, including most notably the pop culture vampire saga sensation *Twilight*. That little factoid put this place on the map, and many folks come here for a glimpse of scenery from the movies.

Those who aren't *Twilight* maniacs will still find plenty to enjoy in St. Helens. The Olde Towne area located along a 3-block stretch of First Street on the waterfront is eclectic and includes shops, restaurants, an old courthouse, and a theater. On a clear day the tops of Mt. St. Helens, Mt. Adams, and Mt. Hood frame the scenery.

getting there

From Scappoose, continue north along the Columbia River on the Lower Columbia River Highway/US 30. St. Helens is 8.5 miles from Scappoose. Turn right on Columbia Boulevard and follow it for 1.5 miles into Olde Towne St. Helens, on the riverfront.

where to go

Captured by Porches Brewery. 40 Cowlitz St., #B; (971) 207-3742; capturedbyporches .com. These beer makers might be a bit tricky to track down, but it's worth it if you can pull it off. All beers from this brewery are made with regionally grown, locally malted organic grain. The Invasive Species IPA is available all year, and there's always at least one other beer available seasonally. Captured by Porches Brewery proper doesn't have a tasting room, but the brewery serves beer from their MoPub Bus, parked in the summertime until Halloween at Kruger's Farm Market (17100 NW Sauvie Island Rd.) on Sauvie Island. Call for details during the rest of the year—the bus is often parked at a Portland food cart pod. About that name—Captured by Porches is what happens when good friends get together with good beer. They end up captured on a porch whiling the night away. Wherever you find these folks, be aware that they probably won't be serving any food—unless you, like so many of us, consider beer a food.

Fishing the Columbia with Dan's Guide Service. Warren; (503) 816-6803; fishwith dan.com. River mouths make excellent fishing grounds because waters of different temperatures collide. There's plenty of that going on here around St. Helens, where several tributaries enter the Columbia River and the Columbia's mouth itself is so close by. Experienced guide Dan Warren loves to take folks fishing in these marvelous waters. Try your luck catching salmon, steelhead, or sturgeon, depending on the season. Guided trips run approximately $175 per person.

Sand Island Marine Park. Not many public parks are in the middle of a river. This 40-acre manmade island is a lovely, developed park totally surrounded by water. But Sand Island has a major catch—you can only access it by boat. If you are ambitious enough to row out, you'll find camping, volleyball, birding, and all manner of artistic inspiration on Sand Island. The ecosystem is a mix of cottonwood forest and grassy areas, and here you'll find campsites, pit toilets, fire pits, picnic tables, nature trails, and one large picnic shelter. Though there are trash barrels scattered around the island, the official policy is "Pack it in, pack it out." Bring your own boat or rent one from Scappoose Bay Kayaking (scappoosebay kayaking.com).

The *Twilight* Tour. Here's what you've all been waiting for—the *Twilight* Tour! (What's that you say? You have no idea what *Twilight* is? Oh. It's a pop culture phenomena of the past decade—a teen vampire romance taking place in the Pacific Northwest.) Several St. Helens locations were used for the filming of *Twilight*. You can find a full list at movie-locations

.com. Here are the top three filming locations plus a *Twilight*-related retail shop to tempt your bloodthirsty little palate.

Filming Locations:

Edward Saves Bella Honorary Parking Lot. 225 S 1st St. This parking lot has views of local murals and was the location of Edward's brave saving of Bella from a gang of threatening thugs. It's also a great place to park your car while you tour St. Helens.

Bella's House. 184 S 6th St. The quaint home where Bella lived with her father is actually a private residence on a dead end. Please park at the bottom of the hill and walk up to take pictures from the street.

Thunderbird and Whale Bookstore. 260 S 2nd St. This building served as the bookstore that Bella visited to research vampire life, but in real life it's a private business. Observe from a distance.

Shop:

Jilly's Beverly Hills Shopping. 294 S 1st St.; (503) 396-5488; jillyssthelens.com. Women's outfits and accessories ranging from modern to the '50s, hippie to bellydancer, Old Hollywood to New Wave. Jilly's prom dresses and fairy wings were used in the *Twilight* dress shop scene, when Bella and her friends were shopping for prom dresses. Jilly is usually in the shop, and she loves Twilighters and telling stories about how she met Robert Pattinson.

where to eat

Dockside Steak and Pasta. 343 S 1st St.; (503) 366-0877. Right near Columbia View Park is this restaurant, with a menu that extends to fine seafood dishes, classic Italian entrees, steaks, great burgers, and interesting nightly specials. The patio has views of the Columbia River and the Cascade Range. Open Mon through Sat 11 a.m. to 9 p.m. and Sun 4 to 8 p.m. $$.

Houlton Bakery. 2155 Columbia Blvd.; (503) 366-2648. This sweet little bakery serves fabulous pastries, lovely lunches like roast pork loin with caramelized apples and corned beef and braised red cabbage, fresh baked bread, and Pacific Northwest coffee. This is a good place to take a breather from downtown strolling, and also to take the kids. Open Tues through Sat 9 a.m. to 3:30 p.m. $.

Klondike Restaurant and Bar. 71 Cowlitz St.; (503) 366-2634; klondikerestaurant.com. Serving the finest American food including sandwiches, seafood, steaks, mashed potatoes, and baked potatoes with the works in cozy, warm surroundings with charm and history. Fabulous house-made desserts are here to tempt you, too. $$–$$$.

where to stay

Nob Hill B&B. 285 South 2nd St.; (503) 396-5555; nobhillbb.com. Listed on the National Register of Historic Places, this home was built in 1900, giving it historic charm, yet it has been updated with modern conveniences and transformed into an inviting bed-and-breakfast. Guests have the choice of three romantic guest suites, each of which is luxurious and beautiful. The home also offers large gathering rooms with cozy couches. A full gourmet organic breakfast is served each morning in the formal dining room. $$.

worth more time

Vernonia. The charming little community of Vernonia is about 20 miles west of St. Helens as the crow flies. This quaint little town that sits at the lower elevation of the Coast Range mountains is a very popular day trip destination, particularly for road cyclists, who find the barely traveled roads that lead here to be friendly for their sport. Additionally, two trails designed for biking (as well as walking or running) terminate here—the Banks-Vernonia Trail (21 miles of tree-lined, easy-grade pathway through glades and across streams), which begins in Banks, and the Crown-Zellerbach Trail, which begins in Scappoose (17 miles along the placid, bird-rich banks of Multnomah Channel to the outer reaches of the Coast Range).

Whether you arrive by car or by bike, you've earned the right to lunch at the **Blue House Cafe** (919 Bridge St.; 503-429-4350; blue-house-cafe.com), which serves Greek and Mediterranean foods in a light, open space. Vegetarian and meat dishes with organic and local ingredients make everyone happy here.

If you decide you want to sleep over, try **Rock Creek Bed and Breakfast** (1162 State Ave.; 503-429-2503; rockcreekbb.com). This 2-story vintage mill house is an attractive, appealing spot to spend the night, and its surrounding perennial gardens are simply gorgeous.

To get to Vernonia from St. Helens, return to Scappoose on US 30 and take a right on the Scappoose-Vernonia Highway. After 20 miles, take a left on OR 47/Nehalem Highway N, and continue 5 miles into Vernonia.

northeast

day trip 01

northeast

living volcanoes:
silver lake, wa; toutle, wa

silver lake

Once upon a time Mt. St. Helens was known for its perfect shape. Now it's known for its massive crater. On May 18, 1980, the beautiful mountain in the North Cascade Range blew its top. Everyone who was living in the Pacific Northwest remembers that event—ash fell in a radius of hundreds of miles. The eruption caused the largest landslide in recorded history. Winds reached over 300 miles per hour, and the valley below the mountain was instantly scoured by heat, wind, ash, and rock. Many folks lost their lives, as did countless wild animals.

Today, Mt. St. Helens is still treated with the reverence and awe that it earned that cataclysmic day. But in the 30-plus years that have passed, the area has also become a testament to the power and beauty of nature and the ability of the land to make a rapid recovery. Earth that was once practically annihilated has transformed into a green landscape once more, and bright flowers and green seedlings have taken their place where once there was only ash and mud.

Silver Lake is the first town off I-5 en route to Mt. St. Helens. Though it's just a few miles off the very busy north-south interstate between Portland and Seattle, this small town feels alpine and rustic. You can feel the weight of the vast wilderness ahead, pulling you out of the city and into a terrain that is both lush and austere.

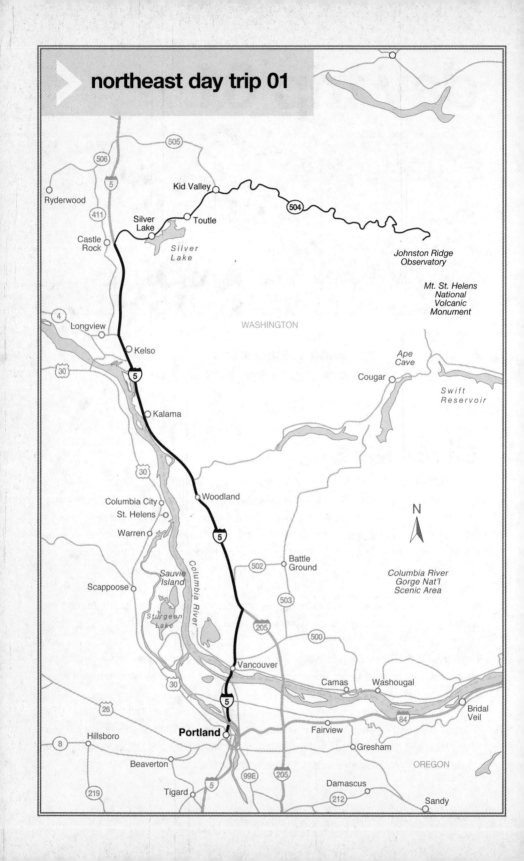

northeast day trip 01

Though in a different way than years ago, Silver Lake remains a recreational playground. Visitors come here every year for skiing, spelunking, hiking, camping, horseback riding, and more. Fishing is very popular—Silver Lake is one of the best largemouth bass lakes in Western Washington, and also boasts crappie, bluegill, trout, catfish, and edible carp. Tourism thrives here—thousands of people a year find that they just have to get a glimpse of that amazing Mt. St. Helens.

getting there

From Portland, take I-5 north toward Seattle. Continue for 55 miles. Look for WA 411 S/WA 504 E exit, exit 49, toward Castle Rock/Toutle. Turn right onto WA 504/Mt. St. Helens Way NE/Spirit Lake Highway. Continue for 6 miles into Silver Lake.

where to go

Silver Lake/Mt. St. Helens Visitors Center. Milepost 5 on WA 504. This is the first of four Mt. St. Helens Visitor Centers, and one of the most convenient for its proximity to I-5. The center features walk-through interpretive exhibits and award-winning theater programs that educate the visitor on events before, during, and after the 1980 eruption. Kids love the walk-through volcano model, and grown-ups love the bookstore, which offers books on flora and fauna local to the area and the Washington Cascades and, of course, the natural history of Mt. St. Helens. Nearby, a 1-mile nature trail and the Silver Lake wetlands provide opportunities to observe waterfowl, wildlife, and native vegetation against the backdrop of Mt. St. Helens. Open daily 9 a.m. to 5 p.m. from May 16 through Sept 30. Open daily 9 a.m. to 4 p.m. from Oct 1 through May 15 (except for Jan through Mar, when the center is closed Tues and Wed). Closed major holidays.

Seaquest State Park. 3030 Spirit Lake Hwy.; (888) 226-7688. Seaquest State Park is a 475-acre, year-round camping park on Silver Lake. The beautifully forested park hugs over a mile of Silver Lake shoreline. Visitors enjoy 1 mile of trail on this shallow wetland 3,000-acre lake and 6 miles of woodland trails for hiking and bicycling. There are spectacular views of wildlife, Silver Lake, and the surrounding area from the campground and surrounds, as well as children's play areas and playing fields. Great seasonal fishing, boating, and swimming are available nearby.

where to stay

Blue Heron Chateau. 2846 Spirit Lake Hwy.; (360) 274-9595; blueheronchateau.com. Choose from 7 intimate, beautiful guest rooms, each featuring simple floral decor, a queen-size bed, a full bath, and a private balcony overlooking Mt. St. Helens. A spacious parlor offers a fireplace to relax next to and comfy chairs to sit in. With the room comes a full country breakfast, served each morning in the expansive dining room. $$.

Lakeview Lodgings. 240 Lakeview Dr.; (360) 274-7482; mtsthelenslodging.com. This cozy lodging offers 3 cabins at very affordable rates. Done up in western mountain decor with wood paneling and deer and elk patterned fabrics, these rustic cabins have log beds and fireplaces. Views of Mt. St. Helens are lovely from this Silver Lake–front location. $–$$.

Silver Cove RV Resort. 351 Hall Rd.; (877) 380-7278; silvercoveresort.com. Open to the public year-round, this is one of the nicer RV parks you'll visit. Large lots with hookups for RVers are here, of course, but there are also cabins for rent and a recreational facility with laundry, kitchen, and restrooms. Silver Cove itself has several canals, big enough for small watercrafts, that lead to Silver Lake. $.

Silver Lake Resort. 3201 Spirit Lake Hwy.; (360) 274-6141; silverlake-resort.com. This motel is basic in decor and amenities but has many charms. Views of Silver Lake, Mt. St. Helens, and the surrounding forest are pleasant. Some rooms have spa tubs and fireplaces. But the pièce de résistance is that because the resort is quite literally on the lake, you can fish directly from your balcony. Now that's living. $$.

toutle

Once a thriving timber town, these days Toutle survives primarily on tourism. Like Silver Lake, Toutle is one of the last outposts before the secluded grandeur of Mt. St. Helens and its surrounds. With a population of less than 1,000, Toutle is a quiet place most of the time, but summer brings throngs of visitors.

For your purposes, day tripper, Toutle is essentially the last place to pick up food and gas to keep you going on your journey to the famous mountaintop. It's also the site of overnight lodging, a couple of restaurants, a quirky roadside attraction or two, and plenty of scenic beauty.

getting there

From Silver Lake, travel east on Spirit Lake Highway/WA 504, 5 miles to Toutle.

Keep in mind that should you choose to drive to the rim of Mt. St. Helens, you will continue another 41 miles past Toutle. Aside from the last small town, Kid Valley, just a few miles past Toutle, you won't find any more towns. Therefore, the destinations in this Toutle section are not all in Toutle proper, but extend along WA 504 past Toutle. Not all destinations use street addresses per se; we've used milepost designations when appropriate to help you keep your bearings. (The listings here remain in alphabetical order by section, as is the style of this book, so be aware that they won't read in the order you will pass them on the road.) There is only the one road, however, so you are highly unlikely to get lost.

Note: Kid Valley, just past Toutle, is the last place to gas up on the way to Mt. St. Helens.

> ## cloudy with a chance of a ruined day trip
>
> *In 1980, when I was a child living with my family on the Oregon Coast, the explosion had been positively major news. Not only was it the primary story in the papers and on television for weeks, but, although we were 300 miles from the mythic mountain, volcanic ash fell in my own backyard.*
>
> *By the time I finally ventured to Mt. St. Helens as an adult, a visit to the West Coast's most famous volcano was long overdue. A friend and I drove north from Portland on I-5 on a fair day in June, wound our way through the mountainous terrain of WA 504, and emerged at the rim to gaze upon . . . a thick bank of low-hanging clouds completely enveloping the crater. We couldn't see a thing. This is, after all, the Pacific Northwest. Clouds happen.*
>
> *One of the advantages to today's world is that there are high-tech tools to use to check the weather in advance of a much anticipated day trip. Check noaa.com for general weather conditions in the Mt. St. Helens region or try the Mt. St. Helens Volcano Cam, fs.fed.us/gpnf/volcanocams/msh, for an image of the crater itself in live time. Things might change during your drive, but at least you'll have a better shot at getting a crystal clear view of that awesome crater.*

where to go

Bigfoot and the Buried A-Frame. Milepost 20 on WA 504, Kid Valley. This is definitely the spot to fill up your own personal quirk quota. First off is the Mt. St. Helens Bigfoot statue—a 28-foot-tall, concrete statue of the famous Sasquatch (who some say lives here, and others say was killed in the volcanic eruption), with detailed fur and a goofy grin. After you've had your photo taken with the big guy, check out the buried A-frame house nearby. The mud from the Mt. St. Helens eruption reached speeds of up to 70 miles per hour on its way down the mountain. By the time it reached Kid Valley, it had slowed to a leisurely 20 miles per hour—still plenty fast enough to destroy homes in this forest. This A-frame house—newly built at the time—wasn't destroyed, but was filled with 200 tons of silt, mud, water, and ash. Today you can see it stuck in place half underground as it was nearly 35 years ago, and even venture inside.

Coldwater Lake Recreation Area. Milepost 45 on WA 504. Before the eruption of Mt. St. Helens, Coldwater Lake didn't exist. A massive landslide created a natural dam that henceforth collected water: voilà, a lake. Coldwater Lake Recreation Area offers opportunities to explore the lake's origins and current flora and fauna. Restrooms and picnic tables are available. Several hikes originate here, as well. The Birth of a Lake Trail is a leisurely quarter-mile

the road(s) less traveled

This day trip focuses on the northern rim of Mt. St. Helens and attractions en route, along WA 504. This is the most popular route to the mythic mountain, but be aware that there are two other roads that access Mt. St. Helens. WA 503 comes in from the southwest and offers the opportunity to see the historic Cedar Creek Grist Mill, hike to the summit of Mt. St. Helens, and explore Ape Cave, a natural wonder consisting of two tubes through which lava traveled below the Earth's surface. WA 99 provides access to the mountain from the northeast, and allows visitors access to spectacular Spirit Lake and other hiking and explora-tion options. See visitmtsthelens.com or a good Washington State map for more details.

stroll on an interpretive boardwalk. The Hummocks Trail is a 2.4-mile loop through house-sized boulders. The Lakes Trail is a 9-mile round trip to the end of Coldwater Lake and back.

The Forest Learning Center. Milepost 33 on WA 504; (360) 274-7750; mountsthelens .com/Forest-Learning-Center. Within months of the 1980 eruption of Mt. St. Helens, Weyer-haeuser Corporation began hand-planting 18 million seedlings. Today, the Forest Learning Center allows visitors to walk through a lifelike forest, experience an eruption chamber, and learn about forest recovery, reforestation, and conservation of forest resources. Interactive exhibits and a virtual helicopter tour video are indoor attractions; outdoors is a volcano playground for the kids. Open Fri through Sun from mid-May through Labor Day weekend from 10 a.m. to 4 p.m. Admission is free. The gift shop, restrooms, elk viewing, and play area are open from Mar to the end of Oct from 10 a.m. to 6 p.m.

Hoffstadt Bluffs Visitor Center. Milepost 27 on WA 504; 15000 Spirit Lake Hwy.; (360) 274-5200; hoffstadtbluffs.com. This grand lodge-like facility is one of the largest post and beam structures on the West Coast and offers a family-friendly restaurant, expansive gift shop, meeting rooms, and event space all overlooking the gorgeous Toutle River Valley and Mt. St. Helens. Inside the center is the Memories of a Lost Landscape exhibit, which interprets what life was like at Mt. St. Helens before the blast. Outside, a paved walking path will take you through a memorial grove planted in 2000 in memory of the 57 people who perished in the May 18, 1980, eruption. The gift shop offers apparel, Mt. St. Helens jewelry, ashware, glassware, and books. This is also the spot to catch a helicopter tour—the Visitors Center partners with Hillsboro Aviation to offer tours from the sky with views of Spirit Lake and the crater of Mt. St. Helens. Helicopter tours are only offered seasonally. Hoffstadt Bluffs Visitor Center is open Thurs through Sun from Oct to March 9 a.m. to 4 p.m.

Johnston Ridge Observatory. Milepost 52 on WA 504; 21500 Spirit Lake Hwy.; (360) 274-2140. Sitting high atop a bluff just 5.5 miles from the Mt. St. Helens crater at an elevation of 4,314 feet is this magnificent visitor center and observatory. This facility is the closest you can get to the mountain by car when driving in from the west, and these are the best views of Mt. St. Helens and much of the 1980 blast zone available, aside from those you'd get in a helicopter. Here you can enjoy spectacular scenery including the lava dome, crater, pumice plain, and landslide deposit. A wide-screen theater presentation and interpretive displays depict the sequence of geologic events that changed the landscape. Discover the art and science of monitoring an active volcano and predicting eruptions through various displays and also read eyewitness accounts from eruption survivors. This is also the place to access the eruption trail—a 1-mile hike that offers a picture perfect view of the 1-mile-wide and 2,000-foot-deep crater. The visitor center is open daily from 10 a.m. to 6 p.m. May through Oct. Closed in winter. A Monument Pass is required and can be obtained at the center.

Wineries. Pacific Northwest wineries are everywhere these days—even on the slopes of Mt. St. Helens. Give these a try on your trip through:

Harmony Wines. 555 Kroll Rd., Castle Rock; (360) 274-7235; harmonywineswa .com. Beginning with a planting of Interlaken, a green seedless table grape, this winery has grown to produce many light, fruity blends. Open daily 11 a.m. to 7 p.m., weather permitting. It's a good idea to call ahead and make sure the roads are clear.

Mt. St. Helens Cellars. Tasting Room: 1254 Mount Saint Helens Way NE, Castle Rock; Winery: 211 Morning Star Dr., Silverlake; (360) 967-2257; mtsthelenscellars .com. Owners Gary and June left Washington State for California for a while, only to return to native soil to plant some pinot noir vines. Taste the fruits of their labors here. Open Fri noon to 6 p.m., Sat noon to 5 p.m. and Sun 1 to 4 p.m..

where to shop

Drew's Grocery and Service Station. 5304 Spirit Lake Hwy.; (360) 274-8920. This full grocery store and service station in Toutle has been turned into a hot spot by location alone. It's basically the last place to get hot deli food (to include the best chicken on a stick), hunting and fishing licenses, beer and wine, an ATM machine, fresh coffee, and ice before the meandering drive to Mt. St. Helens. Stop in for some road food or a picnic lunch and fill up the gas tank.

where to eat

Castle Rock Bakery. 160 Huntington Ave. N, Castle Rock; (360) 274-7787. Custard filled Bismarks, baked donuts with chocolate frosting and sprinkles, frosted sugar cookies with colorful icing—what more do you need from an easy-to-locate bakery on your road trip? $.

Fire Mountain Grill. Milepost 27 on WA 504; 15000 Spirit Lake Hwy.; (360) 274-5217; hoffstadtbluffs.com. High-backed booths and wooden floors adorn the inside of this spacious restaurant at Hoffstadt Bluffs Visitor Center. In the summertime, sit outside on the spacious patio with umbrella-shaded tables. The menu offers burgers, salads, coconut prawns, and sandwiches like BLTs and grilled turkey and cheddar. If you're brave, try the Bigfoot Burger Challenge: 5 beef patties, 5 slices of cheese, onion rings, cheese sticks, lettuce, tomatoes, pickles, and a Bigfoot-size fistful of fries. If you devour it in 30 minutes, you get a free Mt. St. Helens Bucket List T-shirt. Closed in the winter (Nov to Mar); open 11 a.m. to 7 p.m. in the summer. $.

19 Mile House. 9440 Spirit Lake Hwy., Kid Valley; (360) 274-8779. As the name implies, this restaurant is located at the 19-mile mark of WA 504. It's a rustic riverside joint with lots of atmosphere. The kitchen turns out good food, including the specialty/monstrosity the St. Helens Burger, which consists of a quarter-pound beef patty, a fried egg, a slab of ham, both cheddar and pepper jack cheeses, a pile of fresh local greens, onions, tomato, and a special house sauce. But make sure you save room for dessert—the 19 Mile House is famous for their fresh cobblers, including blackberry and strawberry-rhubarb. Yum. In good weather, eat outside on the veranda and gaze upon the Toutle River. Open seasonally. $.

Parkers Steak House. 1300 Mt. St. Helens Way NE, Castle Rock; (360) 967-2333; parkers steakhouse.com. This place has it all—breakfast, lunch, and dinner in huge portions from a huge menu with a wide variety of items including omelets, hand-cut steaks, fresh made pastas, daily chopped salads, succulent seafood dishes, and plenty of dessert. $–$$.

where to stay

Eco Park Resort. 14000 Spirit Lake Hwy.; (360) 274-7007; ecoparkresort.com. Cabins, RV spots, tent sites, and yurts are all options at this lodging, the closest to the blast zone. Everything is clean and very inviting. Horseback tours are available along with helicopter tours, and many hiking trails are an easy access from the resort. The restaurant goes by the amusing name Eco Park Backwoods Café and serves hearty, delicious food to prove it. Great burgers, logger stew, and rib eye steaks will keep you going, whatever Mt. St. Helens adventure you pursue. Don't miss a bite of the homemade pie. Reservations are required via the website or by phone. $–$$.

Kid Valley Campground. 9360 Spirit Lake Hwy.; (360) 274 9060; kidvalley.com. Full RV hookups, partial hookups, tent sites, picnic area, bath house with showers, forested hiking trail on site, and a convenience store and gas station nearby make this lovely campground a popular destination. The Toutle River, adjacent, and Green River, nearby, have both recovered from the volcanic mudflows and offer great steelhead and salmon fishing. $.

east

day trip 01

east

wonderful waterfalls:
bridal veil, cascade locks,
stevenson, wa

bridal veil

Bridal Veil is a blink-and-you'll-miss-it sort of place, with a good excuse. The natural spectacle that is the Historic Columbia River Highway sizzles with enough powerful beauty to distract even the most astute visitor from the services and amenities of a township. Boasting a dozen waterfalls, views of the magnificent Columbia Gorge, and a lush green Pacific Northwest forest, the drive along the historic highway is not to be missed.

It's also a drive with history. In the early 1900s, Samuel Hill, the "Father of the Columbia River Highway," invited Samuel C. Lancaster, a renowned engineer from Tennessee, to assist him in the construction of a road that would allow travelers to pass as close to the river and the gorge as possible. Both men agreed on one thing—the natural splendor of nature should not be marred by the road, but instead enhanced. As many lovely spots should be accessed as possible. They stayed true to this vision, and therefore the road is a narrow and meandering one that was ultimately abandoned by most travelers for the smooth sailing of the faster, newer I-84.

However, the romance of the Columbia River Highway remains undeniable, and many travelers enjoy this passageway each year. It is absolutely one of the most scenic drives in the Pacific Northwest.

This day trip begins at the start of the Historic Columbia River Highway in Troutdale, passes through the small town of Bridal Veil, and continues for the duration of the west

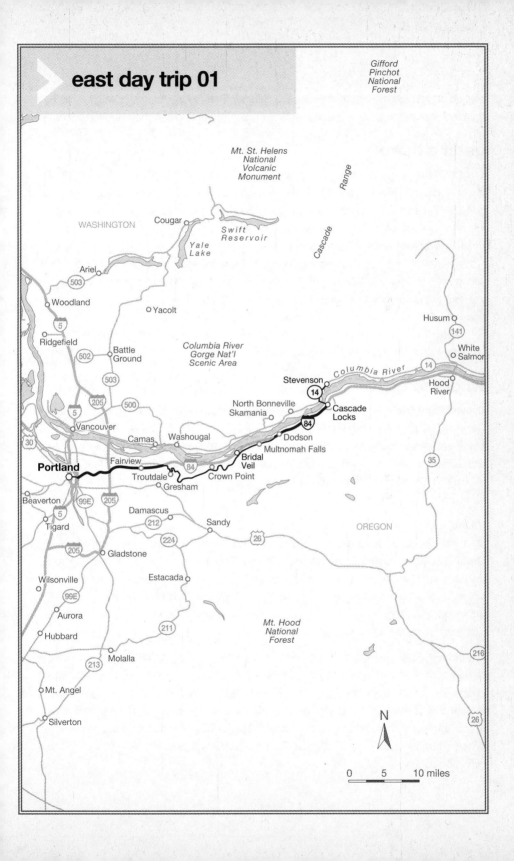

Gifford
Pinchot
National
Forest

Mt. St. Helens
National
Volcanic
Monument

Cascade Range

WASHINGTON

Cougar

Swift
Reservoir

Yale
Lake

Ariel

503

Woodland

Yacolt

5

Ridgefield

Husum

141

Battle
Ground

502

Columbia River
Gorge Nat'l
Scenic Area

White
Salmon

503

Columbia River

14

205

500

Stevenson

14

Hood
River

5

North Bonneville
Skamania

Cascade
Locks

Vancouver

Camas

Washougal

84

Dodson

35

Fairview

84

Multnomah Falls

30

Bridal
Veil

Portland

Troutdale

Crown Point

Gresham

Beaverton

99E

205

Damascus

212

Sandy

OREGON

5

Tigard

224

26

205

Gladstone

Wilsonville

Estacada

99E

Aurora

211

Hubbard

Mt. Hood
National
Forest

216

213

Molalla

Mt. Angel

Silverton

N

26

0   5   10 miles

section of the highway before crossing the Bridge of the Gods and looping back west on the other side of the Columbia Gorge in Washington State. You can make the trip a loop.

getting there

The Columbia Gorge Highway begins in Troutdale. To follow it in its entirety, take I-84 E out of Portland, and then take the 257th Drive exit (exit number 17/Kane Road). Turn right on NE 257th and watch for signs for the Columbia Gorge Highway, which will be a left turn just after the Outlet Mall. From that location, in Troutdale, Bridal Veil is 15 miles past Crown Point (or a total of 29 miles from Portland).

Alternately, to proceed directly to Bridal Veil without seeing Crown Point or the first section of the Columbia Gorge Highway, take exit 28 off of I-84 and turn right into Bridal Veil. But this is not recommended. This trip is meant to be Sunday-drive-style—take it slow and easy and don't skip scenery for speed.

Note: This road is one of those that might be closed in inclement weather. If you are traveling in the winter, check tripcheck.com ahead of time for road condition information.

where to go

Crown Point Vista House. Eleven miles east of Troutdale on US 30; (503) 695-2240. Crown Point is a promontory that stands 733 feet above the Columbia River and offers stunning panoramic views. The Vista House, built in 1916, is a lovely masterpiece with a marble interior and brass fixtures. Here you will find a public restroom—in fact, that's about all you'll find, save for expansive beauty. It's enough. Hours vary by season and according to weather.

Hiking. The Columbia River Gorge is Portland's hiking mecca. In addition to trails associated with the waterfalls (below), the **Eagle Creek Trail** (12 miles round-trip), **Herman Creek Trail,** and **Pacific Crest National Scenic Trail** are all accessible from this part of the Historic Columbia Gorge Highway. Pick up a map at the Multnomah Falls Lodge or grab one in town before you leave to plan a hike of the duration and difficulty for which you are in the mood. In addition to food, water, and good shoes, bring a jacket—it is often rainy and windy in the gorge, in all seasons.

Multnomah Falls Lodge. 50,000 Historic Columbia River Hwy.; (503) 695-2376; multnomah fallslodge.com. At this lovely old lodge at the base of Multnomah Falls, you'll find a visitor center, where you can learn natural and cultural history of the Columbia Gorge and pick up tips about hiking and other recreation in the area. If it's meal time, visit the restaurant, where authentic Northwest cuisine is served in a rustic, romantic environment. Open 7 days a week, but hours vary seasonally. Call for details. *Note:* This is not an overnight lodge, only a day lodge.

Waterfalls. One of the most famous aspects of the Columbia Gorge Highway is its string of beautiful waterfalls, many of which are accessible by car. Some require a short hike, and, in fact, each of these is a great excuse for a short hike. Many of these trails are well traveled and family friendly. Pick up a map from Multnomah Falls Lodge for hiking trail details. Rather than list these waterfalls alphabetically as is the style standard for this book, here they are listed in the order you will encounter them, assuming you are driving east on the highway from Portland. This isn't a comprehensive list, either—see waterfallswest.com for more falls and hikes.

Latourell Falls. This falls is unique among the best-known Columbia Gorge waterfalls, as it plunges over a rocky cliff, falling straight down from an overhanging basalt cliff instead of tumbling over rocks. From the parking area, walk a short distance up the trail to a viewpoint or walk about 0.1 mile to the base of the falls.

Bridal Veil Falls. As pretty as its name, and probably the second most popular waterfall in the gorge. A short hike from the parking lot will take you to a viewpoint.

Multnomah Falls. As the granddaddy of the Columbia Gorge waterfalls, Multnomah Falls is one of the most visited destinations in the state of Oregon. This means that, while you shouldn't miss stopping here, don't expect to be alone. Walk to the viewing area located in a carved-out opening in the rock face, or for an even closer view, walk another several hundred feet up the paved trail to reach Benson Bridge, which spans the falls at the first tier. For a little more solitude, hike up to the top of the waterfall (2 miles round-trip), where you can catch a glimpse of other waterfalls and the spectacular Columbia River.

Oneonta Gorge. A trail climbs up this gorge and leads to Lower Oneonta Falls, Middle Oneonta Falls, Upper Oneonta Falls, and Triple Falls. Worth the hike if you have time.

Horsetail Falls. Easily accessed and including a swimming-sized pond, Horsetail Falls is a great place for a picnic. From here, hike a quarter-mile up the trail to reach the lovely Ponytail Falls.

where to shop

Columbia Gorge Premium Outlets. 450 NW 257th, Troutdale; (503) 669-8060; premium outlets.com. On your way to witness scenic beauty and a glimpse of the history of the Northwest, why not do a little shopping? You are going to have to drive right past this outlet mall and its 45 outlet stores, including Harry & David, Tommy Hilfiger, and Jones New York, anyway. Just try to resist. Open Mon through Sat from 10 a.m. to 8 p.m. and Sun from 10 a.m. to 6 p.m. Extended hours during the holidays.

where to eat

Tad's Chicken 'n Dumplins. 1325 E Historic Columbia River Hwy.; (503) 666-5337; tads chicdump.com. Known for comfort food with a view since the 1940s, Tad's offers favorites like their signature chicken and dumplings, pan-fried chicken, house smoked salmon, Willapa bay oysters, lobster, homemade salad dressings, hand-cut fries, and pan-fried chicken livers. This is one of the last remaining roadhouses on the Historic Columbia River Highway, with a view of the Sandy River. Open for dinner 7 nights a week. $$–$$$.

Shirley's Tippy Canoe Bar and Grill. 28242 E Historic Columbia River Hwy.; (503) 492-2220; shirleysfood.com. This place has been around forever, as evidenced by the rough-hewn wood paneling and old-school Native American motif. But this roadside tavern-turned-family-friendly place has been renovated and is under new ownership. You'll find friendly service and excellent seafood, though it can be expensive. In the summer, Tippy Canoe offers outdoor seating. Open 7 days a week 8 a.m. to close. $$–$$$.

where to stay

Bridal Veil Lodge. 46650 E Historic Columbia River Hwy.; (503) 695-2333; bridalveil lodge.com. Bridal Veil Lodge was a popular stopping point in the heyday of early motor touring. Back in the day, which was right around 1926, it was called Bridal Veil Lodge and Auto Camp and 50 cents would get a good hot meal of roast pork, mashed potatoes, and vegetables fresh out of the garden. For another buck-fifty, you could pull the Ford around back and pitch a tent, or tuck your family into one of the snug cabins or rooms in the lodge. Today the lodge welcomes guests with the same warmth and hospitality, and a bit more modern style. $$.

McMenamins Edgefield. 2126 SW Halsey, Troutdale; (503) 669-8610; mcmenamins .com. The McMenamin brothers have been busy these past 25 years sweeping the Pacific Northwest for abandoned buildings with lots of heart and potential, which they harness, renovate, and transform into masterpieces of hospitality. Edgefield is one such place, and plenty of reason to make your day trip an overnighter. This sprawling facility was built in 1911 as the county poor farm. Poor no longer, today Edgefield is a National Historic Landmark and destination for thousands of visitors every year. The hotel oozes charm and houses more than 100 European guest rooms, fine dining in the Black Rabbit restaurant, 2 golf courses, pampering at Ruby's Spa, an on-site glass blower, and a full-sized music venue. There's always a party happening somewhere here. $–$$.

cascade locks

Cascade Locks is one of the oldest towns on the Columbia River, first taking root in 1853 when three white families settled here alongside the Indian families who already lived here.

chauffeured day trippin'

Here's your day-trip-with-personal-driver option. Martin's Gorge Tours offers wine, wildflower, and waterfall tours of the Columbia River Gorge, and will even pick you up at a handful of Portland downtown hotels or the gorge hotel, Skamania, and Bonneville Hot Springs Resort. Afternoon wine tours of the Gorge and Hood River Valley are offered daily, year-round; Morning Wildflower Tours are offered weekends from Mar through June; and morning waterfall tours are offered mid-week year-round and weekends July through Feb. Tours run from $49 to $99 per person. For more information contact Martin's Gorge Tours at (503) 349-1323 or see martins gorgetours.com.

For as long as there had been people in the Pacific Northwest, Cascade Locks had already been a destination.

Before the installation of the Bonneville Dam, a massive stretch of rapids ran by Cascade Locks on the Columbia River, described by Lewis and Clark as the "great rapids of the Columbia." Native Americans used the site to fish in the frothy water created by the falls. The river also served as the region's main highway, clear up until the 1930s when the first roads were built. Travelers heading west by water would be forced to stop here to portage—the churning waters were 2.5 miles long and so vicious that even seasoned Indian canoers and French-Canadian trappers often had to pull out of this part of the river. Some early Oregon settlers tried to run the rapids on makeshift rafts, atop which they'd perched their wagons. Many lost the supplies they had brought all the way across the continent—others lost their lives.

Today, Cascade Locks is still primarily a stopover for the weary traveler, as well as a quiet and scenic mountain village home to about 1,000 people. For the day tripper, it's the site of the lovely Bridge of the Gods and the impressive Bonneville Dam.

getting there

From Bridal Veil, continue east on the Historic Columbia River Highway to its terminus, just before Dodson. Merge onto I-84 E and continue east to Cascade Locks/US 30 exit, number 44, and continue into Cascade Locks. Total mileage from Bridal Veil to Cascade Locks is 17 miles.

where to go

The Bridge of the Gods. The original bridge of the gods was formed about 29,000 years ago when a mountain on the Oregon side of the river near Cascade Locks caved in, letting loose a massive slide that filled the river with 270 feet of debris. This event blocked the Columbia River and created a natural dam. Over the years, erosion slowly dug at the base of this dam, eventually tunneling through and leaving a natural bridge above. These events gave rise to a local Native American legend about the "bridge of the gods." The modern-day Bridge of the Gods is a manmade structure, completed in 1926 as the third oldest bridge on the Columbia River. Its high perch above the river and delicate appearance, not to mention the fact that it's one of few toll bridges in the Pacific Northwest, make it as legendary as the legend that gave it a name. The bridge is open to motor and foot traffic and crosses from Cascade Locks, Oregon, to Stevenson, Washington. There is a $1 toll for passenger cars, $2 for dual-axle trucks.

Brigham Fish Market. 681 Wanapa St.; (541) 374-9340; brighamfish.com. This Native American–owned year-round fish market offers both fresh and smoked fish, caught right out of the Columbia River. Crab, salmon, sturgeon, and more at this delicious locals-favorite destination.

Bonneville Fish Hatchery. 70543 NE Herman Loop; (541) 374-8393; dfw.state.or.us/resources/visitors/bonneville_hatchery. Located right near Bonneville Lock and Dam, the Bonneville Fish Hatchery receives an average of 1 million visitors a year from all over the world. Built in 1909, the hatchery raises 8 million fall Chinook, 1.2 million coho, 200,000 summer steelhead, and 60,000 winter steelhead annually. Tour the grounds and visit "Herman the Sturgeon" swimming in Kelly's Pond. He's big. Also on-site is the Bonneville Gift Store, open in the summer only, which sells refreshments, gift items, and educational materials about fish, wildlife, and the gorge area. All proceeds benefit Oregon's fish and wildlife. The hatchery is open year-round and is free of charge.

Bonneville Lock and Dam. Accessed from either side of the river: OR 84, exit 40; WA 14, MP 40; (541) 374-8820; nwp.usace.army.mil/locations/bonneville. I once knew a couple who made Bonneville Dam the primary destination of their honeymoon—a concept I found mystifying until I actually saw the place myself. Whatever your opinion of dams as hydroelectric power generators, this place is a sight to behold. Watch fish migrate through underwater fish-ways and roam a five-level facility that includes an observation deck, exhibits, a large theater, and all-glass exterior walls that allow a panoramic view of the Columbia River Gorge. A short walk leads to a viewing area inside the first powerhouse. Open 9 a.m. to 5 p.m. daily.

Cascade Locks Marine Park. 355 WaNaPa St.; (541) 374-8619. This 23-acre marine park and adjacent 3-acre island is on the National Register of Historic Places and is owned and operated by the Port of Cascade Locks. The park includes 3 historic houses that were formerly lock tenders' homes, the *Oregon Pony* (the first steam engine operated in the west), access to fishing on the Columbia River, picnic and pavilion area, a marina, and a visitor center. The marine park is also home to the *Columbia Gorge* Sternwheeler. Within the park is the Cascade Locks Historical Museum, which features information, photos, and artifacts on the history of the Columbia River Gorge. The museum is at Marine Park Port House #1. There is also a cafe and campground in this expansive park.

***Columbia Gorge* Sternwheeler "Landmarks of the Gorge" Cruise.** (503) 224-3900; portlandspirit.com. *Portland Spirit* offers many dinner trip cruises all over the Columbia River. The *Columbia Gorge* Sternwheeler departs from Cascade Locks and provides voyageurs with outrageous views of the gorge from the perspective of the river. Glide past such natural and historic landmarks as Multnomah Falls, Beacon Rock, and Bonneville Lock and Dam. A 5-hour tour runs Wed June through Sept, includes lunch and gratuity, and costs $84 for adults, $64 for seniors and children.

Thunder Island Brewing. 515 NW Portage Rd.; (971) 231-4599; thunderislandbrewing .com. Thunder Island Brewing makes original beers inspired by a love for outdoor adventures, with a nod to local history and a respect for all that the scenic Columbia River Gorge has to offer. Always on tap are an IPA, kolsch, Scotch porter, and pale ale, with seasonals available too. Kids are welcome at this tasting room.

where to eat

The East Wind Drive-In. 395 NW Wanapa St.; (541) 374-8380. The East Wind is a gorge institution, especially in the summer, when hot weather means people want ice cream. Burgers and the like are available here, too—and, by the way, this is the place Cheryl Strayed grabbed a cone at the end of her Pacific Crest Trail hike in her book, *Wild*. $.

stevenson

Stevenson is Cascade Locks' counterpart to the north—another Columbia River city born on servicing travelers. Over 90 percent of Skamania County is protected public land, making this area a beautiful forested retreat. Hiking is great here; the views of the Columbia River and the Oregon side are outstanding. In the summertime, look for huckleberries on the trail you choose to explore.

On Stevenson's waterfront, athletes perform water sports like kiteboarding and windsurfing. In town, you'll see a glimpse of history. Lampposts designed to look like old gas lamps sit out front of old restored buildings that date back to the early 20th century. Stevenson also boasts one of the region's best attractions, the Columbia Gorge Interpretive Center Museum, which provides further insight into this river city's history.

When you've had your fill of the outdoors and education, kick back in one of Stevenson's great restaurants or two luxury resorts and rest up for your next adventure.

getting there

Stevenson is 4 miles north of Cascade Locks across the Columbia River via the Bridge of the Gods. There is a $1 toll for passenger cars.

(To complete this day trip as a loop, after your time in Stevenson, follow SR 14 east to Vancouver and take I-5 south back into Portland, a distance of about 50 total miles from Stevenson.)

where to go

Beacon Rock. Ten miles west of Stevenson on SR 14. This giant monolith, named by Lewis and Clark in 1805, is traversed by a 0.75-mile trail to the top. Despite the steepness, an average hiker can reach the summit in less than 30 minutes, earning the right to spectacular views of the river and gorge. It's a don't-miss.

Columbia Gorge Interpretive Center Museum. 990 SW Rock Creek Dr.; (800) 991-2338; columbiagorge.org. A glimpse of the history of the people of the Columbia Gorge. Exhibits here cover first people, transportation, military, and harvesting resources. There is an enormous fish wheel that sits in a spectacular open, windowed room in this multi-level facility. Open daily 9 a.m. to 5 p.m.

Dog Mountain. Twelve miles east of Stevenson on SR 14. Both intermediate and experienced hikers will enjoy Dog Mountain. This very steep 6.5-mile round-trip hike offers great views of the Columbia River and, come springtime, a gorgeous display of wildflowers.

Hamilton Mountain. Eight miles west of Stevenson on SR 14. This trail offers a 7.5-mile loop for only the most experienced hikers, but families and beginners can walk just 1.25 miles up the trail to view Rodney Falls and the Pool of the Winds.

where to eat

Big River Grill. 192 SW 2nd St.; (509) 427-4888; bigrivergrill.us. The food here has been described as "high-end roadhouse" and "approved by the sturgeon general." Garlic shrimp, spaghetti with homemade meatballs, and Thai peanut chicken are delicious and not fussy, with big, bold flavors and large portions. The chef buys local produce and products when possible. The building, built in 1910 and reportedly once home of a brothel, has oodles of character. $–$$.

Granny's Gedunk Ice Cream Parlor. 196 SW Second St.; (509) 427-4091. An old-fashioned ice cream parlor featuring Umpqua Ice Cream, homemade waffle cones, milk shakes, espresso drinks, and mini doughnuts. This little gem is only open Apr through Sept—call for hours and details. $.

Walking Man Brewery. 240 SW First St.; (509) 427-5520; walkingmanbrewing.com. This little brewpub has yummy beers with original names. Barefoot Brown, Biped Red, Flip-flop Pilsner, and Crosswalk Wheat are made fresh and are available on tap, alongside other examples of Walking Man's best. Ravioli, spring rolls, Greek salad, clam strips, and all kinds of pizzas round out the menu. Open for dinner Wed through Fri, lunch and dinner Sat and Sun. $$.

where to stay

Bonneville Hot Springs Resort and Spa. 1252 E Cascade Dr., North Bonneville; (866) 459-1678, (509) 427-7767; bonnevilleresort.com. This lovely resort offers extravagance and wilderness wrapped up in one. A European spa traps local hot-spring waters, while a central outdoor courtyard with waterfall adds ambience. Each room offers a private balcony; suites have a bubbling mineral water hot tub. There is also an on-site restaurant and lounge and gorgeous gardens. Historic photos line the walls. This resort has been a favorite for many for a long time. $$–$$$.

Skamania Lodge. 1131 SW Skamania Lodge Way, Skamania; (509) 427-7700; skamania .com. Seemingly in the middle of the lovely Pacific Northwest woods is this gorgeous lodge and resort. A majestic building holds 254 guest rooms boasting either a commanding view of the Columbia River Gorge or the lush forests of the Cascade Mountains. The whole place is draped in extravagant native landscaping, and several courtyards offer natural respite. Three restaurants are on-site, including the award-winning Cascade Room with expansive views of the gorge and Columbia River. For lighter fare or a drink, visit the River Rock, which has great views, too. Greenside Grille is located outdoors by the 18-hole golf course. Skamania's great room has towering ceilings, an enormous fireplace, and—you guessed it—great views. This lodge is a very popular site for weddings. If you are lucky, you'll spot a bridal party out the windows while you dine or drink. $$–$$$.

day trip 02

east

fertile valley:
hood river

hood river

Hood River is one of those mythical places—a day trip so excellent that you might just never want to leave. Located on the Columbia River at the intersection of the Cascade Range, Hood River sits smack in the middle of gorgeous scenery and is an outdoor recreation paradise to boot.

The winds here in the Columbia River Gorge reach gale forces, and Hood River has been a world-renowned destination for windsurfing, kiteboarding, kite sailing, and stand-up paddle boarding since the advent of these sports. Mt. Hood looms behind the city, offering opportunities to ski, trek, hike, mountain bike, and more. Mt. Adams is in view to the north. The Hood River itself tumbles fetchingly from the south to the Columbia, providing opportunities to fish as well as kayak and whitewater raft. Across the Columbia is the White Salmon River in Washington State, and even more recreational opportunities.

But Hood River isn't just for the outdoor junkie. The fertile slopes of Mt. Hood as they approach the river give birth to much of Oregon's fruit crop. There are 15,000 acres of orchards in the Hood River Valley, producing mostly apples, pears, and cherries. These are harvested each fall, but those orchards explode with vibrant blooms each spring. Other farm-fresh foods are available in the spring, summer, and early fall.

The town has dozens of lovely historical homes dotting its steep sloped streets. Great little shops and restaurants fill up the charming downtown area, which is great for walking

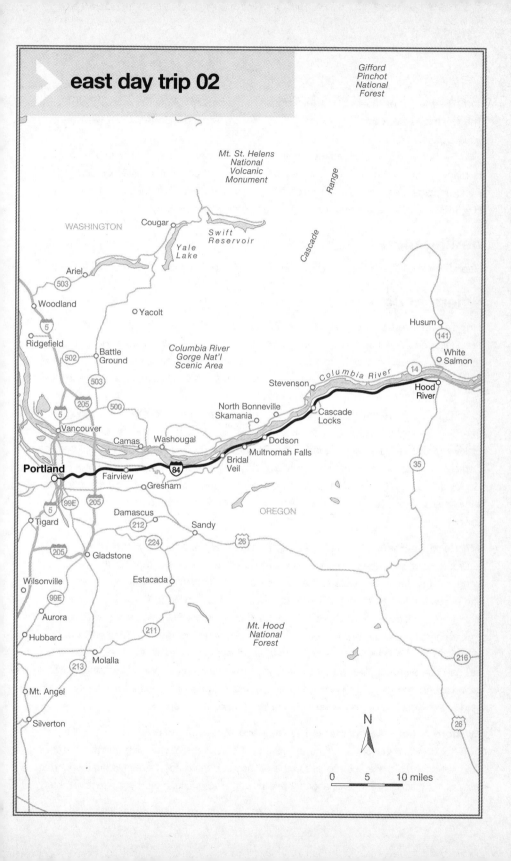

east day trip 02

and offers views of the river from its higher vantage points. Wineries surround the city. The weather is even good—sunnier and warmer more often than this city's west-of-here counterparts.

The many charms of Hood River haven't escaped notice, and the city has been named to many "Best City" and "Top Town" lists, including in *Outside* and *National Geographic Explorer* magazines. Still, the population has grown only modestly in the past 10 years, and Hood River remains a lovely small town in an unbeatable setting.

getting there

Hood River is 60 miles east of Portland on I-84. Take exit 63 toward Hood River/City Center.

where to go

Hood River Fruit Loop. (541) 386-7697; hoodriverfruitloop.com. The Fruit Loop isn't a breakfast cereal—it's a 35-mile scenic drive that begins and ends in Hood River, passing through the valley's orchards, forests, and farmlands. This is a great way to see the Hood River Valley's best bets. Sample delicious fruits and take your favorites home, visit a winery, bury your nose in fields of fragrant lavender, meet a pack of alpacas, and savor delicious baked goods. There are more than 30 destinations listed in this do-it-yourself driving tour, including Lavender Valley Lavender Farm, Browning Blueberries, Packer Orchards and Bakery (seasonal fruit, baked goods), the Gorge White House (you-pick flowers, berries, homemade hard cider, and a wide sampling of gorge wines), Cody Orchards Farm Stand, Smiley's Red Barn (produce), and Cascade Alpacas Yarn and Fiber. Download a map from the website before your day trip or call the phone number above to have one sent to you in advance.

Mt. Hood Railroad. 110 Cascade Ave.; (541) 386-3556; mthoodrr.com. The Mt. Hood Railroad was built in the early 1900s and served as an economic lifeline for the valley, carrying fruit and forest products to market and later functioning as a passenger train. Today the railroad is simply a really fun way to pass an afternoon or an evening. The rail route south out of Hood River offers great views of the Columbia River, forests, meadows, and fruit orchards. Trips are offered day and night, and many include a live narration that covers local history and key points of interest. In addition to standard sightseeing tours, the railroad offers several themed trips, including a murder mystery dinner train and Western train robbery trip for adults and *The Polar Express* experience for kids. Prices vary by trip and age—expect to pay between $25 and $80 for adults. All aboard!

Western Antique Aeroplane and Automobile Museum. 1600 Air Museum Rd.; (541) 308-1600; waaamuseum.org. One of the largest collections of still-flying antique airplanes and still-driving antique automobiles in the country is located right here in Hood River. That makes this place a great destination for the aircraft, automobile, motorcycle, tractor, military jeep, and engine aficionado. Open daily 9 a.m. to 5 p.m. Free admission for active military and children 4 years of age and under.

Windsports. Since the dawn of windsurfing, Hood River has been recognized as one of the world's best spots to catch the wind. Wind sports have flourished and evolved here, into sailboarding, kiteboarding, wakekiting, kite sailing, stand-up paddle boarding, and more. If you want to try one of these sports, this is the place, and there are several vendors to help. Beginners are welcome—in fact, the Hood River Port Commission built a protected harbor for learning windsurfers called The Hook. If the thought of windsurfing terrifies you, or you'd rather just keep your feet on dry terra firma, the waterfront is still a worthy destination. The action on display here is awesome to watch.

For rentals and lessons, check out one of these shops:

Big Winds. 207 Front St.; (541) 386-6086, (888) 509-4210; bigwinds.com. Big Winds is the largest lesson and rental center in the Columbia River Gorge. This is your source for windsurf, kiteboard, and stand up paddling rentals and lessons.

Hood River Water Play. 100 E Port Marina Dr.; (541) 386-9463; hoodriverwater play.com. Windsurfing, kiteboarding, wakekiting, stand-up paddle boarding, and catamaran paddling—these folks offer rentals and lessons for the gamut, and maintain a private beach to do so.

Wineries. There are at least a dozen wineries in the Hood River area and many more in the entire Columbia Gorge—more than we could list here. See columbiagorgewine.com for a complete listing, but here are a few to get you started:

Cathedral Ridge Winery. 4200 Post Canyon Dr.; (800) 516-8710; cathedral ridgewinery.com. Cathedral Ridge was named Oregon Winery of the Year in 2007 and winemaker Michael Sebastiani has been named one of the top winemakers of the year. The winery as a destination has been identified as one of the best for picnics, weddings, and wine tasting. This winery produces chardonnay, rosé, pinot noir, zinfandel, and more. Open daily.

Naked Winery. 102 2nd St.; (541) 386-3700; nakedwinery.com. With labels like Dominatrix Pinot Noir, Shag Chardonnay, and Vixen Syrah, the folks at Naked have proven that they aren't shy. Neither are their wines. Open 7 days a week with live music on the weekends.

Pheasant Valley Vineyard and Winery. 3890 Acree Dr.; (541) 387-3040; pheasantvalleywinery.com. Pheasant Valley is the Hood River Valley's first organic winery and bottles pinot gris, chardonnay and pear wine, pinot noir, zinfandel, and more. There is a small cottage available for lodging on the premises, but it books quickly. Call for details. Open 7 days a week except for the month of Jan, when Pheasant Valley is closed.

Springhouse Cellar. 13 Railroad Ave.; (541) 308-0700; springhousecellar.com. These folks started making wine in the springhouse at their old homestead above the Columbia River. Just a few years later they have a winery and tasting room located in a converted 1920s cannery in downtown Hood River. Every wine they make is available in refillable bottles. Open daily.

where to shop

Anana's Boutique. 206 Oak Ave.; (541) 386-1116; ananas-boutique.com. Custom gowns and dresses for very special occasions are available here, in designs that reflect clean lines, color, and high-quality fabric. Most of Anana's clothes are machine washable and colorfast, and she also stocks other clothes as well as jewelry, shoes, and accessories. Clients can expect direct and honest consultation for which style and colors flatter them.

Made in the Gorge Artist Co-op. 403 Oak St.; (541) 386-2830; angelfire.com/art/made inthegorge. As is true of so many stunning places to live, Hood River is home to many fine and talented artists. This gallery brings many of them together. It's a great spot to find hand-made pieces of art from jewelry to pottery, sculpture to handbags. Open 7 days a week and staffed by a member artist.

Melika. 316 Oak St.; (541) 387-4400; melika.com. Where does the girl kiteboarder buy her clothes? At Melika, where performance activewear, waterwear, and accessories come with plenty of practical style. The Melika mission is to share the inspiration of the Pacific Northwest lifestyle with women everywhere. This Oregon-based company has grown beyond Hood River; shopping at this store is a special treat. Open 7 days a week.

Parts + Labour. 209 Oak St.; (541) 387-2787; parts-labour.com. This little boutique is a modern lifestyle boutique specializing in progressive urban clothing for women by designers from Hood River, Seattle, and Portland. Shoppers who prioritize personal style and artistic expression over conventional fashion will love Parts + Labour. Open daily.

The Ruddy Duck. 504 Oak St.; (541) 386-5050; ruddyduckstore.com. This 2-story family-owned and operated retail store offers the latest in men's, women's, and children's clothing, shoes, toys, gifts, accessories, and housewares. The wooden walkway leading in the front door of this cheerful shop is like a magic carpet—it will take you into a world of wonderful surprises. Open daily.

Silverado. 310 Oak St.; (541) 386-7642; silveradogallery.com. One of my favorite shops anywhere. Silverado has jewelry for everyone, in a wide range of styles and prices. Many local and regional artists are represented and pieces vary from contemporary to traditional.

It's hard to leave this shop without buying something. Come with a Christmas list, and don't forget yourself. Open daily.

Twiggs. 305 Oak Ave.; (541) 386-6188; twiggsonline.com. This art and jewelry store is cool just to walk into, what with all of those vintage displays and an open, modern vibe. Unique jewelry, custom gifts, and home accents are displayed in a series of glass cases that surely holds more treasure than you can carry home. Open daily.

where to eat

Bette's. 416 Oak St.; (541) 386-1880; bettesplace.com. Bette's makes Hood River's breakfast and serves it all day. The huge menu offers eggs Florentine to omelets to cinnamon French toast, as well as sandwiches, soups, and salads. Bette's loves kids and has the extensive children's menu to prove it. Open 5:30 a.m. to 3 p.m. daily. Reservations accepted for large groups. $–$$.

Brian's Pourhouse. 606 Oak St.; (541) 387-4344; brianspourhouse.com. This 1-story Colonial-style white clapboard restaurant exudes small-town charm and high-style class. The atmosphere is dignified and friendly, with oil paintings and fresh flowers in abundance. The eclectic menu boasts porterhouse steak, sushi, and fish tacos. Open for dinner 7 nights a week. Brian's stays open late, until midnight, with a special menu after 10 or 11 p.m. $–$$$.

Celilo. 16 Oak St.; (541) 386-5710; celilorestaurant.com. Seafood, pasta, and steaks are served creatively with an emphasis on local foods at this downtown restaurant. The menu changes with the season but the quality is always top notch. Celilo makes every attempt to buy naturally raised products and organic products when available, and even converts their used vegetable oils into biodiesel to burn in the company car. Open for lunch 11:30 a.m. to 3 p.m. and for dinner starting at 5 p.m. $$–$$$.

Full Sail Brewery. 506 Columbia St.; (541) 386-2247; fullsailbrewing.com. Back in 1987, when the Hood River windsurfing craze was really in full swing and microbreweries were just starting to pop up all over the Pacific Northwest, some folks with a dream bought the old Diamond Fruit cannery in downtown Hood River and turned it into a brewery. Full Sail today brews and bottles lots and lots of beer every year, including an amber ale, IPA, pale ale, and a handful of seasonal brews. The menu at the Tasting Room and Pub offers yummy upscale pub food, including artichoke dip, Thai chicken wings, clam chowder, pulled pork, and bratwurst. If the Imperial Stout brownie served with Tillamook vanilla ice cream and caramel sauce doesn't put you over the edge, the Session Black float with three scoops of Tillamook vanilla ice cream served in a pint glass and topped with award-winning Session Black Lager will. The Tasting Room and Pub is open daily from 11:30 a.m. to 9 p.m. for lunch and dinner. Brewery tours are available daily, free of charge at 1, 2, 3, and 4 p.m. $$.

North Oak Brasserie. 113 3rd St.; (541) 387-2310; hoodriverrestaurants.com. In the cellar of a downtown building is this cozy Italian restaurant, just waiting for you and your hungry tummy. Nosh on roasted garlic and brie soup, garlic mashed potato tacos, grilled lobster ravioli, and veal scaloppini in a warm atmosphere with great service. $$.

Stonehedge Gardens. 3405 Cascade Ave.; (541) 386-3940; stonehedgegardens.com. This romantic restaurant is located on 6 acres not far from downtown. Housed in a restored home, built in 1898, with several intimate dining rooms and a patio featuring more than 6,000 square feet of Italian stone on 5 different levels with seating for up to 200 people. Crab cakes, gorgonzola sirloin, and seared ahi tuna are some menu options. $$–$$$.

3 Rivers Grill. 601 Oak St.; (541) 386-8883; 3riversgrill.com. Northwest cuisine with French flair and award-winning wines can be found at this downtown restaurant. Try the beet salad, seared scallops, gnocchi, or trout piccata. The 3 Rivers Grill strives to use local and organic produce and products whenever available. $$–$$$.

where to stay

Columbia Cliff Villas. 3880 Westcliff Dr.; (866) 912-8366; columbiacliffvillas.com. This spectacular property offers a wide variety of luxury hotel suites and "Euro-style" lodging accommodations. Situated on the edge of a 210-foot cliff, guests can take in the breathtaking views of the Columbia River Gorge National Scenic area from the comfort of their own living room. $$$.

Columbia Gorge Hotel. 4000 Westcliff Dr.; (800) 345-1921; columbiagorgehotel.com. This hotel falls into the "to die for" category. Built in 1921, it's a magnificent villa perched on a scenic cliff over the Columbia River, once a favored retreat for the rich and famous like Clara Bow, Rudolph Valentino, Shirley Temple, and Theodore Roosevelt. Rooms overlook the river or the gardens surrounding Phelps Creek. Each is decorated with Victorian period style artwork and furnishings; some offer brass or canopy beds and fireplaces. The outdoor gardens are themselves a feast for the senses, displaying gorgeous flowers in the spring and adorned with over 500,000 dazzling white lights in the winter. The fine dining restaurant, Simon's, offers breakfast, brunch, lunch, dinner, and happy hour, but open hours and days vary seasonally. If you can't afford a room or dinner or don't have time, stop by for a drink. It's worth it just to see the place and soak up the Gorge's history. $$$.

Hood River Hotel. 102 Oak Ave.; (541) 386-1900; hoodriverhotel.com. This old hotel is on the National Register of Historic Places and many of its original features have been restored, including the lofty ceilings, expansive windows, brass elevator gate, and marble-faced lobby fireplace. Rooms are cozy and done up in Victorian floral decor. The restaurant was set to reopen under new hands at press time, to become the Vintage Grille, specializing in martinis, steaks, and seafood. Hotel: $–$$. Restaurant: $$–$$$.

Inn at the Gorge. 1113 Eugene St.; (541) 386-4429; innatthegorge.com. The Inn at the Gorge is a lovely 1908 Queen Anne house in uptown Hood River with classic furnishings. The back patio is inviting; the wraparound porch is too, and has 23 columns surrounding it. Overnight guests enjoy a full breakfast that might include fresh fruit, tarts, muffins, omelets, or eggs Benedict. *Perk:* Lift tickets to Mt. Hood Meadows ski area are discounted for guests, and the inn even offers storage space for your sports gear. $$.

Oak Street Hotel. 610 Oak St.; (541) 386-3845; oakstreethotel.com. This renovated 1909 beauty is now a classic 9-room hotel and one of the few hotels in Hood River within walking distance to restaurants, cafes, movie theaters, and the marina. Rooms are lovely with hand-forged queen bed frames and oak leaf–adorned bedside tables. Fresh pastries are baked right in the hotel and offered in a buffet style breakfast, along with Oak Street Hotel roast coffee, an assortment of teas, juice, and fresh fruit. $$.

Vagabond Lodge. 4070 Westcliff Dr.; (877) 386-2992; vagabondlodge.com. Located directly above the Columbia River, the Vagabond Lodge—which opened in 1954—has bright, clean rooms at a great price. Set on 5 acres, the grounds are filled with majestic pine trees and native wild flowers. Visitors can enjoy a meal al fresco on the picnic table viewpoint and take a romantic walk on the sunset trail. $.

Villa Columbia. 902 Oak St.; (541) 386-6670, (800) 708-6217; villacolumbia.com. A villa is a large, luxurious house—this 1911 masterpiece fits the bill. Elegant, European-style guest rooms, many of which offer views of the Columbia, are comfortable and lovely. Breakfast is included and can be requested to-go for those itching to get outside and explore the Columbia River Gorge. $$.

worth more time

Husum, Washington, is on the White Salmon River 11 miles north of Hood River and makes for a pretty drive and fun extra jaunt from Hood River. Federally protected as a wild and scenic river, the White Salmon River is one of the most beautiful rivers in the state. Several companies offer whitewater rafting and kayaking journeys here. Try **Wet Planet Rafting** (509-493-8989 or wetplanetwhitewater.com) or **All Adventures** (509-493-3926 or alladventuresrafting.com) to take a ride on these tumultuous waters. Make the trip uphill to **Wind River Cellars** (509-493-2324; windrivercellars.com), which is open daily for tastings. After a touch of wine, have lunch or dinner at **Husum Riverside B&B, Patio Cafe and Icehouse Bar,** which serves heart-healthy and delicious Mediterranean dishes with plenty of meat and vegetarian choices in an old ice house and on a large brick patio. You can stay overnight there, too—it's the former site of the Husum Hotel, founded at the turn of the century (866 WA 141; 509-493-8900; gorgerooms.com). Nearby you'll also find the **Husum Highlands B&B** (70 Postgren Rd.; 509-493-4503; husumhighlands.com). Country charm abounds here, with antique furnishings, wood floors, and high ceilings distinguishing this Victorian home. The grounds are lovely and popular for weddings, with a gazebo and views of the White Salmon Valley. Breakfast is included in a night's stay, and dinner is offered for an additional price.

day trip 03

east

the end of the oregon trail:
the dalles

the dalles

Until the Barlow Toll Road opened over Mt. Hood in 1945, The Dalles was considered the end of the land route of the Oregon Trail. When emigrants reached the mighty Columbia River at this location, they had no choice but to load their wagons onto wooden rafts and float to Oregon City—a dangerous undertaking to say the least. Not surprisingly, some of these travelers chose to simply stay put, and a city was born. First incorporated as Oregon's third city by the Oregon Territorial Government in 1857 as Dalles City, The Dalles ultimately became an economic hub of the Pacific Northwest, linking the Columbia River, the Cascade Mountains, and major transportation routes between Eastern and Southern Oregon and Washington State.

But long before all of that, for at least 10,000 years before emigrants arrived, the site had been a major trade center for Native Americans. Today, the surrounding area, including Horsethief Lake and Wakemap Mound, comprises some of the most significant archaeological regions in North America.

The place earned its name from French-Canadian fur trappers, who noted the tall basalt columns at the site, created by ancient lava flows and the passage of the Columbia River through Celilo Falls, and called them "Dalle"—French for flagstone. These columns are no longer as visible as they once were, and the falls itself is gone—submerged by the

47

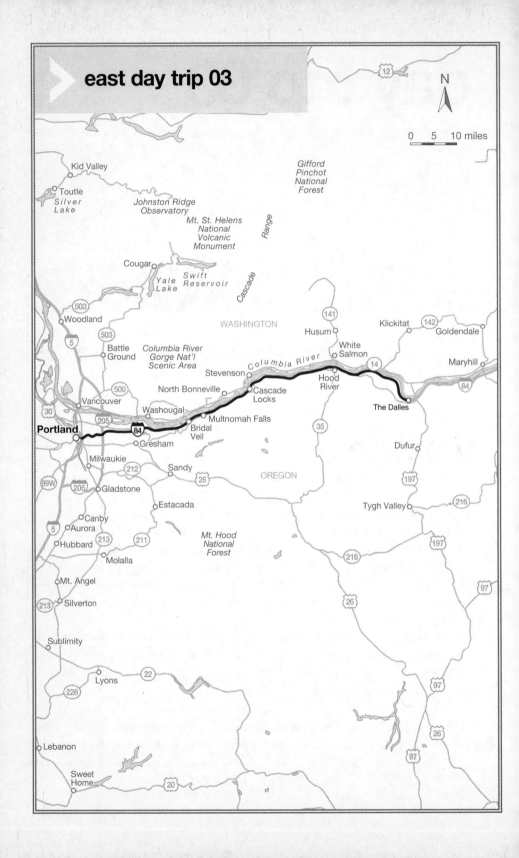

N

0   5   10 miles

Kid Valley

Toutle
*Silver
Lake*

Gifford
Pinchot
National
Forest

Johnston Ridge
Observatory

Mt. St. Helens
National
Volcanic
Monument

Cougar

*Yale
Lake*

*Swift
Reservoir*

Cascade

Range

WASHINGTON

141

503

Woodland

5

503

Battle
Ground

*Columbia River
Gorge Nat'l
Scenic Area*

500

Husum

White
Salmon

Klickitat

142

Goldendale

Maryhill

Columbia River

Stevenson

North Bonneville

Cascade
Locks

14

Hood
River

84

Vancouver

30

205

Washougal

Multnomah Falls

The Dalles

Portland

84

Bridal
Veil

35

Gresham

Milwaukie

212

Sandy

Dufur

99W

205

Gladstone

26

OREGON

Canby

Estacada

197

5

Aurora

Tygh Valley

216

Hubbard

213

211

Mt. Hood
National
Forest

Molalla

216

197

Mt. Angel

26

97

213

Silverton

Sublimity

22

97

Lyons

226

Lebanon

26

Sweet
Home

20

97

creation of the Dalles Dam in 1957. Still, The Dalles remains a destination for history buffs and outdoor recreationalists.

getting there

From Portland, The Dalles is an 81-mile drive due east along the Columbia River on I-84. Take exit 85 toward City Center/The Dalles.

where to go

Columbia Gorge Discovery Center & Museum. 5000 Discovery Dr.; (541) 296-8600; gorgediscovery.org. The structure and surroundings here are as much of a destination as the exhibits and collection. Sitting in one of the oldest continuously occupied areas in North America with immediate proximity to one of the largest rivers on the continent as well as the Lewis and Clark and Oregon Trails is this stunning facility and interpretive center. The building is situated on a 54-acre point of land adjacent to the Columbia River and the Historic Columbia River Highway, and won an American Institute of Architects Honor Award for its appealing design. An incredible stone entryway is cut through by a stylized rock "river" across the floor, which leads to exhibits interpreting 40 million years of natural history, 10,0000 years of cultural history, and 150 years of modern history of the Columbia Gorge. Explore the history of the Columbia, its native peoples, the Lewis and Clark expedition, and travelers on the Oregon Trail. Hundreds of American Indian baskets from throughout the Pacific Northwest are on display, and live raptor shows occur daily. Outdoors, the grounds have been restored with native vegetation and include paved hiking and biking trails, a pond, and scenic overlooks. The Basalt Rock Café serves lunch and snacks; hours vary seasonally. The museum is open 9 a.m. to 5 p.m. 7 days a week year-round.

The Dalles Geocaching. Northern Wasco Parks & Recreation; 414 Washington St.; (541) 296-9533; nwprd.org. Geocaching is a high-tech treasure hunting game played throughout the world by adventure seekers equipped with GPS devices. The Dalles Geocache is a 7-cache password geocache hunt. Pick up a kit (free) at Northern Wasco County Parks & Recreation and follow the hunt!

Fort Dalles Museum and the Anderson Homestead. 500 W 15th St.; (541) 296-4547; fortdallesmuseum.org. When Fort Dalles was established in 1850 as Camp Drum, the site was the only US Army fort on the Oregon Trail between Fort Laramie and Fort Vancouver. Today, a single remaining building endures as Oregon's oldest history museum. Take a tour of the grounds as well as pioneer and military artifacts, antique wagons, and vehicles. On site, visitors can also tour an old-fashioned Swedish log homestead built in 1895. In the summer, Fort Dalles is open daily from 11 a.m. to 4 p.m. Call for details about winter hours.

Klindt's Booksellers. 315 E 2nd St.; (541) 296-3355; klindtsbooks.com. Given that you are holding this actual paper book in your hand instead of travel researching online, I am going to assume that you are at least a little bit of a book junkie. If that's the case, then Klindt's might just be your number one destination in The Dalles. Klindt's first opened its doors in 1870 and is the oldest bookstore in Oregon. The space has all of the charm to prove it. Browse through original bookshelves, cabinets, and squeaky wooden floors to discover all sorts of titles, both brand new and old and out of print. Whether you are searching for mystery or memoir, cooking or cartography, Klindt's automatically provides the history and romance. *Note:* When this book's first edition came out, Klindt's hosted me for a most amazing book signing event, proving that they are as hospitable as they are established. Open daily.

Old St. Peter's Landmark. 405 Lincoln St.; (541) 296-5686; oldstpeterslandmark.org. Built in 1897, dedicated in 1898, and saved from demolition in 1971, this magnificent structure is open free to the public for tours. Gaze on brilliant stained glass windows, listen for the clear melodic tones of the old church bell, feel serenity in the lovely interior of this Gothic brick church. Open Tues through Sat, free admission.

Pulpit Rock. In the intersection of E 12th and Court Streets. This 12-foot-tall rock historically stood next to the Methodist Wascopam Mission, where it was transformed into a natural pulpit by missionary preachers hoping to get their word across to Native Americans. One of the missionaries who preached from Pulpit Rock was mission founder Reverend Jason Lee, whose repeated trips back east in the 1830s and 1840s to spread word of the value of the Oregon Territory are said to have triggered the mass emigration that would follow. Today this rock stands in the middle of the street in the center of The Dalles. Every year at Easter, the surrounding streets are closed and Easter services are offered at the site.

The Riverfront Trail. Access from downtown at Union Street, at the I-84 underpass, and at the Columbia Gorge Discovery Center; nwprd.org/rivertrail. This trail highlight's The Dalles spectacular river setting. Extending for 10 miles along the south bank of the Columbia River

pick a bushel

The major agricultural product of The Dalles is sweet cherries, produced here in quantities of thousands of pounds annually for both domestic and overseas markets. More than 6,000 acres of sweet cherry trees grow around the city, and in the spring, boy, aren't they beautiful. Two local orchards you might visit during harvest season (mid-June through mid-August) are Orchard View Farms Inc. (4055 Skyline Rd.; 541-298-1481) and Sandoz Farm (5755 Mill Creek Rd.; 541-296-3859). Call for details about visiting seasonally to pick up a bushel of Rainiers or Royal Annes.

on The Dalles waterfront, this trail gets you as close to the river as you are going to get and takes bicyclists and pedestrians past Taylor Lakes, The Dalles Marina, and Riverfront Park. Interpretive signs pop up now and then, providing information on the Lewis and Clark Trail, Rock Fort, and The Dalles.

Sunshine Mill & Artisan Plaza. 901 E Second St.; (541) 298-8900; sunshinemill.com. One of The Dalles'—and Oregon's—coolest spots, this unique winery and tasting room is located in a former mill (complete with looming concrete silos) where wheat was milled for more than 130 years. It was the first building in The Dalles to have electricity, powered by a Thomas Edison Motor, still on display. The Sunshine Biscuit Company once owned this property, and the wheat milled here was used to make everyone's favorite cracker, the Cheez-It. With some excellent wines and an eclectic tasting room that incorporates many of the mill's original features and machinery, this is a great place to kick back for a sip and a nibble. Try a cheese, charcuterie, and olive plate with a great flight of wine. In the summer, Sunshine Mills shows family-friendly movies on the side of the silo.

where to eat

Baldwin Saloon. 205 Court St.; (541) 296-5666; baldwinsaloon.com. Launched as a bar to serve workers of the railroad and the Columbia River, the Baldwin Saloon once did a booming business and even had a brothel attached to it. The building served over the years as a restaurant, a steamboat navigational office, a warehouse, a coffin storage site, a state employment office, and a saddle shop. In 1990, a year-long restoration process restored the building to its original purpose (excepting the brothel). The original brick walls and old fir floor were uncovered and given new life, and today mahogany and oak booths and tables, brass fixtures, and turn-of-the-century oil paintings mark the decor. An 18-foot long mahogany backbar made in the early 1900s holds an original mirror trimmed with stained glass panels and a big brass cash register. The menu offers fine dining by way of pastas, seafood, and burgers. Open for lunch and dinner Mon through Sat. $$–$$$.

Clock Tower Ales. 311 Union St.; (541) 705-3590; clocktowerales.com. Taste some local brews at Clock Tower Ales, located in the former Wasco County Courthouse. Built in 1883, the courthouse was home to the last public hanging in the county in 1905. Your visit promises to be far less morbid. Clock Tower has more than 30 local and regional craft brews on tap, plus it offers typical pub food, from burgers to wraps. $–$$.

Cousin's Country Inn and Restaurant. 2116 W 6th St.; (541) 298-5161; cousinscountry inn.com. Northwest hospitality and homestyle cooking in one stop, sprinkled with a good dose of fun. The bright cheery restaurant offers microbrews, locally raised beefsteaks, giant cinnamon rolls, pot roast, and chicken fried steak to weary travelers and locals. The hotel has 3 wings—the Coho, the Steelhead, and the Chinook, each with its own unique style and price range. A heated outdoor swimming pool and a bottomless jar of cookies in the lobby round out your stay. Restaurant open 6 a.m. to 10 p.m. daily (until 9 p.m. in winter). Restaurant: $–$$; Inn: $$–$$$

Montira's Thai Cuisine. 302 W 2nd St.; (541) 769-0500. The best Thai food in the Gorge can be found at this local gem, where the owner and chef Montira herself may meet you at the door with a traditional Thai greeting. Don't miss the pumpkin curry and Thai iced coffee. $–$$.

Petite Provence of the Gorge. 408 E 2nd St.; (541) 506-0037; provence-portland.com. This spinoff of the popular Portland bakery and cafe Petite Provence offers delicious French pastries and yummy breakfast entrees like omelets, brie sausage scramble, and risotto cakes and eggs. For lunch, French onion soup, Monte Carlo sandwiches, and a goat cheese salad entice. There's an espresso bar, too. $.

where to stay

Balch Hotel. 40 S Heimrich St., Dufur; (541) 467-2277; balchhotel.com. This vintage 1908 hotel 15 miles south of The Dalles on US 197 is a favorite for weddings and special occasions. The 3-story brick building has 20 bedrooms plus a magnificent suite on the third floor with a Mount Hood view and private bath with whirlpool tub. Each room is a little bit different, with period furnishings and decor. Some rooms have private baths, some share common baths. $–$$.

Celilo Inn. 3550 E 2nd St.; (541) 769-0001; celiloinn.com. Views of the Columbia River, Mt. Hood, and The Dalles Dam from remodeled rooms in a classic old hotel are the highlight here. Relax with a beverage by the pool after a cooling dip, and enjoy the view of boats going by on the river from the patio. The Celilo Inn offers a free glass of wine at check-in. If that only whets your appetite, try the room package that includes a great day tour of area wineries with an educated guide. Let them do the driving while you do the tasting. $–$$.

The Dalles Inn. 112 W 2nd St.; (541) 296-9107; thedallesinn.com. This is the only hotel in the heart of downtown. Complimentary breakfast, fitness center, heated outdoor pool, and Wi-Fi are all available in this older space that's been recently remodeled. Coffeemakers, refrigerators, and microwaves are in every room, and this hotel is even dog friendly. $–$$.

Fairfield Inn & Suites The Dalles. 2014 W 7th Street; (541) 769-0753; marriott.com. This new 80-room Marriott property, which opened in 2014, is conveniently located at the west end of town, just minutes to downtown. A complimentary breakfast bar, outdoor fire pit, indoor saline pool, and fitness center make it a great spot for vacationing families. It's also extremely pet friendly, allowing dogs and cats in many of its rooms. Four-legged visitors even get a "welcome package" with water/food bowls, treats, and a special blanket! $$

worth more time

If you still have time, cross the Columbia River via The Dalles Bridge and drive another 20 miles east on WA-14 to the **Maryhill Museum of Art** (maryhillmuseum.org) in Goldendale, Washington. Samuel Hill, a successful road builder from the east who was the catalyst behind the Columbia Gorge Highway, purchased 5,300 acres of land along the Columbia River in 1907. Here he formed the Maryhill Land Company, named after his daughter. The location proved too remote, however, and the land company ultimately failed. On the suggestion of a friend, Hill took steps to turn the mansion into an art museum instead, a dream that was not fully realized until 1940, after Hill's death.

Today the gorgeous mansion perched on the hill over the Columbia Gorge holds a diverse collection, including exhibitions on Auguste Rodin (with 80 works, it's one of the largest collections outside of France), the Native People of North America, and international chess sets. Maryhill Museum expanded in 2012 with a new $10 million wing that offers the best new view of the Gorge. Enjoy a snack from the museum cafe while taking in the expansive vista. Open 10 a.m. to 5 p.m. every day, including holidays, Mar 15 through Nov 15.

Equally interesting is the replica of Stonehenge that Samuel Hill built 3 miles east of the museum. Hill duplicated, as nearly as possible, the original size and design of the ancient Neolithic ruin in England, Stonehenge. The Maryhill Stonehenge was dedicated in 1918 and stands today as Hill intended it, as a tribute to those who died in World War I.

southeast

day trip 01

southeast

>>> **the slopes of mt. hood:**
sandy, zigzag & welches,
government camp

sandy

Sandy is located about halfway between Portland and Government Camp at an elevation of 1,000 feet in the Mt. Hood foothills. The town of over 10,000 serves as not only the commercial hub of a rural area of over twice its size, but also as the gateway to Mt. Hood. Sandy is the last semi-major outpost before the string of villages that lead to the iconic mountain itself.

The city's beginnings are rooted in the 1850s, when the fledgling settlement served as a trading post on the Barlow Road, a popular pioneer route and part of the Oregon Trail. Sandy earned its name from travelers who came through here even earlier than that—Lewis and Clark. The explorers originally identified the nearby Sandy River as "Quicksand River." The name "Quicksand" eventually evolved into "Sandy."

Sandy mainly relies on tourism, but also supports many small farms and agricultural pursuits, like the several Christmas tree farms that surround it. This small city has an eclectic flavor—part mountain town, part agricultural town. With Portland only 28 miles away, there's still a touch of urbanity here, too.

getting there

Sandy is 28 miles southeast of Portland on OR 26/US 26 E. Mapquest and similar navigational tools may try to direct you east on Burnside Road from downtown Portland. While

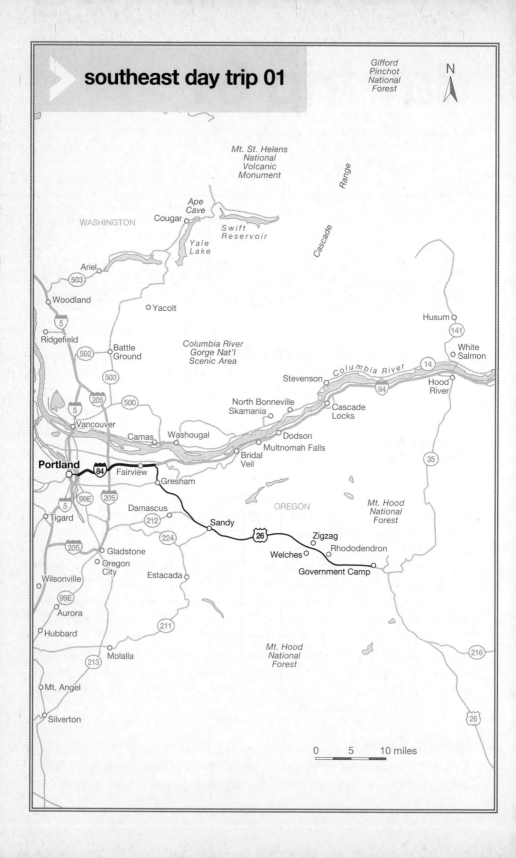

Gifford
Pinchot
National
Forest

N

Mt. St. Helens
National
Volcanic
Monument

Ape
Cave

Cougar

Swift
Reservoir

Cascade

Range

WASHINGTON

Yale
Lake

Ariel

503

Woodland

Yacolt

Husum

141

Ridgefield

5

White
Salmon

Battle
Ground

502

Columbia River
Gorge Nat'l
Scenic Area

Columbia River

14

503

Stevenson

84

Hood
River

205

500

North Bonneville
Skamania

Cascade
Locks

5

Vancouver

Camas

Washougal

Dodson

Multnomah Falls

35

Portland

84

Fairview

Bridal
Veil

Gresham

OREGON

Mt. Hood
National
Forest

5

99E

205

Damascus

212

Sandy

26

Zigzag

Rhododendron

Tigard

224

Welches

205

Gladstone

Government Camp

Oregon
City

Estacada

Wilsonville

99E

Aurora

211

Hubbard

Mt. Hood
National
Forest

213

Molalla

216

Mt. Angel

Silverton

26

0   5   10 miles

Burnside does eventually turn into OR 26, don't take this route! You'll spend your whole day trip going stoplight-to-stoplight. Take I-84 E out of Portland instead, and then take the 257th Drive exit (exit number 17/Kane Road). Follow signs for Mt. Hood/Sandy/Highway 26/US 26E.

where to go

Christmas Tree Farms. mthoodterritory.com. Oregon is the largest producer of Christmas trees in the US, and Mt. Hood Territory is the largest producer in Oregon. Visiting a farm to choose and cut one's own tree during the holiday season is an Oregon tradition. These farms, in and near Sandy, are just two of many in the Mt. Hood region—see the website for more suggestions. Most of these farms are open Thanksgiving to Christmas, but some also are open in the summer, when they offer produce, flowers, and a chance to visit your Christmas tree in advance. Call ahead for details.

> **Alder Creek Farms.** 53895 E OR 26, Sandy; (503) 781-7707. Offers noble and grand fir. Open Nov 26 through Dec 24.

> **Dutcher's Tree Farm.** 33755 SE Compton Rd., Boring; (503) 663-4127. Douglas fir, grand and noble fir, and un-sheared Douglas fir. Open Nov 28 through Dec 23.

Jonsrud Viewpoint Park. In Sandy, north of Highway 26 on Bluff Road. This designated stop on the Oregon Scenic Byway offers spectacular views of Mt. Hood and the Sandy River Valley. Stroll the brick pathways, look through the telescope, and enjoy informational signs about the Barlow Road, part of the Oregon Trail.

Philip Foster Farm. 29912 SE OR 211, Eagle Creek (located 7 miles southwest of Sandy on Eagle Creek–Sandy Highway 172/OR 211); (503) 637-6324; philipfosterfarm.com. Pioneers didn't make it to Oregon without some help. One of the folks who did the helping was Philip Foster, who helped fund, build, and operate the Barlow Road. His work, along with others', paved the way for the thousands of covered wagons that would arrive in the Willamette Valley in the 1850s. Foster made a 640-acre land claim at Eagle Creek, south of Canby, in the late 1840s. The farm he created there served as a welcome sight for pioneers coming down the last hill into the Willamette Valley and the start of a new life. Today the Foster Farm still plays host to many. The farm offers tours and hands-on pioneer activities for the whole family. Walk through beautiful gardens, smell the flowers on the oldest lilac in Oregon, and visit the 1883 farmhouse and 1860 hay barn. Open 11 a.m. to 4 p.m. Saturday in May, June, Sep, and Oct; 11 a.m. to 4 p.m. Tues through Sat from June 21 to August 30.

Rainbow Trout Farm. 52560 E Sylvan Dr.; (503) 622-5223; rainbowtroutfarm.com. Ten ponds brimming with rainbow trout await you and your fishing pole. Actually, you don't even need to bring a pole—the folks at Rainbow Trout Farm will provide one for you, as well as clean and even cook your fish. Enjoy 30 acres of forested beauty, too. Cost is per fish, ranging from $0.75 to $30. Open Mar and April, weekends only, 8 a.m. to dusk; May through October 15, 7 days a week, 8 a.m. to dusk.

Sandy Farm Loop. Try this driving tour of the Sandy area to find farms producing everything from lavender to alpacas, free range eggs to sheep yarn, artisan soaps to pumpkins. Pick up a brochure at the Sandy Area Chamber of Commerce and Visitors Center at 38963 Pioneer Blvd. in downtown Sandy, (503) 668-4006, or print the PDF version from their website, ci.sandy.or.us.

Sandy Historical Museum. 39345 Pioneer Blvd. (next to the City Plaza, which is next to City Hall); (503) 668-3378; sandyhistorical.org. The Sandy Historical Museum's location borders a segment of the famous Barlow Road, which was the last leg of the Oregon Trail that brought thousands of pioneers in covered wagons over the Cascade Mountains to Western Oregon from the mid 1840s until the 1870s. The museum displays maps and information about the Barlow Road and a historical display of the logging industry. Open Mon through Sat 10 a.m. to 4 p.m., Sun noon to 4 p.m. (subject to change).

Sandy Ridge Trail System. 11 miles east of Sandy on East Barlow Trail Road. This world-class mountain biking system has an international draw and over 15 miles of single track trails. Try out the beginner flow trails to narrow advanced technical trails for a day on two wheels with some great scenery.

where to eat

AntFarm Cafe & Bakery. 39140 Proctor Blvd.; (503) 668-9955; antfarm-international .com. An interesting medley of youth support and delicious food, AntFarm started as an organization to provide positive activities for local youth, which grew to include an organic garden and little restaurant at which to serve the food. The menu features diverse and inspired flavors in salads, sandwiches, soups, fresh pastries, gelato, and desserts. $

wy'east

The Multnomah Indian tribe called Mt. Hood Wy'east. In one version of the legend, two sons of the Great Spirit Sahale fell in love with the beautiful maiden Loowit. But she couldn't decide who to choose. The two braves, Wy'east and Klickitat, burned forests and villages in their battle over her. Sahale became enraged and destroyed the three lovers. He erected three mountain peaks to mark where each fell—Mt. St. Helens for Loowit, Mt. Hood for Wy'east, and Mount Adams for the mourning Klickitat.

Ivy Bear. 54735 US 26; (503) 208-9111; ivybear.com. This place is actually a historical landmark. The Ivy Bear was once a restaurant that was also home to a real live tamed bear that would open and drink bottles of Coca-Cola. Today it's a great pizza joint (no live animals necessary). $.

Joe's Donut Shop. 39230 Pioneer Blvd.; (503) 668-7215. What day trip isn't improved by a little sugar? At Joe's, a Sandy icon, fuel up on old-fashioned donuts in an old-fashioned atmosphere. Stop and grab a delectable donut—heck, why not get a dozen? This little shop with checkerboard paint will light up your whole day, and surely you're going to need snacks on the way home, too. Open daily 4 a.m. to 5 p.m. $.

Tollgate Inn. 38100 E US 26; (503) 668-8456; visittollgate.com. Serving a wide range of American-based comfort foods, Tollgate Inn is also a full-service, made-from-scratch bakery. Try their homemade pastries, breads, cakes, and pies. Open every day 6 a.m. to 10 p.m. $–$$.

where to stay

Sandy Salmon Bed and Breakfast Lodge. 61661 E US 26; (503) 622-6699; sandysalmon .com. Named for its location at the point where the Salmon and Sandy Rivers join, the Sandy Salmon is a gorgeous 6,000-square-foot log building and weekend retreat. Wildlife is frequently spotted, including chipmunks, squirrels, raccoons, deer, eagles, osprey, hawks, ducks, geese, herons, woodpeckers, and kingfishers. Fly-fishing opportunities are right out the front door, and simply relaxing in the fresh mountain air is always an option, too. $$$.

zigzag & welches

A string of unincorporated communities stretches between Sandy and Government Camp, the high point of the Mt. Hood pass on US 26 E. These little towns are locally called villages, and collectively known as the Villages at Mt. Hood.

As one drives up the mountain through the villages, the highway becomes increasingly narrow, the fir-dominated forest denser, and the side-of-the-road attractions more intriguing. Little log cabins and colorful pieced-together buildings—brightly painted and puffing smoke out of their oversized chimneys—house restaurants, bars, and lodging. Depending on the time of year, brilliant sunshine filters through leaves, a permeating fog hangs in the trees, or snow buries the rhododendron at roadside. All the while, Mt. Hood, Oregon's tallest mountain, beckons travelers along through a forested corridor.

Zigzag and Welches are two of the Villages at Mt. Hood, located adjacent to each other on US 26 E, the former Barlow Road. Zigzag was named after the nearby Zigzag River, a tributary of the Sandy River. Welches was named after Samuel Welch, a homesteader who settled near Welches Creek in 1882. Both offer respite and refueling along the way up the mountain, and Welches is home to one of Oregon's most popular resorts.

room 217

A year ago, I took my children to Timberline Lodge for the first time. They were blown away by the big old lodge, the steep slopes of Mt. Hood visible through the windows, the many different kinds of animals from eagles to lambs carved into newel posts, and the cozy room we secured for the night. But the exhibit of Timberline history in the lobby held their attention the most—particularly The Shining memorabilia. "Who is that?" my daughter asked, indicating that famous shot of Jack Nicholson looking positively insane. I gave them a very brief and downplayed narrative of the storyline, leaving out most of the blood, murder, and mayhem that ensues when a man goes crazy overwintering in a alpine hotel. I also left out the part that the man who kills his family was a frustrated writer. That might have been a little bit too close to home. Instead, I told my kids they couldn't see the film until they were 18, and scurried them along to the Ram's Head for some French fries.

getting there

Follow US 26 W from Sandy 17 miles to Zigzag, which is right on the highway. Welches is just south of Zigzag, less than a mile, also just off US 26 W.

where to go

Bald Mountain. E Lolo Pass Road, approximately 15 miles north out of Zigzag. Anybody can drive by Mt. Hood, but hiking to Bald Mountain provides a fabulous view of the mountain that not many people see. Even better—it's an easy hike. After the 0.8-mile amble, you hardly feel worthy of the acres of wildflowers and drop-dead-gorgeous view of Oregon's highest mountain that lays before you. Bring your out-of-town friends here to show them what the beauty of Oregon is all about, but don't forget to take a map. You wouldn't want to get your friends lost and become the cause of one of Mt. Hood's infamous recues.

Cascade Streamwatch/Wildwood Recreation Site. 65670 E US 26 E, Welches (on the south side of US 26 between mile posts 39 and 40); (503) 622-3696; blm.org/or. The Bureau of Land Management runs this park, trail, and recreation site, which invites visitors to explore natural streams and wetlands from boardwalks and interpretive trails. Still not sure what the difference is between a salmon and a steelhead? See young examples of both fish through a unique underwater fish-viewing chamber in a stream. Itching to get your toes wet? Wade the waters of the wild and scenic Salmon River. The site is a day-use area and home to family picnic units, several group shelters, playing fields, and access to the Salmon

Huckleberry Wilderness. Park open approximately Mar through Nov (exact dates change every year); $5 per passenger car.

Zigzag Ranger Station. 70220 E Hwy. 26, Zigzag; (503) 622-3191. On the National Register of Historic Places since 1986, 19 of 20 buildings at this forest service compound are historically significant. Many of the buildings were constructed by the Civilian Conservation Corps in the 1930s and 1940s, when the slopes of Mt. Hood were much more remote than they are today. The Forest Service still uses the ranger station as the Zigzag Ranger District headquarters. Also on the grounds you'll find the Wy'East Rhododendron Gardens. Conceived in 1952 as a roadside beautification project, the gardens contain more than 50 types of gorgeous rhododendron plants and many shrubs and trees, including the rare dawn redwood. The grounds are open year-round for self-guided tours. A garden map is available at the Zigzag district office.

where to eat

Altitude Restaurant. The Resort at the Mountain, 68010 E Fairway Ave., Welches; (503) 622-2214; altituderestaurant.com. If you're after swanky upscale dining outside of the city, Altitude is your place. Fresh farm-to-table cuisine with Northwest flair served in a non-stuffy environment is this restaurant's specialty. With 100 wine varietals and a full bar with innovative cocktail menu, Altitude is a great place just to go and have a drink, as well. Open daily for breakfast, lunch, and dinner. $$–$$$.

Rendezvous. 67149 E US 26, Welches; (503) 622-6837; rendezvousgrill.net. Chef/co-owner Kathryn Bliss designs innovative, seasonal menus using many local products, including chanterelle mushrooms and huckleberries. The Rendezvous has developed a reputation for devastating desserts, all prepared freshly in-house. Open daily for lunch and dinner. $$$.

Skyway Bar and Grill. 71545 E US 26, Zigzag; (503) 622-3775; skywaybarandgrill.com. The Skyway looks from the outside as if it's holding its own contest for bold design, and winning. The bright red building with blue accents and a gigantic "Enter" sign will surely catch your attention. Inside, a roadhouse-style interior is home to classic American barbeque food with an Oregon spin. Service and atmosphere are friendly, and live music, karaoke, pool, horseshoes, and a campfire out back make things even more fun. Open Thurs through Sun, dinner only. $–$$.

The Zigzag Inn. 70162 E US 26, Zigzag; (503) 622-4779; zigzaginn.com. The historic Zigzag Inn was built of hand-cut logs in the late 1920s by William John "Bill" Lenz, who also was responsible for many other notable structures in the area. The inn has pleased guests as a family-run restaurant ever since, offering casual, affordable family dining in a lodge-like atmosphere with authentic touches like antler chandeliers. Open 7 days a week for breakfast, lunch, and dinner (call for seasonal hours). $–$$.

where to stay

The Cabins Creekside at Welches. 25086 E Welches Rd., Welches; (503) 622-4275; mthoodcabins.com. These creek-side cabins with vaulted wood ceilings are a cozy place to stay for up to 4 people. Hot tub spa sits over the creek and offers a spectacular view of the forest. $$.

Mt. Hood Vacation Rentals. 67898 E US 26, Welches; (888) 424-9168; mthoodrentals .com. A variety of cozy cabins, romantic cottages, spacious lodges, and beautiful chalets in view, riverfront, and secluded settings. $$.

The Resort at The Mountain. 68010 E Fairway Ave., Welches; (503) 622-3101; theresort .com. Luxury tucked away amongst rural mountain towns is this full resort with golfing, spa, restaurants, and more. There are 157 guest rooms, suites, and villas on 300 acres of evergreen forest and lush mountain flora. $–$$$.

government camp

Government Camp was given its name by settlers traveling the Barlow Road, who discovered several wagons at the location, abandoned by the Regiment of Mounted Riflemen. Today the unincorporated community thrives by way of its location on the south slope on Mt. Hood, where it serves as base camp for a wide range of outdoor activities and adventures. Hikers, mountain bikers, skiers, climbers, campers, birders, snowboarders, and tourists come to Government Camp year-round.

At an elevation of 4,000 feet and with an average snowfall close to 300 inches, Government Camp is as lovely as it is remote and alpine. It's also an old-school skiers and new-school snowboarders kind of hangout, with its own rugged culture.

getting there

From Zigzag, Government Camp is 10 miles east directly on US 26 W.

where to go

Mt. Hood Adventure. 88335 E Government Camp Loop; (503) 715-2175; mthood adventure.com. This purveyor of recreation tours, outfitting, and rentals truly provides every adventure possible in the Mt. Hood area. Whether you are set on trying your hand at rock climbing or bird watching, kayaking or inner-tubing, hiking or sleigh rides, moonlit snowshoeing or snowmobiling, these folks can hook you up. Prices vary.

Mt. Hood Cultural Center and Museum. 88900 E US 26; (503) 272-3301; mthood museum.org. Six galleries interpret natural history, fine arts, the evolution of skiing on Mt. Hood, mountain climbing, and the Forest Service and Mt. Hood. Located on the old Barlow

picture perfect

Trillium Lake is the quintessential alpine lake—crystal blue water, enchanting for-ested perimeter, incredible volcanic peak as backdrop—which is probably why it's been photographed so very much. Even if you've never been here, you've likely seen the lake on a postcard. Trillium Lake is popular for fishing and picnicking, but our family memory of Trillium is of one day when my daughters were little, and spent an entire afternoon playing in the mud. The grown-ups weren't so interested in the mud, but with Mt. Hood to gaze upon and the sun overhead on a leisurely summer day, no one was complaining. Three miles past Government Camp, take a right off US 26 onto Trillium Lake Road. There is also a campground here. In the winter, a popular cross-country ski and snowshoe trail passes through here. Just don't forget the camera.

Road. Museum bookstore, art sales gallery, visitor information services, and Internet access on-site. Open daily 9 a.m. to 5 p.m., except holidays. Free.

Mt. Hood Skibowl Summer Adventure Park & Alpine Slide. 87000 E US 26; (503) 222-BOWL; skibowl.com. During winter months, take the kids to the slopes of Portland's closest ski resort, which boasts more night skiing than any other resort in the country, a nearby tubing hill, and hundreds of miles of family-friendly cross-country Nordic trails in the Mt. Hood National Forest. Relatively new are a Snow Tube and Adventure Park with some major attractions, including a 2-acre adult and kiddy snowmobile track and cosmic tubing, which combines lights and music to create a party on the snow. When the snow melts, Skibowl turns into a Summer Adventure Park with more than 20 attractions including a half-mile dual alpine slide, mountain bike park with more than 40 miles of trails, bike rentals and tours, automated batting cages, disc golf, ziplining, 18-hole mini golf, and horseback riding. Prices vary.

where to eat

Charlie's Mountain View. Government Camp Loop Rd.; (503) 272-3333; charliesmountain view.com. Here's where to find an old-school Government Camp experience. Classic ski town cuisine meets fresh produce and high-quality meats at Charlie's, where après-ski means an Original Mountain cheeseburger, waffle fries, prime rib, or a Caesar salad. Char-lie's is known for nightlife and offers live music on weekends. Extensive beer and wine list, too. $–$$.

Glacier Haus Bistro. 88817 E Government Camp Loop Rd.; (503) 272-3471; glacierhaus
.com. Homemade sandwiches, salads, and pizzas using fresh, quality ingredients served
in an old country store. Dinners feature classic European dishes including wiener schnitzel,
sauerbraten, Hungarian beef goulash, and other specialties. $–$$.

Mt. Hood Brewing Co. 87304 E Government Camp Loop Rd.; (503) 272-3172; mthood
brewing.com. "A brewery with an altitude." The menu offers such tasty treats as deviled
eggs, poutine, and Oregon leg of lamb. The brewers believe in brewing small handcrafted
batches of beer, sold for consumption close to the source. Because the source is beautiful
Mt. Hood, all the better for you. $–$$.

where to stay

Collins Lake Resort. 88149 E Creek Ridge Rd.; (503) 928-3498; collinslakeresort.com.
The comfort and luxury of a small resort in the heart of ski paradise, Collins Lake Resort
offers chalets with 2 to 3 bedrooms, 2.5 baths, well-equipped gas kitchens, and an open
great room with a stone fireplace. Many units also have gas barbecues on the private outdoor deck. Chalets have a mountain view, creek view, or forest view, each with tall windows
to allow you to take advantage of beautiful views. $$$.

Huckleberry Inn. 88611 E Government Camp Loop Rd.; (503) 272-3325; huckleberry-inn
.com. Huckleberry Inn offers easy access to ski areas and cross-country paths; and in the
summer, hiking trails and mountain lakes. Sixteen lodging rooms as well as dorm-style
facilities for ski or tour groups make this a convenient place to stay; the steakhouse (open
during the holiday week and ski season weekends) and the 24-hour family-style restaurant
are very popular. Cafe: $. Steakhouse: $$. Lodging: $–$$.

Timberline Lodge. 27500 E Timberline Rd.; (503) 231-7979; timberlinelodge.com. Mt.
Hood's Timberline Lodge, which sits at an elevation of 6,000 feet on the flanks of Mt. Hood,
is legendary. The massive, imposing wood structure was built in 1937 and immediately
became a Pacific Northwest icon. Even if you've somehow missed hearing about Timberline
or seeing a picture, you'll still recognize the exterior if you've seen the movie *The Shining*.
Don't worry—the inside isn't haunted by the spirit of Jack Nicholson's character, Jack Tor-
rance, a troubled writer who snaps during a winter at an isolated hotel. Your stay promises
to be much more pleasant. The National Historic Landmark is warm and spacious, with a
stone and wood interior that's steeped in rich Pacific Northwest history. From the Ram's
Head Bar, watch skiers take to the slopes and climbers set out for the summit—Mt. Hood
is one of the most popular mountains to climb in the Pacific Northwest. The rooms can be
small but have been renovated and are charming. You don't need to be a guest to enjoy
Timberline—45-minute tours are offered by US Forest Service rangers for free and available
to everyone. Call for seasonal tour hours. Dining: $–$$$. Lodging: $$–$$$.

day trip 02

southeast

columbia river basalt country:
maupin

maupin

Maupin is a little outpost in the rolling high desert hills of the lower Columbia River basin that might have been left to a few lonely ranchers if it weren't for the lively river that flows through town. The section of the Deschutes River that passes through here is one of the most popular waterways in the state of Oregon for rafters and kayakers. The climate, access to great rapids, and predictable water flows make the Deschutes ideal for river rats, and thousands flock here each summer to get a taste of Boxcar and Elevator rapids. Beginning in May and continuing through the warmer months, this place bustles with activity.

In the winter, it's pretty quiet around here. But the ranchers are still around. In fact, many of the ranches in these parts have been worked by the same family for generations. If there is one thing anyone who has ever run or worked a ranch knows, it's that farm country might be quiet, but it is never boring. Nor is it unattractive. The skies are wide open and blue here most of the year, and the rolling sage and rabbit brush plains allow for picturesque and sweeping views.

The weather is nice, too. A little known secret about this part of the state is that when it's raining in Portland, it's often sunny and hot in Maupin. Because of the high desert weather in Maupin, summers start earlier and end later. The busiest time of the year for rafting is July and August, but savvy river rats know that the best time of year to go rafting is September and October. During the fall, there are fewer folks on the river and the experience with the environment and the guide is much more personal.

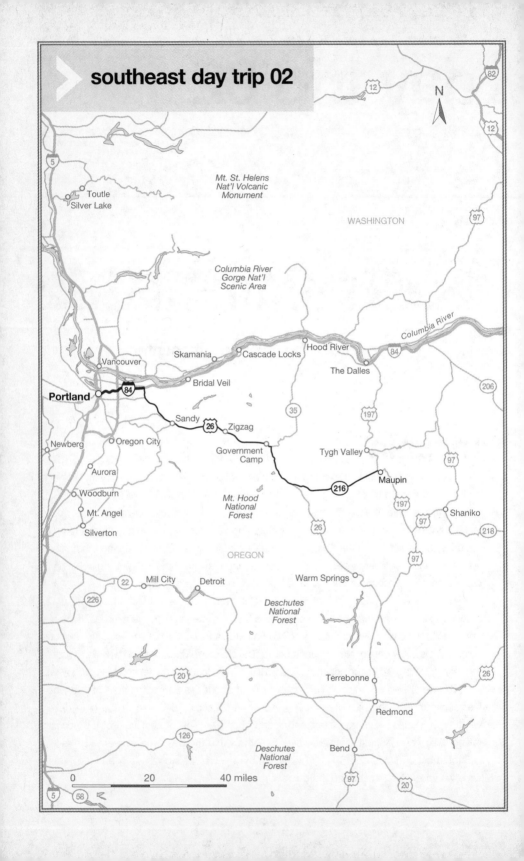

N

82

12

12

5

Toutle
Silver Lake

Mt. St. Helens
Nat'l Volcanic
Monument

WASHINGTON

97

Columbia River
Gorge Nat'l
Scenic Area

Columbia River

Skamania   Cascade Locks   Hood River

Vancouver   84

The Dalles   206

Bridal Veil

Portland   84

Sandy   197

26 Zigzag

Newberg   Oregon City   35

Government
Camp   Tygh Valley   97

Aurora   216   Maupin

Woodburn

Mt. Angel   Mt. Hood
National
Forest   26   197   Shaniko   97

Silverton   218

OREGON   97

Mill City   Detroit   Warm Springs   97

22

226   Deschutes
National
Forest

20   Terrebonne   26

126   Redmond

Deschutes
National
Forest   Bend

5   58   0   20   40 miles   97   20

Some of the locations in this day trip are located (as noted) in Tygh Valley, a little town in a gorgeous valley just 10 miles north of Maupin on US 197. Climb out of the Deschutes River canyon through wheat fields to this forested, mountainous community.

getting there

Take I-84 E out of Portland to the Kane Road exit, exit 17, 257th Drive. Follow 257th and signs for US 26 E. Drive 55 miles on US 26 E. Turn left onto OR 216 E. Drive 26 miles. Turn right onto US 197/The Dalles-California Highway. Drive 3 miles to Maupin.

where to go

Rafting. Whitewater rafting can be a very awakening experience, placing a person in a vulnerable state and allowing for an awesome adrenaline rush. The Deschutes River attracts hundreds of thousands of people in search of this experience from all over the country and beyond each year.

The Deschutes River originates high in the Cascade Mountains, south of Maupin 100 miles. The river carves its path through 250 miles of high desert before flowing into the Columbia River to the north. The section of the Deschutes River known as the Lower Deschutes is the 100-mile section from Pelton Dam (near Lake Billy Chinook) to the mouth of the Deschutes. The lower river offers a beautiful desert canyon filled with sagebrush, osprey, incredible basalt rock formations, and plenty of exciting rapids.

Rafting season takes off in late May/early June and continues until October. The most common raft trip is the day trip, a 13-mile stretch from Harpham Flat to Sandy Beach. This trip takes about 3.5 hours (or longer if you pull over to swim, have lunch, and explore river rock slides). Floaters on this stretch of the river will experience Class III and IV rapids. Several companies exist to get tourists out on the water. Some only offer guided trips and others offer do-it-yourself trips. The Deschutes River is relatively easy to raft or kayak if one isn't an expert, but a guide is always a good way to go if you've never rafted before. Guided day trips typically run about $75 to $95 per person.

Here are a few outfitters and guide services to help you experience the Deschutes:

Deschutes River Adventures. 602 Deschutes Ave.; (541) 395-2238; 800-rafting .com. Deschutes River Adventures is one of the pioneer raft shops in Maupin, launched 30 years ago to rent rafts to people coming over for day trips from Portland. DRA offers guided day trips, as well as day and overnight do-it-yourself raft rentals (with no guide).

Deschutes U-Boat. 501 Hwy. 197 S; (541) 395-2503; deschutesuboat.com. This is another long-time family-run raft business that has been in Maupin since the rafting phenomenon began. Deschutes U-Boat offers raft and kayak rentals and guided day trips.

River Drifters. 405 Deschutes Ave.; (800) 972-0430; riverdrifters.net. River Drifters offers a number of trips on the Lower Deschutes, from half-day journeys to 5-day vacations. One of the more popular trips is the full-day trip, which covers more than 14 river miles and takes between 5 and 6 hours to complete.

Sage Canyon Raft Company. 502 Deschutes Ave.; (800) 538-RAFT; sagecanyon riverco.com. Sage Canyon offers the regular gamut of Deschutes trips—half-day, full-day, etc. This outfitter is particularly good for overnight rafting trips. Trips can be anywhere from 2 nights to 5 nights, and include food, site preparation, river history, and fishing guiding along the way. Overnight trips run $250 to $375 per person.

Fishing. The Deschutes River is as rewarding for fishing as it is for whitewater rafting and kayaking. Salmon and steelhead have always been a huge life source for Maupin and South Wasco County residents. Salmon runs hit in the spring and fall, and attract eager fishermen ready to test their skill and luck. With a limit of 2 salmon per day, a fortuitous fisherman can go home with 30 pounds of fish and feed a lot of happy friends and family. The steelhead run hits September to November, also attracting droves of people. Both fly and spinner fishing are world class on the Deschutes River.

Deschutes Angler. 504 Deschutes Ave.; (541) 395-0995; deschutesangler.com. This shop and guide service provides fly-fishing retail products and services, Deschutes River fishing trips, and private lake guided fly-fishing trips.

Deschutes Canyon Fly Shop. 599 S Hwy. 197; (541) 395-2565; flyfishing deschutes.com. Since 1985, the folks at Deschutes Canyon Fly Shop have aimed to provide the best products, guided trips, and accurate information about river and fishing conditions possible. Customized fly-fishing guided services are available to help you decipher the river, improve technique, and increase effective fishing time. Deschutes Canyon has a private trophy lake, too. Guided trips run $250 to $595. Call for details.

Hunting. While not for everyone, hunting has a long history in this region and continues to be a very popular and productive activity in the Maupin and Tygh Valley area. Upland bird hunting season begins in the fall and runs through January. Deer, elk, antelope, bighorn sheep, bear, and bird are just some of the game available for tag holders in this area. While hunters need not employ a guide, it is crucial to understand the regulations and safety requirements of hunting. Contact the Oregon Department of Fish and Wildlife, dfw.state.or .us, or hire one of these guides for your hunting adventure:

River Runner Outfitters. (541) 978-0152; fishdeschutes.com. These guides specialize in upland bird hunts. Or try a "cast and blast"—a local's favorite that involves hiking the canyon for wild chukar and walking the river's banks for pheasant, intermingled with fishing the river.

White River Hunt Club. 84060 Fred Ashley Rd., Tygh Valley; (541) 483-2115; whiteriverhunt.com. This family-owned ranch consists of more than 1,200 acres of varying terrain on which to hunt. More than 3 miles of White River frontage make this place very beautiful, as well.

where to eat

Anglers Restaurant and Lounge. 34 N Mariposa Dr., Tygh Valley; (541) 544-2299; anglersrestaurantandlounge.com. Comfort food and drink are served here alongside spectacular views of Mt. Hood and Pine Hollow Reservoir. Steak, seafood, pasta, pizza, and nightly specials keep the crowds happy, and lunch boxes to go are available for fishermen. There's nothing too fancy about Anglers—just homestyle food and a great Western bar experience. Open for breakfast, lunch, and dinner 7 days a week. $.

The Rainbow Tavern. 411 Deschutes Ave.; (541) 395-2497. The Rainbow, or "The Bow," as locals call it, is a Maupin icon. If you are in the mood for cheap drinks, a juke box, Hamm's on tap, a dance floor, pool tables, and real-life cowboy sightings, this is your spot. And anyway, it's really the only spot to go for any sort of nightlife in Maupin. This authentic cowboy bar offers up live music in the summer every Fri and Sat night. Weekends are usually packed during the summer, but with a stimulating mix of folks from guides to tourists to locals to rafters. Homestyle country food is at the ready. The Bow is not swanky but it can be a whole lot of fun. $$.

Sportsman's Pub and Grub. 56826 Wamic Market Rd., Tygh Valley; (541) 544-3011. Authentic cowboy bars are a dime a dozen around here, apparently. This one, past Tygh Valley on OR 48/Wamic Market Road, offers a full-service bar, a pool table, and all Oregon Lottery games. If you like to sing, come here for karaoke every Fri and Sat night starting at 8 p.m. The Sportsman's Pub and Grub also offers breakfast, lunch, dinner, pizza, catering, and orders to go. $–$$.

where to stay

Camping. Maupin is the sort of place that simply calls out for camping. There's nothing much better than hearing the river roll by as you gaze into a sky full of stars and stay up late around a campfire in the high desert. Here are a few options:

BLM. (503) 808-6002; blm.gov/or. The Bureau of Land Management offers several first-come, first-served camp sites along the Deschutes River in the Maupin area. Oasis, Blue Hole, and Oak Springs are a few popular sites. There are several more, too; see the web for details. Prices range from $8 to $35.

Hunt Park. 81849 Fairgrounds Rd., Tygh Valley; (541) 483-2288. Near the fairgrounds, this park can accommodate up to 1,000 overnight campers. The park has 120 RV hookups with power, water, high-speed Internet, and a shared dump station. Tent campers can choose from multiple camping locations with convenient bathrooms and showers. Sites are $15 to $20. $.

Maupin City Park. 206 Bakeoven Rd. (541) 395-2252; cityofmaupin.com. Pitch a tent or park an RV right in town. On-site amenities include restrooms with showers, full hookups for RV sites, an on-site park supervisor, free Wi-Fi, and a community building available to rent with a kitchen. Make a reservation in advance if you'd like. Sites cost $15 to $35. $.

Imperial River Company. 304 Bakeoven Rd.; (800) 395-3903; deschutesriver.com. Located right on the Deschutes River, the Imperial River Company is arguably the most luxurious lodging in Maupin. There are 25 Oregon history-themed guest rooms, each with scenic views of the river, that provide a comfortable and interesting place to lay your head. Choose a river-view room with a private balcony and a jet tub, or take a ground-level room for easy access to and from the Deschutes. Many rooms have private decks; the lodge lobby has a communal fireplace to hunker near. The restaurant is a popular spot, too. The dining room provides delicious and hearty meals like fresh-cut steak and baby back ribs. Their all-natural, range-grown Angus beef comes from the Imperial Stock Ranch, nearby in Shaniko. Imperial River Company also organizes rafting, hunting, and fishing trips for guests. $–$$.

buckin' broncos

There are rodeos, and then there are authentic, down-home, small-town, truly Western rodeos. The Wasco County Fair and Rodeo is one of the latter. Held the third weekend in August in Tygh Valley, this event is an honest hometown rodeo complete with clowns, cows, and plenty of action. The fair offers up all that county fairs should—4-H exhibits, livestock, carnival rides, entertainment, and food. The corollary event—a demolition derby—adds to the wild and crazy good times. The entire affair is a highlight of the year in this part of the state, for locals and tourists alike. Bring some boots because there are fences to hop and cow pies to traverse. Don't miss the funnel cakes—they are beyond compare. See wascofair.com or call (541) 483-2288; 81849 Fairgrounds Rd. in Tygh Valley.

The Oasis Resort. 609 US 197 S; (541) 395-2611; deschutesriveroasis.com. The Oasis Resort offers overnight lodging, Deschutes River fly-fishing for trout and steelhead, and cozy, comfortable accommodations. Private cottages are circled around a lush, green lawn and are very affordable to rent. The restaurant serves up delicious breakfast, lunch, and dinner. Most famous for old-fashioned, hard ice cream milk shakes, terrific burgers, and ribs, the Oasis Cafe offers a diverse menu ranging from large farm-style breakfasts to full dinners. An extensive selection of microbrews and Northwest wines accents your meal. Browse the historic photos and memorabilia (including Mike's "world's smallest fly-fishing museum") and see why the Oasis has been the favorite of fly-fishers since 1928. A fly-fishing package offers lodging, food, and a guided fishing trip. The Oasis also runs a campground, just 1/8 mile upriver, with grassy tent and RV spaces. $.

The River Run Lodge. 1210 Hartman Ave.; (877) 335-8867; riverrunlodge.net. This casual, country-style lodge offers 6 simply decorated rooms, each with fish-printed bedspreads, wall art, and decor. Located in the heart of Maupin's recreation district, River Run Lodge offers easy access to the river, restaurants, and other local amenities. $.

worth more time

Shaniko. At its heyday, the city of Shaniko was a transportation hub and considered the "Wool Capital of the World." Located at the center of 20,000 square miles of wool, wheat, cattle, and sheep production, 150 years ago Shaniko was a boom town. Today, it's practically a ghost town. The last census turned up a population of fewer than 30 people. But that doesn't mean there isn't anything to see here. Preservation of this historic town has been spearheaded by investments from Robert B. Pamplin Jr., a businessman and founder of the *Portland Tribune* and Columbia Empire Farms. The **Shaniko Historic District** includes the **Shaniko Schoolhouse,** the **Shaniko Jailhouse,** and the **Shaniko Historic Center,** all of which have been restored. Most folks just drive through Shaniko these days, but it's worth getting out and taking a stroll around, looking at the old buildings and pondering change.

Nearby, the **Imperial Stock Ranch Headquarters** (imperialstockranch.com/ranch /history) has been a working ranch since before 1900. The owners have taken pains to preserve the ranch and sheep ranching in innovative ways; in 2014, wool from their sheep was used in US Olympic team sweaters.

To reach Shaniko from Maupin, head south 21 miles on US 197 to the intersection with US 97. Turn left onto US 97 and continue another 12 miles to Shaniko.

day trip 03

southeast

crags & ag:
terrebonne

terrebonne

Terrebonne is hard to define. At first glance the area north of Redmond looks like just another stretch of arid high desert, a blip on the map in a sea of sagebrush. But there's more going on here than meets the eye. Terrebonne serves as paradise on earth to an eclectic group of visitors and residents, from world-class athletes to ranchers to wealthy retirees to vintners.

Some are drawn to the incredible rock formation Smith Rock, which is hard to miss even from the highway. Some come for the good soil. All, probably, love the killer views of the Cascade Range. There's something special about the climate here, too. During the time of the year when the rest of Central Oregon has frost nipping at its heels and is getting snowed upon, Terrebonne seems to stay a little bit warmer and drier. On those wet, cold spring days when everyone is dying to dry out and warm up, Smith Rock is a great place to be.

Get off the highway and you'll see Terrebonne's diversity and charms. Next to brand new multimillion-dollar homes are century-old farms selling pumpkins and free-range beef. Socioeconomic and cultural differences abound, but everyone who lives and visits here agrees that Terrebonne (which means "good earth" in French) is a little slice of heaven.

Terrebonne is still rural, and you won't find many services, but there are a few gems tucked away here and there.

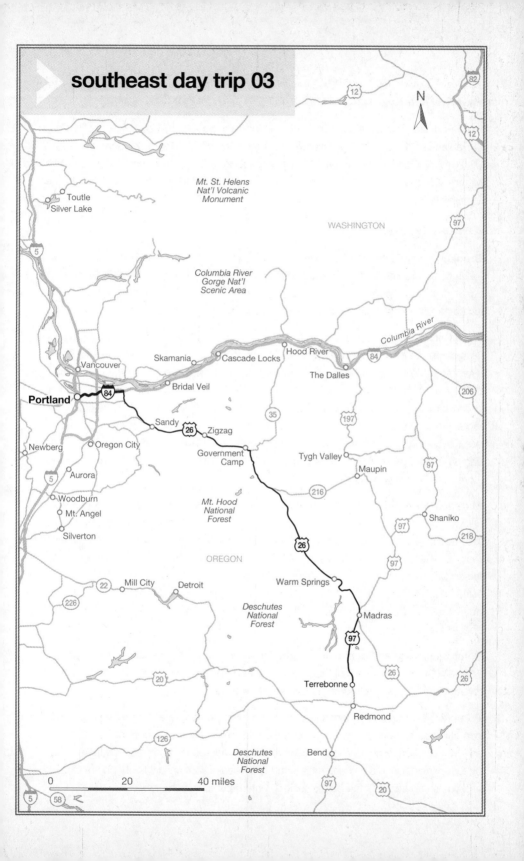

getting there

From Portland, Terrebonne is beyond Mt. Hood to the south and east. Take I-894 E out of Portland to the 257th Drive exit (exit number 17/Kane Road). Follow signs for OR 26/ US 26 E/Mt. Hood. Continue past Mt Hood on US 26 until it merges with OR 97/US 97 at Madras, 63 miles south and east of Government Camp. Continue south on US 97 another 21 miles to Terrebonne.

where to go

Crooked River Ranch Golf Course. 5195 Club House Rd.; (800) 833-6343; crookedriver ranch.com. The fifth hole at this fabulous golf course has been recognized as the most beautiful golf hole in Oregon. There are fabulous canyon, rimrock, mountain, and river views, not to mention the wildlife. You'll have a hard time keeping your eye on the ball.

Lake Billy Chinook. Located about 20 miles west of Culver off of the Culver Highway; lakebillychinook.com. Lake Billy Chinook is a spectacular lake created by the nexus of three rivers—the Metolius, the Deschutes, and the Crooked—put in place by the Round Butte Dam. With 72 miles of shoreline and 6 square miles of water, the lake is a popular desti-nation for many recreational activities, including fishing, hiking, waterskiing, camping, and more. For the truly passionate, rent a houseboat and spend several days on the lake. Day-use permits are required and can be purchased at the Cove Palisades State Park office, campground registration booths (summer only), and local sporting goods and convenience stores. See website for details.

Maragas Winery. 15523 SW US 97, Culver; (541) 546-5464; maragaswinery.com. People said you couldn't grow wine grapes in Central Oregon. Doug Maragas proved them wrong. This boutique winery produces hearty Bordeaux-style reds and southern European-style muscats, German-style pinot gris, and a new-age style of chardonnay. Since planting Jef-ferson County's first vineyard in 2007, the Maragas family has hosted several events a year in their big red barn, celebrating good wine and good people. Tours, tasting, and patio open Tues or Wed through Sun 11 a.m. to 5 p.m. depending on season. See website for special events.

Peter Skene Ogden Scenic Viewpoint. Three miles north of Terrebonne on US 97; (800) 551-6949. If you enjoy vertical basalt cliffs and scenic river canyons, the Ogden Wayside is for you. The park is perched at the top of a striking canyon. Bring a camera!

Pumpkin Patches. Terrebonne is one of the most amazing places in Oregon to visit a pumpkin patch, if only for the views and the sun. These two farms both have Smith Rock as epic backdrop, and there's something about the wide-open sky that makes the light here picture-perfect. Bring a camera—this is the spot to take your annual family photo. Oh, yes, and you surely can pick the perfect jack-o'-lantern pumpkin here, too.

Central Oregon Pumpkin Co. 1250 NE Wilcox Ave.; (541) 504-1414; themaize .com. Pumpkin patch and so much more, including zoo rides, a pumpkin cannon, hay fort, harvest market, wagon rides, pumpkin launcher, and more. The best part is "the maize"—a maze made of corn that's a different design every year. Open 7 days a week in Oct. Free entry; fees for maize and pumpkin purchase.

DD Ranch. 3836 NE Smith Rock Way; (541) 548-1432. The DD Ranch is a family-owned venture. What was all about the pumpkins has expanded over the years. You can still come here for a fabulous pumpkin patch outing every October—there's a petting zoo, hayrides, and a harvest market, as well as rows and rows of the big round gourds we love to carve. But the DD has started hosting a Christmas event, too, with trees for sale and Santa hanging around offering up "ho ho hos." The DD is also a great place to buy free-range, hormone-free pork and beef, and they have a community-supported-agriculture produce-buying program, too. Free entry; fees for pumpkins and some activities. Open the entire month of Oct; call for seasonal hours.

Rockhard/Juniper Junction. 9297 NE Crooked River Dr.; (541) 548-4786. Only in Terrebonne would climbing and mountaineering equipment coexist with world-famous fresh wild huckleberry ice cream in a ramshackle wood-shingled building. But don't miss the chance to stop in—ice cream this good is never a bad idea, even if it's 10 a.m. Hours vary seasonally; even if it looks closed, give a knock.

Smith Rock State Park. 9241 NE Crooked River Dr. (off US 97, 14 miles south of Warm Springs); (800) 551-6949; oregonstateparks.org. Smith Rock is something everyone should witness at least once. It's true that you can see the wondrous multicolored majesty of welded tuff volcanic rock from US 97, but Smith Rock is best experienced close up. Most people come here for the rock climbing, which is world famous. There are hundreds of

the nose knows

Madras, the community that sits between Warm Springs and Terrebonne, is one of the richest agricultural areas east of the Cascade Range in Oregon. Jefferson County leads the world in carrot seed production, and other commercial crops include vegetable, grass, and flower seeds; garlic; mint; and sugar beets. As you pass through this part of the state, roll down your window—often the smell of garlic or mint is in the air, and guessing which can be a fun road trip game. In the spring, keep an eye out for wild asparagus growing in the roadside ditches. Fruit stands and roadside veggie vendors pop up seasonally, too.

routes, some that are extremely difficult, and climbers from practically everywhere on earth have been summoned here to prove their mettle. If you're a newbie, consider taking a private or group lesson with Chockstone Climbing Guides (541-318-7170; chockstoneclimbing .com) or First Ascent Climbing Services (541-318-7170; goclimbing.com). But, if scaling a rock wall is not your cup of tea, come to hike, picnic, view wildlife like deer, beavers, and eagles along the Crooked River, or summit the trail known as Misery Ridge. It's steep, but entirely walkable, requiring no ropes or any of the skill the rock climbers you'll see on the way need. At the top, take in a stunning view of the Cascade Range, the river below, and surrounding ranches and farms. It will blow your mind. Oregon State Parks charge a fee to park—purchase a day-use, 12- or 24-month pass.

where to eat

La Siesta Cafe and Cantina. 8320 N US 97; (541) 548-4848. Darn good Mexican food in a simple, homey establishment, with a motley collection of art on the walls and all the chips and salsa you can eat. The margaritas are dandy, and there are several local brews on tap, too. $.

Pump House Bar and Grill. 8320 US 97; (541) 548-4990. Traditional saloon with steaks, ribs, chicken fried steak, pasta, seafood, burgers, and more. Open for lunch and dinner 7 days a week. Live music some weekend nights. $–$$.

Terrebonne Depot. 400 NW Smith Rock Way; (541) 548-5030; terrebonnedepot.com. Constructed in 1911 for the Oregon Trunk Railroad, the Terrebonne Oregon Trunk Passenger Depot was left abandoned for much of the latter half of the 20th century. A total renovation in 2005 restored the historic structure and transformed it into a lovely restaurant serving steaks, pastas, pizza, sandwiches, and burgers. New American cuisine is prepared according to season and showcases the wonderful variety of flavors found in the Cascade region. The spacious, well-lit space includes a massive, elegant bar carved by local artisans from old-growth fir blocks that once supported the depot's floor. Outdoor seating puts you up close and personal with the trains that still pass by. Open Wed through Sun for lunch and dinner. $$.

where to stay

Sunview Motel and Resort. 5010 SW Clubhouse Rd.; (800) 282-0944; sunviewmoteland resort.com. About five miles northwest of Terrebonne is the Crooked River Golf Course, adjacent to which is this little motel. Clean, standard rooms have great views of the high desert landscape and the rimrock canyon of the Crooked River. There's a volleyball court, tetherball, and a horseshoe pit on site. A tennis court, basketball court, and free outdoor swimming pool are nearby. $–$$.

worth more time

The Warm Springs Reservation was established by the Treaty of 1855 on a small reserve of land in north-central Oregon where several tribes had lived for thousands of years. In 1937, the Wasco, Paiute, and Warm Springs Tribes organized as the Confederated Tribes of Warm Springs and became a sovereign, self-governing nation. **The Museum at Warm Springs** (541-553-3331; museumatwarmsprings.org) was created by the Tribes to preserve their traditions and to keep their legacy alive. Tribal-inspired architecture created this 25,000-square-foot, award-winning museum located along Shitike Creek. Explore traditional dwellings including a tule mat lodge, wickiup, and plankhouse that have been meticulously constructed to show life in this landscape long ago. There's a great basket collection, and many lovely beaded objects. You may listen to ceremonial songs and traditional languages, witness a Wasco wedding exchange, or watch yourself on camera as you try the hoop dance. Open from 9 a.m. to 5 p.m. daily from Mar to Nov; the museum is closed on Mon and Tues from Nov through Feb.

day trip 04

southeast

high & dry:
bend

bend

Bend is a bit of a stretch distance-wise as a day trip from Portland, but don't tell that to all of the people who day trip to this high desert town every year. The charms of Central Oregon are just too powerful to resist for many Portlanders, never mind the 3-hour drive each way. Wide open, sunshiny skies and unlimited recreational opportunities lure thousands of visitors to Bend each year, no matter how much time they can spare.

Bend was born a logging town over a century ago and remained small, rural, and fairly isolated until the 1990s. Then word got out. Oregon might be known for rain, but that weather phenomenon mostly stays clear of the state's "dry side"—the area east of the Cascade Range that includes Central Oregon. Bend gets about 12 inches of precipitation a year, compared to the nearly 40 annual inches that fall on Portland. Tourists and fans of Mt. Bachelor ski resort from around the Pacific Northwest had been hip to Bend's charisma for a long time, but about 15 years ago, word traveled to the rest of the nation. The population boomed. Culture and amenities multiplied. Bend was reborn as a classy, happening destination—which still offers a lion's share of the best recreational options in the state.

As a day tripper, your primary challenge will be figuring out what to do first. You'll have no shortage of options. World-class skiing, hiking, cycling, golf, fishing, mountaineering, paddling, shopping, dining, and festival-going are all at your fingertips, not to mention the

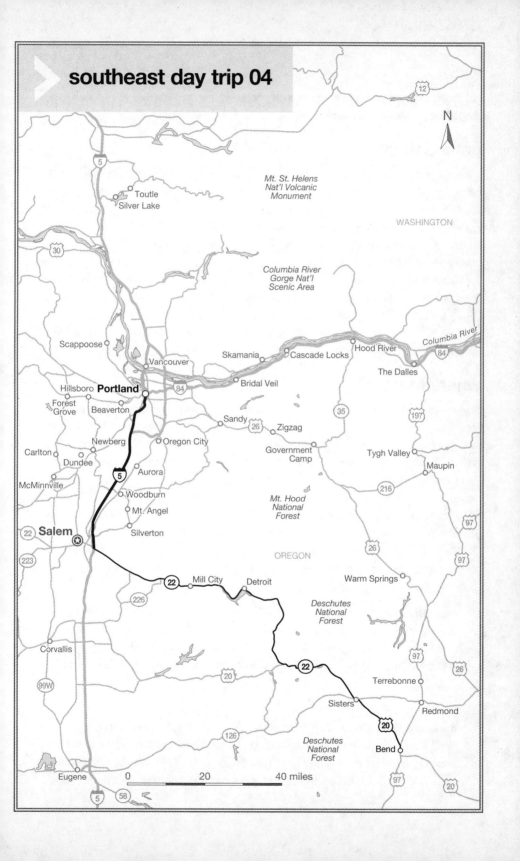

southeast day trip 04

N

Mt. St. Helens
Nat'l Volcanic
Monument

WASHINGTON

12

5

Toutle
Silver Lake

30

Columbia River
Gorge Nat'l
Scenic Area

Scappoose

Vancouver

Skamania   Cascade Locks   Hood River   Columbia River

84

The Dalles

Hillsboro   **Portland**

Forest
Grove   Beaverton

Bridal Veil

Sandy

35

197

84

Carlton

Newberg

Dundee

Oregon City

Zigzag

26

5

Aurora

Government
Camp

Tygh Valley

McMinnville

Woodburn

Maupin

Mt. Angel

216

Salem

22

Silverton

Mt. Hood
National
Forest

97

223

OREGON

26

Mill City

Detroit

Warm Springs

26

97

22

226

Deschutes
National
Forest

Corvallis

20

22

97

26

99W

Terrebonne

Sisters

Redmond

126

20

Deschutes
National
Forest

Bend

Eugene   0   20   40 miles

97

20

5   58

fact that Bend has become a world-famous craft brew mecca. Whatever you choose to do, chances are it will include beer.

getting there

There are two primary routes to choose from between Portland and Bend, and folks tend to be loyalists about which path is best. Either way you need to cross the Cascade Range— you can choose to do so via Mt. Hood and Blue Box pass or via Salem and the Santiam Pass. I personally prefer the latter, to avoid the suburbs of Gresham and busy ski traffic on Mt. Hood. In the winter, it's a good idea to check tripcheck.com to see if one route or the other is clearer of weather challenges.

From Portland via Salem, head south out of Portland on I-5. Just south of Salem, watch for the OR 22 exit, exit 253, towards Detroit Lake/Bend. Turn left (east) onto OR 22. OR 22 becomes North Santiam Highway. Continue to follow this route east until it merges into US 20 E. Travel through Sisters and another 20 miles to Bend. Total mileage from Portland is 175 miles.

where to go

Breweries. Bend is a craft brew–lovers' dream. In fact, while the microbrewery phenomenon didn't exactly begin here, it sure sunk its teeth in. Since Deschutes Brewery was founded in 1988, 18 more breweries have opened in Central Oregon, with more on the horizon. Beer and Bend are so intertwined that there's a popular activity in town, called the Bend Ale Trail. See visitbend.com for a map and passport that will guide you on a journey through Bend's breweries. (For extra credit, visit the breweries in Sisters, Sunriver, Prineville, and Redmond—whew!). Then return to the Visit Bend Welcome Center (917 NW Harriman St.) to receive a free silipint (a silicone pint glass for people on the go).

Or simply pick and choose from this partial list, no overachieving necessary. All but one of these establishments are also restaurants; each serves a variation on pub-style comfort food.

Bend Brewing Company. 1019 NW Brooks St.; (541) 383-1599; bendbrewing .com. Bend's second-oldest brewery and brewpub sits on the Deschutes River downtown and offers outdoor seating in the summertime. This is the only brewery in Central Oregon to have won Small Brewpub Champion of the Year at the World Beer Cup (2008). The beers here are little delicious award-winners. Brewery tours by appointment. Open daily for lunch and dinner.

Boneyard Beer Co. 37 NW Lake Place; (541) 323-2325; boneyardbeer.com. Bend's toughest brewery operates out of an old warehouse tucked away in a little neighborhood near downtown. Their facility only offers tastings and beer sales—no food. Still, Boneyard has nurtured a growing reputation for themselves as purveyors of great beer, and you'll see it on tap around the state. Open 11 a.m. to 6 p.m. 7 days a week.

Crux Fermentation Project. 50 SW Division St.; (541) 385-3333; cruxfermenta tion.com. Located in the center of Bend and drawing on the talent of longtime Deschutes brewer Larry Sidor, Crux offers tasty beers in a building that used to be an auto garage. Killer views of the Cascade Range inspired Crux's innovation on happy hour—"Sundowner," the hour following sunset, when beer and food specials are offered. Tours by appointment. Open daily for lunch and dinner.

Deschutes Brewery. Brewery: 901 SW Simpson Ave.; (541) 385-8606; Public House: 1044 Bond St.; deschutesbrewery.com. The granddaddy of Bend breweries distributes today all over the country, but the magic still happens here at the Brewery on Bend's west side. Tours are offered Mon through Sun at 1, 2, 3, and 4 p.m. and will leave you wiser and more appreciative of beer—especially after you've tried the free samples. There is also a tasting room here, open 7 days a week from noon to 5 p.m. The Public House and restaurant is located downtown and serves up all of Deschutes' beers as well as lots of food. Open daily for lunch and dinner.

Good Life Brewing Co. 70 SW Century Drive; (541) 728-0749; goodlifebrewing .com. Since opening in a warehouse in mid-June 2011, GoodLife Brewing Co. has become a neighborhood favorite, the cornerstone of the new Century Center complex on Bend's west side. It's also home to the Bend Cycle Pub—a multi-person pedal-powered beer tour on wheels. Open daily noon to 10 p.m.

McMenamins Old St. Francis School. 700 NW Bond St.; (541) 382-5174; mcmenamins.com. The McMenamin brothers strike again with this converted Catholic school in downtown Bend. The brewery is in the basement and sports some fun and funky murals on the walls and tanks. Beers on tap vary by season, but there's always something great flowing. Tours by appointment. Open daily for breakfast, lunch, and dinner.

Silver Moon Brewing. 24 NW Greenwood Ave.; (541) 388-8331; silvermoon brewing.com. Award-winning signature beers and seasonal specials are served at this brewpub and restaurant, also a popular spot for live music and entertainment. The decor here is eclectic, the vibe laid back and old school—play a game of pool or kick back in mismatched chairs and hang out as long as you like. Open 7 days a week for lunch and dinner.

10 Barrel Brewing Co. 1135 NW Galveston Ave.; (541) 678-5228; 10barrel .com. The 10 Barrel brewpub is the hip cool kid on the brewery scene, offering up really fabulous beers on Bend's west side. The outdoor fire pit is the center of the action summer or winter; indoors, imperial pints are served with pizza, burgers, and more. Open for lunch and dinner 7 days a week.

Worthy Brewing. 495 Bellevue Dr.; (541) 639-4776; worthybrewing.com. When Worthy Brewing opened in 2013 on Bend's east side, it did things a little bit differently from the start. The huge campus includes solar energy, a greenhouse in which to grow hops, bocce ball, space for live music and—oh yes—great food and beer. Open for lunch and dinner 7 days a week.

Deschutes River Trail. Bend Parks and Recreation District, 799 SW Columbia St.; (541) 389-7275; bendparksandrec.org. This trail is the crowning jewel in a local parks system that consists of dozens of gorgeous, well-planned parks. The River Trail consists of almost 19 miles of paved and dirt trail, and provides nearly uninterrupted access to the Deschutes River, which runs through the heart of Bend. Pick up a map at parks headquarters (address listed here) or simply head for the river, pick up the trail, and walk as far as you'd like.

Golf. Bend is home to more golf courses per capita than any other Oregon region. The good news is that many of them are open nearly all year. The bad news is that they aren't all open to the public. Here are three that are:

Rivers Edge Golf Course. 400 NW Pro Shop Dr.; (541) 389-2828; riverhouse.com.

Tetherow. 61240 Skyline Ranch Rd.; (541) 388-2582; tetherow.com.

Widgi Creek Golf Club. 18707 Century Dr.; (541) 382-4449; widgi.com.

The High Desert Museum. 59800 S US 97; (541) 382-4754; highdesertmuseum.org. Since it opened in 1982, the High Desert Museum has been introducing people to the history, natural history, and culture of the high desert region. This sprawling museum has exhibits indoors and out that include live animals throughout, from lizards to sturgeon, porcupines to burrowing owls, lynxes to black widow spiders. Exhibits interpret the history of the West, Native American culture, the forest, birds of prey, and more. There is a cafe and really fabulous gift shop, too. Open every day except Thanksgiving, Christmas, and New Year's Day. Open 9 a.m. to 5 p.m. May 1 through October 31; 10 a.m. to 4 p.m. daily, November 1 through April 30. Admission is $15 for adults, $12 for seniors, and $9 for youth, with discounts in the winter.

Mt. Bachelor. SW Century Drive, 21 miles west of Bend; (541) 382-2442; mtbachelor .com. Skiers, snowboarders, and Nordic skiers flock here each winter, but that's not the only reason to visit Central Oregon's most popular volcano. In the summer, lifts run to the summit and give an inimitable view of the Cascade Range and a bike park operates with 10 miles of trails. The Cascade Lakes Highway, also called SW Century Drive, along which Mt. Bachelor is located, is one of the most beautiful drives in the state and passes by a handful of alpine lakes, many of which have beaches and campgrounds; Elk Lake has a lodge and restaurant, too. In the winter, Century Drive closes just past Mt. Bachelor; stay at the mountain and enjoy 3,683 acres of ski-able terrain, 88 runs, and 56 kilometers of groomed Nordic trail, all covered in plenty of ski-able, board-able, sled-able snow.

Pilot Butte. OR 20/Greenwood Avenue just east of NE 12th Street. This cinder cone stands 500 feet over the middle of town and is equal parts landmark and destination. It served as a beacon in the high desert 100 to 200 years ago, guiding travelers working their way to Bend or further west. Today there is both a trail and a road to the top; millions of visitors ascend every year. From the top, the entire city of Bend is visible as well as many mountains in the Cascade Range. Fireworks are launched from the top each Fourth of July. The road closes seasonally, but the trail is always open. It's steep but worth the climb.

where to shop

Bend has two primary, distinct shopping districts, each with its own style and more shops than we can list here.

Downtown. (541) 788-3628; downtownbend.org. Bend's downtown has transformed in 20 years from quiet and sedated to booming and happening. All varieties of wonderful shopping opportunities are here, from fresh flowers to haute couture to antiques to books. Make sure to visit **Lulu's** (150 NW Minnesota Ave.) for fabulous women's clothing, **Dudley's** (135 NW Minnesota Ave.) for new and used books as well as coffee and snacks, **The Feather's Edge** (113 NW Minnesota Ave.) for outstanding gifts, **John Paul Design** (1006 NW Bond St.) for original world-class jewelry, and **Patagonia @ Bend** (1000 Wall St.) for fine outdoor clothing. The first Friday of each month, downtown hosts an art walk—the streets are packed with activity.

The Old Mill District. 520 SW Powerhouse Dr.; theoldmill.com. Formerly just what it sounds like—the site of Bend's original lumber mills—the Old Mill District is located on the Deschutes River and is a beautiful, upscale outdoor mall. There are many chain stores here as well as local shops and restaurants. The Gap and Banana Republic are here, and don't miss REI and Strictly Organic Coffee. A cinema and walking trail are here, too; across the river on a footbridge is the Les Schwab Amphitheater, which books great music acts all summer season. Minimum store hours for the Old Mill District are Mon through Sat 10 a.m. to 8 p.m. and Sun 11 a.m. to 6 p.m. Longer hours during the holidays.

where to eat

Anthony's Home Port. 475 SW Powerhouse Dr.; (541) 389-9998; anthonys.com. The menu here features delicious fresh Northwest seafood flown in directly from the ocean, but the real attraction is this restaurant's location. The spectacular view of the Deschutes River as well as Mt. Bachelor and the Three Sisters Mountains provides such a stunning backdrop you'll hardly care what you eat (and it's all fabulous anyway). Make a reservation for sunset;

> # festival heaven

One thing that Bend's population and culture boom spawned is a flurry of festivals. Between May and November, there's something fabulous happening every weekend—often more than one thing simultaneously; even the off-season is full of activity. The first Friday of every month brings a hoppin' art walk to downtown (downtownbend.org). In the summer, free concerts are held every Sunday afternoon at Les Schwab Amphitheater (theoldmill.com). There are children's festivals, hot air balloon festivals, cycling festivals, beer festivals, live music festivals, antiques festivals, car festivals, and Oktoberfests. My very favorite festival by far is the BendFilm Fest, held the second weekend of October each year. Four days of independent films, parties, workshops, lectures, and the camaraderie of festival become more than the sum of their parts. This event brings people together to talk about the things great films can urge us to consider—the mysteries and joys of life, pain and joy and happiness, and the ways we are all alike and yet unique. Like all forms of great art, independent films can make us see anew the beauty and connection that is around us already. See bendfilm.org for more information on the BendFilm Fest. For a complete listing of Bend's festivals, see visitbend.com.

in the summer, sit outdoors and watch the reflection off the river. Open for lunch and dinner 7 days a week; brunch on Sun. $$–$$$.

5 Fusion. 821 NW Wall St.; (541) 323-2328; 5fusion.com. 5 Fusion Chef Joe Kim was nominated in 2014 as Best Chef in the Northwest by the James Beard Foundation, for good reason. The sushi and Asian fusion entrees here are simply amazing. The modern hip ambience is great for date night or a casual evening at the bar (they have a wonderful happy hour). $$–$$$.

Hola! Old Mill District; (541) 647-2711; holabend.com. The very best Peruvian Mexican food you will eat, including ceviche, mole, chile relleno, and amazing seafood enchiladas, all with fabulous flavor and freshness. The full bar provides amazing margaritas, the space is colorful and vibrant, the service really friendly. This place gets the food right clear down to the desserts—the pièce de résistance is bananas flameadas, which consists of sliced bananas pan fried with butter, brown sugar, and cinnamon, fired up with rum, and served on top of vanilla ice cream. It's made right at your table. Open 7 days a week for lunch and dinner. $$.

Jackson's Corner. 845 NW Delaware Ave.; (541) 647-2198; jacksonscornerbend.com. This is the place to go if you want to feel like a local. This old market in a residential neighborhood near Bend's downtown does many things, and does them all well. There is a small deli and grocery section that stocks great beers, prepackaged foods, and a few staples. In the back, an espresso stand serves up truly excellent coffee all day. At the counter, order meals that defy expectations of counter service. The kitchen here produces excellent food, often prepared from local and organic products. Seating is casual and sometimes communal. There is some outside seating in the summer. Hang out here as long as you want—everyone feels at home at Jackson's Corner. Open 7 days a week for breakfast, lunch, and dinner. $–$$.

Joolz. 916 NW Wall St.; (541) 388-5094; joolzbend.com. "Where the mezza meets the mesa." Enjoy happy hour, a cozy nightcap, or late night snack at Joolz, Bend's sole Lebanese restaurant and one of the most charming dining spaces in town. The decor is a colorful blend of artistry and whimsy (with a large collection of hookahs) and the food and drinks are incredibly flavorful and inspired. Try the forbidden rice bowl—simple and delicious. $$.

The Lot. 745 NW Columbia St.; (541) 610-4969. Definitely the most innovative dining space to pop up in recent years, the Lot is a collection of food carts surrounding covered, heated seating and a taproom. Food choices range from Mexican to Hawaiian to Thai, and 16 taps offer the best in Bend's beer as well as selections from throughout the Northwest. Fire pits and heated concrete seats keep visitors warm all year. $.

Pine Tavern. 967 NW Brooks St.; (541) 382-5581; pinetavern.com. This restaurant has anchored downtown Bend on the Deschutes River since 1936. Known for the Ponderosa pine tree growing through the center of the dining room, sourdough scones with honey butter served before every meal, and the most picturesque patio in town, the Pine Tavern serves Pacific Northwest food like smoked salmon salad with pears and crumbled blue cheese and pork tenderloin. The food and service are simple, rooted in the past, and excellent. Open for lunch Mon through Sat and dinner 7 nights a week. $$.

Sparrow Bakery. 50 SE Scott St., #22; (541) 330-6321; thesparrowbakery.com. This little French bakery is a bit off the beaten path, but finding it will make your taste buds happy. The pastries here are divine—don't miss the Ocean Roll, which is like a cinnamon roll only much better, and the hand-folded croissants. Grilled sandwiches and salads are served at lunchtime, and often include local produce and products as ingredients. Open Tues through Sat 7 a.m. to 2 p.m. $.

Victorian Cafe. 1404 Northwest Galveston Ave.; (541) 382-6411. With something like 9 different kinds of eggs Benedict on the menu, the Victorian has earned itself the title of best Bend breakfast many times over. There's often a line outside this old house on Bend's west side, but the wait is made more tolerable by a fire pit and the availability of Bloody Marys. Beyond poached eggs topped with everything from smoked salmon to mangos, choose from pancakes, omelets, and all the usual breakfast fare. Lunch brings fabulous sandwiches and salads, but breakfast is served all day and is really how this place shines. The menu is pretty expensive, but it's worth it. In the summer, sit outside on the patio. $$.

Zydeco. 919 Bond St.; (541) 312-2899; zydecokitchen.com. Cajun cooking with a Pacific Northwest flair is served at this cool downtown restaurant. The scene is modern and hip, the food spicy and scrumptious. The blackened catfish with Zydeco sauce, Dungeness crabmeat, sautéed spinach, and mashed potatoes will melt in your mouth. Open for lunch Mon through Fri 11 a.m. to 2 p.m. and dinner 7 days a week from 5 p.m. to close. $$–$$$.

where to stay

Lara House Lodge. 640 NW Congress St.; (800) 766-4064; larahouse.com. If romance and a prime location across from Bend's Drake Park are what you are after, this bed-and-breakfast will suit your needs. Six guest rooms have attractive mission-style furnishings, exquisite linens, and down comforters, all with private baths. Guests relax by the cozy fireplace, beautiful sunroom, and candlelit front porch. Every evening, there is a wine hour featuring Pacific Northwest wines paired nicely with delicious hors d'oeuvres and gourmet cheeses. In the morning, a sumptuous multicourse breakfast will get your day started right. It's all fairly expensive here, great for a special occasion. $$$.

McMenamins Old St. Francis School. 700 NW Bond St.; (541) 382-5174; mcmenamins .com. What was once a private Catholic school is now a whimsical, fun hotel, restaurant, bar, theater, and music venue. These brick buildings in downtown Bend are full of old memorabilia, murals, and 19 cozy guest rooms that used to be classrooms (additional rooms are under construction). There is also a fabulous soaking pool that's open to the outdoors through a hole in the ceiling and tiled beautifully by a local artist. Don't miss O'Kane's Pub, a stand-alone building studded with gorgeous stained glass and surrounded by a courtyard, specializing in scotch. There is often live music on weekends and for special celebrations. Don't worry about the nuns—they are all gone. $$.

Mt. Bachelor Village Resort. 19717 Mount Bachelor Dr.; (800) 547-5204; mtbachelorvillage .com. This resort combines the convenience of being in town with the peace and quiet of a forested, riverfront location. Spectacular Deschutes River views are available from the River Ridge suites, which also have gas fireplaces and private hot tubs on a deck overlooking all of that spectacular river and forest. The Ski House condominiums are less expensive but not nearly as nice—spring for the River Ridge suite. You won't regret it. Tennis and a swimming pool on-site, too. $$$.

The Oxford Hotel and 10 Below. 10 NW Minnesota Ave.; (877) 440-8436, (541) 382-1010; oxfordhotelbend.com. The restaurant in the new Oxford Hotel, Bend's only four-star boutique lodging, is tucked away in the basement. But that secluded location only makes this bright space feel all the more singular from the rest of the world. The chic urban restaurant put itself out on a limb in terms of decor—and you might feel like you are out on a limb surrounded by tree cross-sections on the wall, tree motifs on the curtains, and shades of green all around. The food is top-notch, as well. If you're here for lunch, don't miss the

BLTA. The grilled rustic toast, thick-cut bacon, tomato, avocado, and smear of maple aioli is a perfect example of why sweet, fat, and salt have always been some of our favorite things. Open for breakfast, lunch, and dinner daily (even holidays). The hotel rooms are also absolutely metropolitan, done up in rich earth tones with flashes of white and silver, with touches like opaque etched-glass screens and local French presses and fresh coffee in the rooms, and organic bath and body products in the bath. The beds are divine. The Oxford prides itself on its sustainable practices, and is one of the only hotels in the state to use non-chemical-based cleaning products. $$–$$$.

Tetherow Lodges. 61240 Skyline Ranch Rd.; (541) 388-2582; tetherow.com. Open in 2014, this lodging offers a fantastic view, and one that isn't much like others in Bend. Facing north over rolling high desert landscape, the view takes in the David McLay Kidd golf course, the Cascade Range in the distance, the Paulina Range to the east, and Pilot Butte right in town. Tetherow has two restaurants on-site and is located between the forest and town—maybe the best of both worlds. $$–$$$.

south

day trip 01

south

oregon's beginnings:
oregon city

oregon city

Oregon City is located 13 miles southeast of Portland on the east side of the Willamette River, just below Willamette Falls. The town is part of the Portland metro area, and there is no obvious division between Oregon City and the other suburbs that surround Portland. But don't dare suggest to an Oregon City resident that they live in Portland. Residents of this town take their distinction seriously. That might be in part because of Oregon City's history.

The city played a significant role in Oregon's beginnings. Established by Dr. John McLoughlin of the Hudson Bay Company in 1829, Oregon City was the first city in the US west of the Rocky Mountains to be incorporated. Oregon Territory was officially created in 1848 and Oregon City was designated as the territory's first capital, an honor it held until the capital was moved to Salem in 1852.

Oregon City remained a vibrant community, if a little quieter, after Oregon was granted statehood in 1859. In later years, Oregon City's economy rested on the forest industry, until harvest dried up in the 1980s.

Today, Oregon City's appeal resides in history—the center of the city retains part of its historic character through the preservation of houses and other buildings from the era of the city's founding. Oregon City residents are very proud of their gritty, authentic downtown revival. Appeal also rests in Oregon City's unique geographical placement at the confluence of the Clackamas River and the Willamette River. This unique topography includes three

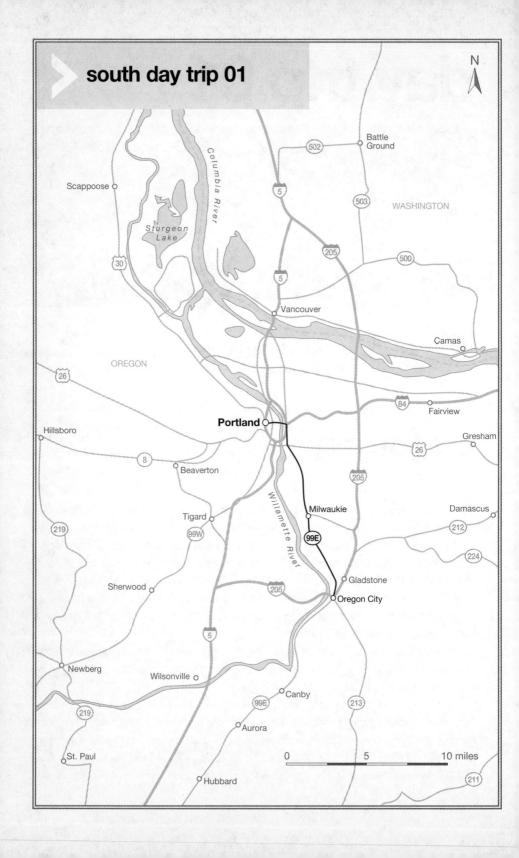

N

Battle Ground
502
5
503
WASHINGTON
Scappoose
205
500
30
Sturgeon
Lake
Columbia River
5
Vancouver
Camas
OREGON
26
84
Fairview
Portland
Hillsboro
Gresham
8
26
Beaverton
205
Milwaukie
Damascus
Tigard
212
99W
99E
224
Willamette River
Sherwood
Gladstone
205
Oregon City
5
219
Newberg
Wilsonville
Canby
99E
213
Aurora
219
St. Paul
0   5   10 miles
Hubbard
211

terraces that rise above the river, creating an elevation range from about 50 feet above sea level at the riverbank to more than 250 feet above sea level on the upper terrace. The lowest terrace, on which the earliest development occurred, is only 2 blocks or 3 streets wide, but stretches northward from the falls for several blocks. This is where you'll want to begin your day of exploration, though Oregon City offers many other pleasures, too.

getting there

Oregon City is located 13 miles south of Portland. Take exit 9 off of I-205 from the north or south, or take OR 99 E/McLoughlin Boulevard south from Milwaukie. McLoughlin Boulevard can be very slow going during high volume traffic hours—avoid at these times.

where to go

The Bike Concierge. (503) 314-6095; thebikeconcierge.com. Oregon in the last few years has seen a boom in bicycle tourism. This business was created to remove the obstacles to bicycle exploration that might exist for visitors. The Bike Concierge provides gear, ride support, route suggestions from partial day to multi-day, and even emergency pick up. No more excuses to not see the greater Portland area by bike.

Dream Ridge Stables. 20524 S Ridge Rd.; (503) 631-8466; dreamridgestable.com. Need a horse fix? Horse rides at Dream Ridge begin with basic instruction in an indoor riding arena and then move to an outdoor field filled with barrels, cones, poles, small jumps, and wide open spaces. Owner Karen Bower then leads the way through beautiful trails with views of the Viola valley and the lower Cascade Mountains. Prices vary.

The End of the Oregon Trail Interpretive & Visitor Information Center. 1726 Washington St.; (503) 657-9336; historicoregoncity.org. The End of the Oregon Trail Interpretive Center reopened in July 2013 with a featured film, *Bound for Oregon*, interactive learning programs and exhibits, and some great outdoor amenities including a heritage garden. The visitor center also offers changing displays on the Oregon Trail and Clackamas County history, as well as a great selection of local products and gifts in the Country Store. The kids will love loading the wagon and making candles. Open daily except major holidays.

John McLoughlin House. 713 Center St.; (503) 656-5146. The Canadian-born Dr. John McLoughlin has been called the Father of Oregon, and he was certainly the father of Oregon City. The fur trade was booming in 1824 when Dr. McLoughlin crossed the Rockies, establishing Ft. Vancouver on the Columbia River a year later. Beaver fur hats had become a popular item the world over, and British, French, and American trappers descended on the west. McLoughlin served as chief factor, or superintendent, of the British Hudson's Bay Company at the fort for many years, befriending Native Americans and lending a hand to pioneers. Though it was miles south of the fort, McLoughlin took to the Oregon City site, founding a city here and eventually retiring in this house. In 1941, the McLoughlin House was designated by Congress as the first National Historic Site in the West. Open for tours Wed through Sun. Free admission. ***Note:*** There is a relatively newly established Willamette Falls Heritage Trail, which takes the curious, self-guided, past 30 heritage and cultural sites in Oregon City, West Linn, and Lake Oswego, including this one. See mthoodterritory.com/willamette-falls-heritage-trail for more info.

Oregon City Municipal Elevator. 300 7th St. (official address is 610 Bluff St., but main street entrance is on 7th St.); (503) 657-0891. Oregon City is divided into upper and lower areas; the lower area is on a geologic bench next to the Willamette River, and the upper area sits atop a bluff. Trails connected the two before stairs were built in the 1800s. In 1915, modernity came to town and the city built the Oregon City Municipal Elevator to ferry residents between their town's two tiers. The elevator continues to operate as one of only four municipal elevators in the world and "Elevator Street" remains the only vertical street in North America. Open to the public 7 days a week; no charge.

Oregon City Farmers Market. 2051 Kaen Rd. off Beavercreek Road; orcityfarmersmarket .com. From May through Oct on Sat and Wed, 9 a.m. to 2 p.m., visit for fresh produce, pastured meats, farm eggs, wines, honey, preserves, breads, flowers, plants, goat's milk soaps, and gelato from local farmers and vendors. Chefs from local restaurants offer demonstrations; live music lifts spirits. Park and ride the Historic Trolley to the Market. ***Note:*** Also check out Oregon City's Summer Downtown Wednesday Market and the Downtown Winter Saturday Market.

The Oregon Lavender Farm. 20949 S Harris Rd.; (800) 289-8427; libertynatural.com, oregonlavenderfestival.com. The Oregon Lavender Farm hosts the Annual Clackamas County Lavender Festival the last Saturday and Sunday in June each year. Wine tasting, food, music, distillation demonstration, and much more occur on the farm's 10 acres of lavender angustifolia "Buena Vista," developed for its super blue color and superior fragrance. The farm is the home of Liberty Natural Products, Inc. a primary supplier of more than 1,000 botanical extracts, and also participates in the Oregon Lavender Festival—an event with multiple locations—every July.

Spirits of Oregon City Walking Tour. (503) 679-4464; nwghosttours.com. Pass by some of Oregon City's most spirited places and hear their ghost stories. Who knows—maybe you'll meet your very own ghost. Two different tours in Oregon City: McLoughlin Neighborhood and Downtown Oregon City.

Stevens-Crawford Heritage House. 603 6th St.; (503) 655-2866; clackamashistory.org. Wagon master Medorem Crawford, who brought pioneers across the Oregon Trail, built this house in 1907–08. A classic example of Foursquare architecture, this house, amazingly, contains all of its original furniture. Open Thurs through Sat for tours.

speed with a view

Want to see Oregon City and Willamette Falls from a totally unique perspective? Try a Willamette Jet Boat tour. The history, wildlife, and Willamette Falls tour leaves from Portland, near OMSI (Oregon Museum of Science and Industry), and jets upriver to Willamette Falls and back, offering views you'd never get from land. May through Sept. Call (888) JETBOAT; willamettejet.com. Another river-tour option is to take a cruise on the Portland Spirit, *a 98-foot custom-built yacht. See portlandspirit.com.*

Willamette Falls/McLoughlin Promenade. Runs along McLoughlin Boulevard; access at 7th and Center Streets. This 7.8-acre linear park on the bluff above downtown provides spectacular views of the Willamette River, Willamette Falls, and downtown Oregon City. The charming concrete walkway was originally constructed in 1937 as a Works Progress Administration project and was recently restored. Seating, picnic areas, and historical markers along the way are lovely and helpful, but the real attraction is the view of the second-largest waterfall in the United States, a former gathering place of Native American tribes and Oregon's early pioneers.

Wineries. Like so much of this region, Oregon City has seen wineries pop up like rainstorms in spring. Check out these four:

Christopher Bridge Wines. 12770 S Casto Rd.; (503) 263-6267; christopher bridgewines.com. The Carlberg family purchased this nearly 80-acre farm in 1952 primarily for its stunning Willamette Valley views and close proximity to Portland. Today the family continues a love of the land with an estate winery. Open by appointment and for special events.

Forest Edge Vineyards. 15640 S Spangler Rd.; (503) 632-9463; forestedge vineyard.com. Practicing sustainability and permaculture, this winery makes several whites and red blends. Open weekends year-round.

King's Raven. 11603 S New Era Rd.; (503) 505-6873; kingsravenwine.com. This family-owned parcel creates over a dozen red and white wines a year, with a half-acre amphitheater on site for events of all sorts. Open weekends.

Villa Catalana Cellars. 11900 S Criteser Rd.; (503) 780-6200; villacatalanacellars .com. This small winery produces less than 500 cases a year from an estate. The home and tasting room were inspired by San Clemente de Tahull, a 12th-century romanesque church in Catalonia, Spain. Open Sat 1 to 4 p.m.

where to shop

Oregon City Main Street. Downtown Oregon City is a charming place to wander and shop. Check out Denim Salvage (611 Main St.; denimsalvage.com) for recycled denim for the whole family; The Flat Boutique (719 Main St.; theflatboutique.com) for apparel, art, and home decor; Christmas at the Zoo (524 Main St.; christmasatthezoo.com) for holiday decor and plush animals; and You Can Leave Your Hat On (212 7th St.; hatshopinoregoncity.com) for an awesome collection of hats of all sorts.

where to eat

Highland Still House Pub. 201 S 2nd St.; (503) 723-6789; highlandstillhouse.com. Looking for Portland's widest selection of single-malt scotch? Here's your spot. This friendly Scottish-style pub features a cozy old-world atmosphere with antique furnishings from England and Scotland, and cooks up traditional Scottish fare with a Northwest influence for lunch and dinner 6 days a week. Outdoor seating with views of the Willamette Falls is significant perk. Closed Mon. $$.

Singer Hill Cafe. 623 7th St.; (503) 656-5252; singerhill.com. Cafe, bakery, and community hub, with innovative demonstration garden out back and live music spring and summer Friday and Saturday. This place is a real local's favorite. Open 7 a.m. to 6 p.m. Mon through Sat, 9 a.m. to 5 p.m. Sun. $.

The Stone Cliff Inn. 17900 S Clackamas River Dr.; (503) 631-7900; stonecliffinn.com. Located on the historic Baker Rock Quarry site, this fine dining establishment and log structure is nestled amid old growth trees on cliffs overlooking the Clackamas River, with stunning views from the outside deck, and the option of doing some bouldering on the rocks before or after your meal. Northwest cuisine pleases all. Claim to fame: The Stone Cliff Inn was one filming site of the *Twilight* movie. Lunch and dinner 7 days a week. Reservations recommended. $$$.

Tony's Smokehouse & Cannery. 1316 Washington St.; (503) 656-7512; tonysfishmarket .net. Tony's has been selling high-quality smoked fish and seafood products to an eager public since 1936, but they now serve lunch too. Try the fish and chips, Baja tacos, or salmon chowder. Take home some fresh crab. $–$$.

Nebbiolo Wine Bar. 800 Main St.; (503) 344-6090; nebbiolowinebar.biz. This classy joint features the high ceilings and brick walls of downtown's best buildings. Menu items range from calamari to cannoli, tapas to tenderloin, malbec to martinis, allowing Nebbiolo to satisfy a diverse appetite. $–$$.

where to stay

Sandes of Time Bed and Breakfast. 16022 SE River Rd., Portland; (503) 654-8813; sandesoftime.com. If driving all the way back to Portland is just too much to bear after a day spent slowing down to the pace of lovely Oregon City, book a room at the Sandes of Time Bed and Breakfast in Milwaukie, halfway between Oregon City and Portland. This wonderful old home was completed in 1907 atop a rocky knoll on 3 park-like acres. Recently restored and renovated, it now includes 4 downright lovely guest rooms and 3 covered porches with porch swings—the perfect place to while away the evening. $$.

worth more time

North of Oregon City 10 or 15 minutes is Milwaukie, home to a few Oregon gems. **Bob's Red Mill Whole Grain Store and Visitors Center** (503-607-6455; bobsredmill.com) produces more than 400 flours, cereals, and baking mixes, including certified gluten-free and certified organic products. The store features a bakery, deli, cafe, 18-foot operating waterwheel, and historic milling equipment. **Dave's Killer Bread** (503-335-8077; daves killerbread.com) is across the street and sells Dave's truly killer, delicious, organic whole grain breads at a discount. **Pendleton Woolen Mills** (503-535-5786; pendleton-usa .com) has been making fine blankets in classic designs for 140 years, and this shop is your source for first quality Pendleton fabrics, remnants, yarn, buttons, notions, and patterns at unbelievable prices.

day trip 02

south

treasure hunting:
woodburn, aurora

woodburn

Woodburn earned its name literally. A slash burn, set after the railroad line had been laid in the 1880s, burned out of control and destroyed a woodlot here. Voilà—a city was named.

Today, however, that which was once burned black is green. Nurseries and farms abound in this part of the Willamette Valley, many of which you can visit. Everything from pumpkins to lawn seed to fruit trees to strawberries is cultivated here, and buying it from the source always a fun, rewarding option.

Aside from flora, Woodburn is known for shopping. The Woodburn Company Stores is Oregon's number one tourist attraction, with 4 million visitors per year to its more than 100 outlet shops. While the stores are located right on Oregon's busiest thoroughfare, I-5, and represent the height of modern commerce and style, venture into Woodburn proper and you might see a glimpse of the past. Woodburn has been home to a sizable community of Russian Orthodox Old Believers since the 1950s, when this Christian reformed church escaped persecution from the official Russian Orthodox Church and moved to the US from Turkey. On the streets of Woodburn, one might see women in long skirts and scarves and men with beards.

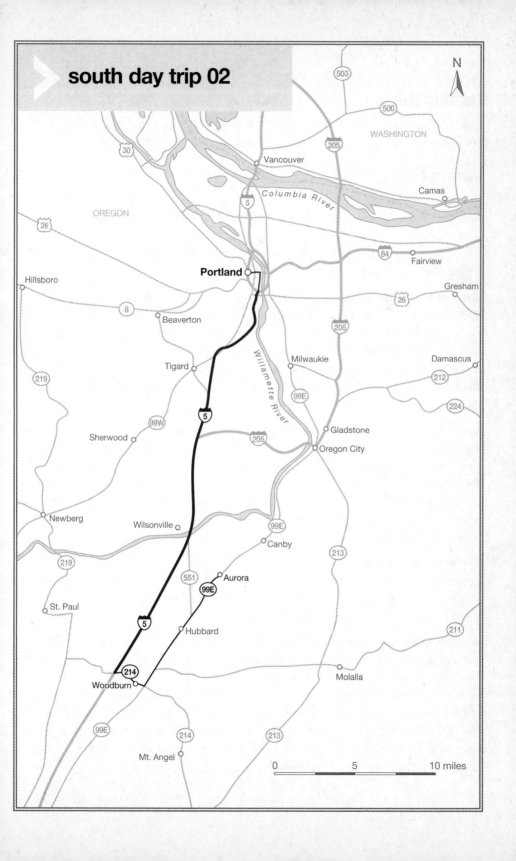

getting there

Take I-5 south from Portland for 29 miles. Take the OR 214 exit, exit 271, toward Woodburn/Silverton. Turn left onto OR 214 and proceed directly into Woodburn.

where to go

Al's Garden Center. 1220 N Pacific Hwy.; (503) 981-1245; als-gardencenter.com. Awarded Garden Center of the Year in 2006 by Garden Centers of America, Al's produces 6 million plants a year. The Garden Center also offers several seminars and special events a year, like Kid's Bulb Day. Check the website for details. Open Mon through Fri 10 a.m. to 6 p.m., Sat 9 a.m. to 6 p.m., Sun 10 a.m. to 5 p.m.

Bauman Farms. 12989 Howell Prairie Rd. (off OR 99 E south of Woodburn); (503) 792-3524; baumanfarms.com. Bauman family matriarch Great Grandmother Elizabeth Bauman started farming here in 1894, but things didn't really take off commerce-wise for this small farm for nearly 100 years. Today Bauman Farms is home to a nursery, bakery, and vegetable farm that attract hundreds of visitors a year. Host to many seasonal events, including an Easter egg hunt and a pumpkin patch in the fall, Bauman Farms also offers homemade zucchini bread, donuts, and pie. Hours vary annually.

Garden World. 10506 Broadacres Rd.; (503) 982-2380; gardenworldonline.com. A big sign on I-5 alerts passers-by to this amazing garden store's existence, but the freeway view has nothing on an up-close-and-personal visit. Whether you are after a one-stop plant shopping trip, a tour with your designer or contractor, or field trip with the kids or garden club, Garden World is your destination. Ten acres and 1,000 varieties of locally grown plant material including 100 different Japanese maples, rare and unusual conifers, and many sizes of shade and flowering trees make this place pretty as well as productive.

Settlemier House. 355 N Settlemier Ave.; (503) 982-1897; settlemierhouse.com. This Victorian/Craftsman house was built in 1892 and sits on nearly 3 acres of beautifully landscaped grounds. A very popular spot to host private events, and tours are offered to the public on the first Sunday of each month.

Wooden Shoe Tulip Farm. 33814 S Meridian Rd.; (503) 634-2243; woodenshoe.com. The Wooden Shoe Tulip Farm has been around since 1986, but the Iverson family has been growing tulips even longer than that. Why not, when they are so beautiful? Today the operation includes bulbs, cut flowers, potted tulips, a gift shop, other plants, and all sorts of food and activities on weekends. In recent years, owners have planted a vineyard and now offer wine tasting on-site. In April, Wooden Shoe opens their 40 acres of tulips and daffodils for an entire month for the Tulip Fest. In October, it's all about the Pumpkin Fest. See the website for details.

where to shop

Woodburn Company Stores. 1001 Arney Rd.; (503) 981-1900; shop-woodburn.com. Here, it is entirely possible—possibly even inevitable—to shop until you drop. More than 100 outlet stores are here in one enormous complex, including Adidas, Banana Republic, Liz Claiborne, Nautica, Carter's, Levi, and more and more and more. When you can't take it anymore, grab some refreshment at Cold Stone Creamery or Pan Asian Express, and then get back at it. Around Christmastime, this place is jamming, but given that it's been ranked one of the most popular tourist destinations in the state, you can count on it being pretty busy all year long, especially weekends. The parking lot can be a zoo, but that's just the price to pay for great prices. If you apply yourself, you can take care of your entire holiday list in one powerful day. Open Mon through Sat 10 a.m. to 8 p.m., Sun 10 a.m. to 7 p.m.

where to eat

Luis's Taqueria. 523 N Front St.; (503) 981-8437; luisstaqueria.com. This family-owned and -oriented establishment has been serving Michoacan-style Mexican food since 1993. Luis's is locally loved and well known for its delicious hand-made corn tortillas and famous dishes—and guests: President Barack Obama ate at Luis's when he was on the campaign trail in 2008. $.

Orchards Grille at OGA Golf Course. 2850 Hazelnut Dr.; (503) 981-4653; ogagolfcourse .com. Good food, gracious service, and one of the best picturesque settings in the North Willamette Valley. Restaurant serves American food with Italian influences 7 days a week for lunch; lounge and deli selections offered from dawn until dusk. By the way, the golf course is great to play as well. $–$$.

Vitality Food and Spirits. 1475 Mt. Hood Ave.; (971) 983-5280; iamvitality.com. Located at the Spa at Wellspring, this restaurant offers delicious foods and an extensive menu, including heart-healthy, organic, and gluten-free dishes. Open for breakfast, lunch, and dinner Mon through Sat. $–$$$.

aurora

Visiting Aurora is a little bit like taking a time machine 150 years into the past. Known as Oregon's Antiques Capital, this lush, rural town is home to dozens of antiques shops, as well as many examples of distinctive original architecture and one of the state's premier National Historic Districts. It's antiquated here, but in the very best possible way.

Founded as a religious commune in 1856 by Dr. William Keil, who named the settlement after his daughter, Aurora has become a destination for those seeking everything from a turn-of-the-century chiffarobe to a piece of hazelnut candy to simply a taste of the 19th century.

getting there

Aurora is 8 miles north of Woodburn on US 99 E/OR 99 E.

where to go

Old Aurora Colony Museum and Historical Society. 15018 2nd St. NE; (503) 678-5754; auroracolony.org. The Aurora Colony was a Christian commune that existed from 1856 to 1883. Nearly 600 people, almost all German and Swiss immigrants, lived together here, subsisting on farming and manufacturing, making most of their own products including furniture, textiles, and baskets. The houses and buildings from the Aurora Colony represent one of the largest concentrations of structures built by German craftsmen in the Pacific Northwest. Today visitors can see inside the Ox Barn, Steinbach Cabin, Kraus House, Will Family Summer Kitchen, and Tie Shed, and several other buildings can be viewed as part of a walking tour. Self-guided and guided tours are available, and throughout the year several special events occur, featuring quilts, craft demonstrations, and hands-on activities for adults and children. Open Tues through Sat 11 a.m. to 4 p.m. (closed for the month of Jan and on all major holidays).

where to shop

Antiques. There are nearly 20 antiques shops in the Aurora area. Here we mention a few, but as any good antiques hunter knows, your best bet is to make a day of it, wander around, hit every shop you can, and leave no stone unturned.

Antique Village. 21581 Main St. NE, #A; (503) 678-1007; antiquesoregon.com. Furniture, fine and costume jewelry, glass, decor, pottery, and collectibles. Open Tues through Sun 11 a.m. to 5 p.m.

Aurora Mills Architectural. 14971 1st St. NE; (503) 678-6083; auroramills .com. This store is a must-see for anyone interested in architectural salvage. A big warehouse is filled with unique, historic, and vintage architectural materials, such as stained and beveled glass, lighting, fireplace mantels, ornamental cast iron, clawfoot tubs, Victorian hardware, terra cotta, rustic timbers, and old growth flooring. Open Tues through Sun 10 a.m. to 5 p.m.

Home Again Antiques. 21631 Main St. NE; (503) 678-0227. Very nice store, featuring primitives.

Main Street Mercantile. 21610 Main St. NE; (503) 678-1044. One of the largest antiques stores in town with possibly the best selection from multiple dealers including furniture and books. Open Tues through Sun.

Pacific Hazelnut Candy Factory. 14673 Ottaway Ave.; (800) 634-7344; pacifichazelnut .com. A whopping 98 percent of all hazelnuts grown in the United States are from the Willamette Valley, and the folks at the Pacific Hazelnut Candy Factory know how to turn them into delectable sweets. In addition to roasting and seasoning nuts, the Pacific Hazelnut Candy Factory also chocolate coats hazelnuts, almonds, walnuts, prunes, and pretzels. The hazelnut toffee they developed was featured in *Bon Appetit* magazine. Open Mon through Fri 9 a.m. to 4:30 p.m. and Sat 10 a.m. to 4 p.m.

where to eat

The Colony Pub. 21568 US 99 E; (503) 678-9994. Cold and hot sandwiches, seafood specials, fresh soups, salads, and burgers are available in this classic pub along with pool table, jukebox, and lottery games. The food is much better than the average pub usually manages to produce. $–$$.

White Rabbit Bakery. 21368 US 99 E; (503) 267-9044; whiterabbitbakery.com. A gem of a place in a little old town, the White Rabbit Bakery offers mostly gluten-free pastries, cookies, bread, sandwiches, and cakes with names like the Tulgey Wood, the Mad Hatter, and the Fat Elvis. Owner Emily Arreola aims to bring a little comfort to folks who are missing it in the form of sweet, warm, buttery, sugary, fresh, and decadent delectables. Why White Rabbit? Arreola says it's all about following your dreams and the way life gets indisputably curiouser and curiouser. Famous for their wide variety of gluten-free offerings. Open Tues through Fri 6:30 a.m. to 4 p.m., Sat and Sun 8 a.m. to 4 p.m. $.

where to stay

Feller House Bed and Breakfast. 21625 Butteville Rd. NE; (503) 678-0268; thefeller house.com. This historic farmhouse was built in the 1880s on what is known as French Prairie. Now this old homestead is a bed-and-breakfast, offering 2 rooms. Breakfast is a wholesome meal with a gourmet touch featuring homegrown and local produce in season, served at the table near the woodstove in the kitchen, graced with cut flowers from the property. $$.

day trip 03

south

capital city:
salem

salem

Salem was originally called Chemeketa, by the Kalapuyan people, which means meeting
or resting place. It was a portentous denotation, as Salem went on to become the Oregon
state capital and therefore a most important meeting place to this day for Oregonians.

"Chemeketa" went through many more name changes before becoming Salem,
including The Mill, for its location on Mill Creek. The origin of Salem is uncertain: Was it an
Anglicized version of the biblical word Shalom, the last five letters of Jerusalem, or after
Salem, Massachusetts? In any case, Salem was founded in 1842, became the capital of
the Oregon Territory in 1851, and was incorporated in 1857.

Today, Salem is the third largest city in the state, after Portland and Eugene. Its location on the Willamette River was and still is an important part of Salem's appeal; the fact
that Salem is on I-5 under an hour south of Portland makes it conveniently accessible.
Many folks travel to Salem for state business; and though it's not commonly considered a
tourist destination, Salem offers many cultural, historical, and natural destinations worthy of
exploration.

getting there

Salem is 47 miles south of Portland on I-5.

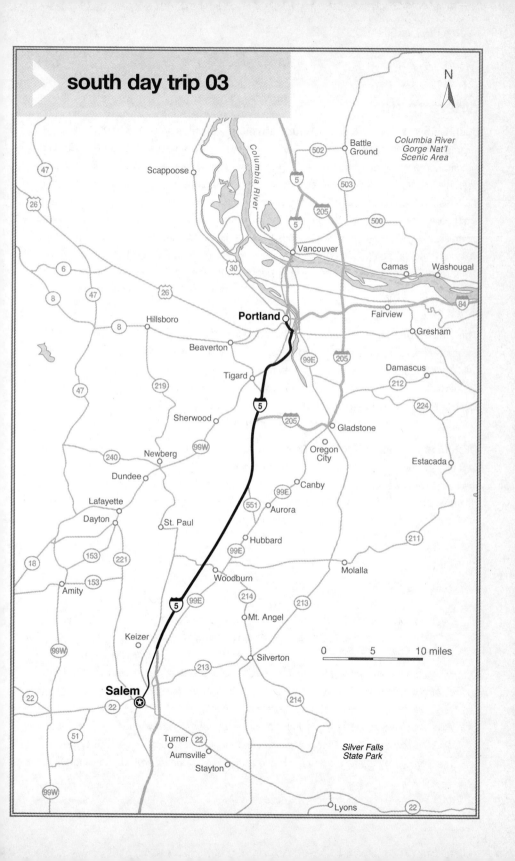

south day trip 03

N

Scappoose

Columbia River

Columbia River
Gorge Nat'l
Scenic Area

Battle
Ground

502

503

5

205

5

500

Vancouver

30

Camas   Washougal

84

Fairview

Portland

Gresham

Hillsboro

Beaverton

8

Tigard

99E

205

Damascus

212

Sherwood

219

5

205

224

Newberg

99W

Gladstone

Oregon
City

Estacada

Dundee

240

Canby

99E

Lafayette

551

Aurora

211

Dayton

St. Paul

153

221

Hubbard

99E

Molalla

Amity

153

Woodburn

18

5

99E

214

213

Mt. Angel

Keizer

Salem

Silverton

213

214

22

Turner   22

Aumsville

Stayton

Silver Falls
State Park

99W

Lyons   22

0   5   10 miles

where to go

Bush Barn Art Center & Bush House Museum. 600 Mission St. SE; (503) 581-2228; salemart.org. Built in 1878 for Asahel Bush and his family, the Bush House Museum is a historic home interpreting and preserving the lives, legacy, and art collection of these pioneering Oregonians. Explore the recently restored 1882 conservatory, the second oldest in the West. In the home's old barn is the Bush Barn Art Center, featuring three galleries and a gift gallery exhibiting and interpreting works of 20th- and 21st-century fine art and crafts by artists living or working in the Pacific Northwest. Both destinations are in historic Bush's Pasture Park, 90 acres featuring walking trails, a civic rose garden, and several children's play areas. The art center is open Tue through Fri, 10 a.m. to 5 p.m.; Sat and Sun, noon to 5. The museum offers tours March 1 through December 23, Wed through Sun at 1, 2, 3, and 4 p.m.

The Hallie Ford Museum of Art. Willamette University, 700 State St.; (503) 370-6855; willamette.edu/arts. This is the third largest art museum in the state, yet remains fairly unknown. It is truly a lovely museum that reflects the rich, diverse culture of the Northwest and explores the history of art around the world. Hallie Ford features outstanding rotating exhibits as well as permanent galleries of Asian, European, and Native American art. Open Tues through Sat 10 a.m. to 5 p.m., and Sun 1 to 5 p.m.

Oregon State Capitol. 900 Court St. NE; (800) 332-2313; oregonlegislature.gov. The current Oregon State Capitol building—constructed in 1936–1938 and expanded in 1977—is the third to house the Oregon state government in Salem. Two former capitol buildings were destroyed by fire, one in 1855 and the other in 1935. A visit here is a great opportunity, whether to learn about Oregon's rich history or the legislative process. Tours are available,

take a hike

Minto-Brown Island Park is a 1,200-acre natural park located within the city limits. On an island in the Willamette River between West Salem and downtown, the park includes open and wooded areas with many trails for walking, jogging, biking, and in-line skating. It also has a 15-acre off-leash dog park—an excellent spot for visitors traveling with their 4-legged family members. Furthermore, plans are under way to construct a pedestrian bridge to connect Minto-Brown Island Park with Riverfront Park—making the connected park system larger than Central Park in New York City. That project is scheduled for construction in 2015. In the meantime, both parks are still open and available for your vast exploration. cityof salem.net.

including staff-guided, self-guided, or video. Art, interactive, and historical exhibits are also on-site. Open weekdays 8 a.m. to 5 p.m.; admission is free.

The Oregon State Hospital Museum of Mental Health. 2600 Center St. NE; (971) 599-1674; oshmuseum.org. One of only a handful of museums of its kind in the world, this amazing place is dedicated to telling the stories of the many people who lived and worked at Oregon's State Hospital from the late 1800s on, and the history of how mental illness was defined and treated in the state's history. The museum is connected to two films, as well—first, it is the site for the filming of the movie *One Flew Over the Cuckoo's Nest,* based on Ken Kesey's novel, and there is a permanent display dedicated to the film and its writers, director, and cast. Second, the fascinating, short documentary film *Library of Dust* chronicles the discovery of over 3,500 copper canisters of cremains of people who had lived in Oregon institutions, and the subsequent quest to learn who they were, to reunify them with family members, and to create a memorial of their lives. Open Tues, Fri, and Sat noon to 2 p.m. Admission $4.

Salem's Riverfront Park. 101 Front St. NE; downtown Salem; (503) 588-6261; cityof salem.net. Salem's Riverfront Park is 23 acres along the Willamette River. A former logging operation site, the city bought the land from Boise Cascade and began restoring it in the 1980s. Now it offers many trails and greens, and is home to **Salem's Riverfront Carou- sel** (salemcarousel.wix.com) and **A.C. Gilbert's Discovery Village Children's Museum** (acgilbert.org). A highlight is **Eco Globe,** a beautiful spherical piece of art that includes 86,000 tiles depicting the entire planet Earth that was originally a large pressurized tank used by Boise Cascade to hold acids that were used to "cook" wood chips into pulp. It was a 5-year process to transform this "acid ball" into public art, featuring tiles made by local artists and schoolchildren.

Willamette Heritage Center. 1313 Mill St. SE; (503) 585-7012; willametteheritage.org. Here is a fascinating look at Oregon pioneer history. This 5-acre campus is home to 14 beautifully preserved historic buildings, including the 1841 Jason Lee House, thought to be one of the oldest and best preserved homes west of the Rockies. The campus is also home to the Thomas Kay Woolen Mills, the pre-cursor to the famous Pendleton Woolen Mills. Open to visitors Mon through Sat 10 a.m. to 5 p.m.

Willamette Valley Cheese Company. 8105 Wallace Rd.; (503) 399-9806; wvcheeseco .com. This artisan cheese company was created by owner Rod Volbeda, who spent more than a decade nurturing his herd of Jersey cows and perfecting cheese recipes. The result is more than 30 varieties of buttery, handcrafted cheeses. At the tasting room, learn more about the cheese-making process and sample each variety. Open Tues through Sat 10 a.m. to 5 p.m.

Willamette Valley Vineyards. 8800 Enchanted Way SE, Turner; (503) 588-9463; wvv .com. Willamette Valley Vineyards has several tasting rooms around Oregon, but this is the granddaddy, and the site of the main vineyards. A new tasting room remodel in 2014 features a huge central fireplace, 3 tasting bars, and a chef's station where visitors can watch chefs whip up delicious bites to accompany the award-winning wines. Stunning views overlooking the vineyards, toward Jory Hill and the Coast Range, and a new deck and courtyard area are perfect for summertime sipping. Open daily 11 a.m. to 6 p.m.

where to eat

Adam's BBQ. 1210 State St.; (503) 362-2194; adams-rib-smoke-house.com. Specializing in Santa Maria–style barbecue, Adam's creates burgers, gumbo, salads, and smoked meats in every iteration from sandwiches to combos. Locals swear by this little joint in west Salem. $–$$.

Amadeus Cafe. 135 Liberty St.; (503) 362-8830; amadeussalem.com. "A fork to mouth restaurant" in downtown Salem, Amadeus is a lovely destination for lunch or dinner. A generous happy hour covers dishes from short ribs to pizza to poutine to "petit le mac," backed by a nice wine list and full-service bar. There's a huge dessert list, too. Chic, modern decor and attentive staff round out the experience. Open Tues through Sat for lunch and dinner. $$.

Busick Court Restaurant. 250 Court St.; (503) 787-1204; busickcourt.com. This downtown Salem breakfast, lunch, and brunch destination is in an old brick building with huge windows. Cozy, colorful, and serving huge portions, Busick Court is a local's favorite, especially for Sunday brunch. Try the cinnamon raisin french toast. Open for breakfast and lunch 7 days a week; breakfast served all day. $.

Christo's Pizza. 1108 Broadway St. NE; (503) 371-2892; christospizzasalem.com. Delicious pizza in many combinations, from garlic lover's to mozzarella and clams. Christo's makes a relish of parsley, garlic, olive oil, and "a few secrets"—it's a delicious crust dipper. The lounge offers live music. $–$$.

Da Vinci Ristorante. 180 High St. SE; (503) 399-1413; davincisofsalem.com. Fine dining for dinner, Italian style. Pizza, pasta, risotto, steak, seafood, a full bar, and a lovely atmosphere are highlights at this restaurant. Grab a seat at the crescent marble bar for happy hour or secure a table for two (or more). Open for dinner every night but Sun. $$–$$$.

Gamberetti's Italian Restaurant. 325 High St. SE; (503) 339-7446; gamberettis.com. Approachable Italian fare in a comfortable restaurant space (with lots of windows) in Pringle Park Plaza in downtown Salem. In the summer, many tables in a park-like setting make for great outdoor dining. Open for lunch and dinner Mon through Fri; dinner Sat. $–$$.

Gilgamesh Brewing Company, The Campus Restaurant and Brewpub. 2065 Madrona Ave. SE; (503) 584-1789; gilgameshbrewing.com. The three Radtke brothers and their father, Lee, spent the summer of 2012 renovating a former grass seed warehouse

one enchanted afternoon

The Enchanted Forest is part Oregon legend, part every kid's fantasy day trip. This attraction built into a forested hillside just off I-5 near Turner has been a part of the local scenery and culture since the 1970s. It's much more than a theme park. Within its magical boundaries are a log ride, dragons, monsters, a storybook lane, a Western town, a kiddie train, bumper cars, a haunted house, an English village, gnomes, cowboys, princesses, and Humpty Dumpty. It's all a little bit quirky—no flashy over-produced style here. That vibe is what makes the place so special. Kids love it, and adults are charmed, too. When I took my children there for the first time a few years ago, all three of us were grinning through the entire visit (even when my oldest vanished into Alice's underground rabbit hole for what seemed like a beat too long). The whole project remains in the hands of its creator, Roger Tofte, and his family. That love and undivided attention shows. Prices vary by attraction but are generally very reasonable. The Enchanted Forest is located at 8462 Enchanted Way Southeast in Turner. Use exit 248. Because of its convenient location on I-5 between Salem and Albany, a visit to this fun park would be easy to include in a couple of other day trips in this book, including Albany, Eugene, and Mill City. See enchantedforest.com or call (503) 363-3060 for more information.

and its office into a full-scale brewery and handcrafted restaurant. Their motto is "a beer for everyone" and the range of selections provides the delicious proof, alongside a sizable menu with all the best brewpub foods. A patio overlooks Pringle Creek, providing great al fresco dining in the summertime. Tours of the brewing facilities are offered regularly on weekends. $–$$.

Roberts Crossing. 3635 River Rd. S; (503) 584-1035; robertscrossing.com. Roberts Crossing was originally built in 1916 as "The Query Store" and later became known as the Roberts Store. The restaurant opened in 2009 in this historic building. Old photos hang on the walls depicting the old store and saloon. A menu of classic American dishes, a full-service bar, and nice wine list make this a good family destination. Located in scenic Southeast Salem. Open for dinner every day but Mon. $$.

The Wild Pear. 372 State St.; (503) 378-7515; wildpearcatering.com. Sisters Jessica James and Cecilia Ritter-James cook up fresh, delicious Northwest cuisine in this chic little downtown cafe. Dishes like a lobster and seafood melt, Caesar salad, and a selection of wraps are nicely prepared and delicious; try the carrot ginger curry soup and their signature Wild Pear salad. Open for lunch and happy hour Mon through Sat. $.

Word of Mouth Bistro. 140 17th St. NE; (503) 930-4285; wordofsalem.com. In a quaint house retrofitted to accommodate the restaurant, this place offers some of the best breakfast, brunch, and lunch fare in the Mid-Willamette Valley. You'll wait in line to get in, especially on weekends, but it's worth it! Filet mignon chicken fried steak and eggs and cinnamon roll pancakes—wow. $.

where to shop

The Fussy Duck. 3170 Commercial St. SE; (503) 910-5639; facebook.com/TheFussy Duck. Huge shop featuring vintage-style decor, gifts, home decor, and lots more, with a kind of "shabby chic" feel to it. This shop moved in 2014 to a new, larger location in South Salem and has quickly becoming a local favorite.

One Fair World. 474 Court St. NE; (503) 585-1636; onefairworld.org. Salem's only fair trade, nonprofit retailer brings unique, beautiful, and delicious products from around the world to downtown. Featuring a great selection of quality, artisan-crafted jewelry, home decor, and accessories as well as fair trade coffees, teas, and chocolates. Open 7 days a week.

Red Raven Art Gallery. 440 Ferry St. SE; (503) 798-9973; redravengallery.com. An artists' cooperative offering an eclectic mix of fine art in every price range, including textiles, paintings, bronze and ceramic sculptures, glass work, functional pottery, wood and stone sculptures, artisan jewelry, and woven wearable art. Red Raven is a terrific place to find all kinds of great gifts by local artists.

Reed Opera House Mall. 189 Liberty St. NE; (503) 391-4481; reedoperahouse.com. This circa 1870s building was once home to vaudeville theater. Later, it housed a couple of department stores. Today, it's the state's oldest surviving theater and home to funky, eclectic shops like SLAB Soap Company, The Kilt & Thistle Scottish Shoppe, a crystal shop, and even a tattoo parlor. Also in the Reed are small restaurants like The Little Cannoli Bakery, Sisters Irish Bistro, and Oregon Crepe Company.

Salem Farmers' Markets. Various locations; (503) 585-8264; salemsaturdaymarket.org. Salem offers some truly excellent farmers' markets offering fresh produce, baked goods, artisan wares, live music, and more. The most popular markets are the Wednesday Market, located in downtown Salem, 10 a.m. through 2 p.m., each Wed, Apr through Oct; and the Saturday Market, also downtown, 9 a.m. to 3 p.m., every Sat, Apr through Oct.

where to stay

Century House Bed & Breakfast. 292 17th St. SE; (503) 884-7062; centuryhouseofsalem bandb.com. This charming 4-bedroom bed-and-breakfast is located in a historic home in the heart of downtown Salem. Proprietor Jean Brougher offers friendly, personalized service in this very cozy, comfy old home, including a delicious breakfast served in the morning. Cyclists love this place for its locked carriage house for storing bikes overnight. $–$$.

The Grand Hotel. 201 Liberty St. SE; (503) 540-7800; grandhotelsalem.com. Most definitely Salem's finest lodging, this beautifully appointed, 193-room hotel is the only independent, upscale hotel located in downtown. The Grand Hotel is adjacent to the Salem Convention Center and within easy walking distance of dozens of restaurants, shops, attractions, and the river and parks. On-site dining is available at Bentley's Grill, a spacious restaurant with lots of choices and a great bar. Underground, covered parking and a complimentary breakfast buffet are included in room rates. $$–$$$.

day trip 04

south

farm & garden:
mt. angel, silverton

mt. angel

In 1881, a contingent of Benedictine monks from Engelberg, Switzerland, came to Oregon with hopes of establishing a new American branch of their church. After visiting several locations, the Mt. Angel area was selected as the ideal location for a new abbey. Immigrants from Bavaria and Germany soon followed, and eventually the area became known as Mt. Angel (an English translation of Engelberg).

Mt. Angel Abbey was twice destroyed by fire; the current building, set high above the town on a 300-foot bluff with views of Mt. St. Helens, Mt. Hood, Mt. Adams, and the lush Willamette Valley farmland, was constructed in 1928 and remains a peaceful retreat and destination for many people annually.

The town itself retains a Bavarian old-world flavor—an aura that is encouraged by local businesses who have done up their storefronts to emphasize the city's cultural roots. Mt. Angel's German heritage especially comes to life in September, during Mt. Angel's elaborate Oktoberfest. But all year, visitors enjoy the Mt. Angel Glockenspiel—a life size, authentic work of art and piece of entertainment.

getting there

Take I-5 south out of Portland. Travel for 30 miles to the Woodburn exit, 271. Merge onto OR 214 and travel to the south and east for 10 miles to Mt. Angel.

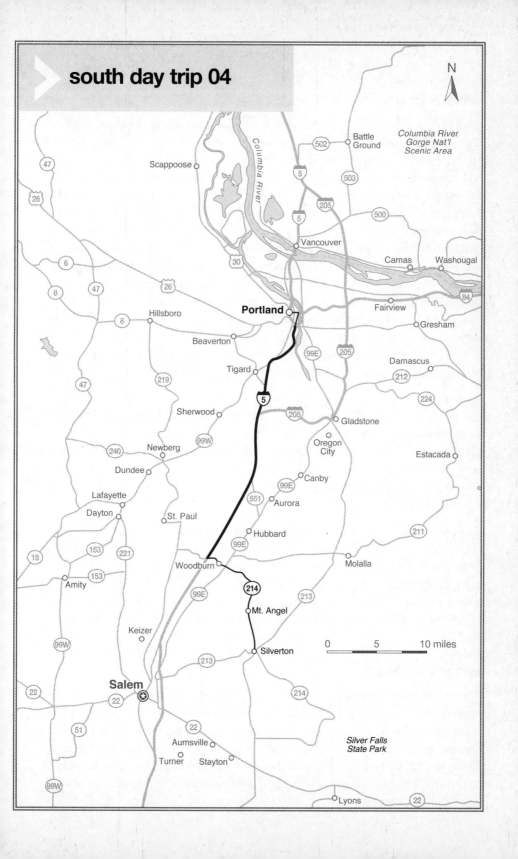

N

Columbia River Gorge Nat'l Scenic Area

Columbia River

47

26

Scappoose

502

Battle Ground

5

503

205

5

500

Vancouver

6

30

Camas

Washougal

8

47

26

84

Hillsboro

Fairview

8

Beaverton

Portland

Gresham

219

Tigard

99E

205

Damascus

212

5

Sherwood

205

Gladstone

224

240

Newberg

99W

Oregon City

Estacada

Dundee

Canby

99E

Lafayette

551

Aurora

211

Dayton

St. Paul

Hubbard

18

153

221

99E

Molalla

Amity

153

Woodburn

214

213

99E

Mt. Angel

213

Keizer

99W

213

Silverton

0   5   10 miles

Salem

22

214

22

51

22

Aumsville

Silver Falls State Park

Turner

Stayton

99W

Lyons

22

where to go

Mt. Angel Abbey. 1 Abbey Dr., St. Benedict (just south and east of Mt. Angel); (503) 845-3066; mountangelabbey.org. In 1883, a group of Swiss Benedictine monks established the Mt. Angel Abbey. Today, a community of monks continues to reside here at this peaceful and exceptionally lovely spot. The abbey itself is a classic beauty of a building in red brick; the grounds are lush with many old hardwood trees, flowers, and huge stretches of lawn. The library, designed by Alvar Aalto, is world-famous and stores a priceless collection of illuminated manuscripts as well as a display of rare, hand-printed books. A seminary school of philosophy and theology operates on the grounds, as does a guest and retreat house. The abbey's gift and bookshop sells books and music, rosaries and medals, greeting cards and art. In a perfect twist of old-meets-new, and an appropriate touch for craft-beer-loving Oregon, the monks of Mt. Angel recently revived the centuries-old tradition of monastic beer-brewing. The Benedictine Brewery now produces and sells bottled monk-brewed beer at the Abbey; a full brewery is coming soon. Bookstore open Mon through Thurs 10 a.m. to 4:30 p.m. Guided tours of other facilities can be arranged by appointment; the library is open to public visitors upon request.

Oktoberfest. Downtown; oktoberfest.org; (503) 845-6882. It only happens once a year, but, boy, is it a doozy. Oregon's oldest and best-loved Oktoberfest began in 1966 as a traditional harvest festival to celebrate the bounty of the earth and the goodness of creation. Today the 4-day event is Oregon's largest folk festival and features continuous live music on 4 stages; free kindergarten with rides and shows; night street dancing; more than 50 alpine food chalets; a large arts and crafts show; traditional biergarten, weingarten, and alpinegarten; and RV and tent camping.

Saint Mary's Church. 575 E College St.; (503) 845-2296; stmarymtangel.org. This gorgeous church has been anchoring downtown Mt. Angel and serving the community since 1912. It is Roman Catholic in faith, but with a Benedictine tradition, reflecting Mt. Angel's roots. Designed and built in the Revival Gothic style, the church is laid out in the form of a Latin cross and boasts 22 stained glass windows. The church is open for viewing upon request, and depending on private events. Of course, you can see the outside just by walking by.

where to eat

The Glockenspiel Restaurant Pub. 190 East Charles St.; (503) 845-6222; glockenspiel restaurant.net. The atmosphere here is comfortable, and the food a fresh mixture of seasonal Northwest cuisine with a hint of Bavaria, including spätzle soup, wiener schnitzel, fondue, and the traditional Friday fish fry (long a Catholic tradition, in accordance with scriptural advisement to avoid meat on Friday). But the real attraction at this restaurant is outdoors. Mt. Angel's Glockenspiel rises 49 feet above the restaurant. This marvel in the center of town celebrates the Native-German-Swiss-Bavarian heritage of the village and Mt. Angel's world-famous Oktoberfest held each fall. Its figures represent Mt. Angel history and dance, sing, and ring bells in celebration. Glockenspiel performances occur daily at 11 a.m. and 1, 4, and 7 p.m., and are free. Restaurant open daily 11 a.m. to 9 p.m. $$.

silverton

Silverton exudes small town charm. A historic downtown district and many old mansions perched on the surrounding hills attract visitors looking for a picturesque slice of America's past every year.

But Silverton does modern, too—the city is home to a thriving arts community with many galleries and unique shops to be discovered downtown. The Silverton Fine Arts Festival draws artists and art lovers to town each August, and transforms this little town into a small artist's enclave.

There's plenty of artistic inspiration to be found here, to be sure, especially from nature. Silverton is nicknamed "Oregon's Garden City," and the Willamette Valley is lush and beautiful here. Silverton has just enough of a hilly aspect to it to offer fabulous views of the countryside. Nearby, Silver Falls State Park boasts 10 waterfalls and is the oldest and biggest state park in Oregon. The Oregon Garden is a newer establishment with just as much beauty—20 specialty gardens bloom on-site, and the only structure in Oregon designed by famous architect Frank Lloyd Wright is here, too.

Right in town, Silver Creek runs through the city, making those historic buildings all the more picturesque.

getting there

Take OR 214 south out of Mt. Angel. Silverton is 5 miles south of Mt. Angel on OR 214.

where to go

Cooley's Gardens. 11553 Silverton Rd. NE; (503) 873-5463; cooleysgardens.com. Founded in 1928 by Rholin and Pauline Cooley, Cooley's Gardens started as a backyard iris hobby. Going on 90 years later, Cooley's grows and ships "The World's Finest Iris" to customers the world over. Cooley's breeds new irises as well as planting classics, and a 4-acre display garden is open to the public. Hundreds of varieties of bearded iris bloom from about May 15 through mid-June.

The Gordon House. 879 W Main St. (next to the Oregon Garden); (503) 874-6006; thegordonhouse.org. Frank Lloyd Wright designed a series of homes in the 1930s and later that he referred to as Usonian—a philosophy of living in harmony with the land of the United States of Northern America (USONA). Designed for Evelyn and Conrad Gordon in 1957 and finished in 1963, this house was one of Frank Lloyd Wright's many creations that ultimately made great impact on the design and architecture of small homes for the middle-class consumer. Originally located in Wilsonville, the Gordon House was moved to this site near the Oregon Garden in 2000 to save it from planned destruction by its owner. It is now registered on the National Register of Historic Places. It is the only building in Oregon designed by Frank Lloyd Wright. Tours of the interior are offered and cover the theories and practices of Frank Lloyd Wright's architecture; the story of how an Oregon farm family commissioned Mr. Wright to design their new home; and the home's rescue, dismantling, moving, and reconstruction. Tours are offered May through Oct from 11 a.m. to 5 p.m. and Nov through Apr noon to 4 p.m., on the hour. Please call for reservations.

The Oregon Garden. 879 W Main St.; (503) 874-8100; oregongarden.org. A whopping 80 acres of specialty gardens is the theme at work here, and isn't it pretty. A Lewis and Clark Garden, Market Garden, Rose Garden, Oak Grove, Northwest Garden, Tropical Garden, and much more are here waiting to be explored. The Children's Garden is complete with an in-ground hobbit house, a tree fort, and furniture filled with colorful annuals. There are also waterfalls, quiet ponds, fountains, beautiful vistas, and art. A motorized tram provides visitors with an excellent overview of the garden's many features. Passengers have unlimited on-off privileges at 6 stopping points. The tram is designed for passengers with limited mobility and operates from Apr to Oct. Garden hours: May to Sept 9 a.m. to 6 p.m.; Oct to Apr 10 a.m. to 4 p.m. Admission is $5 to $10 and varies by season.

Silver Falls State Park. 20024 Silver Falls Hwy. (OR 214, 26 miles east of Salem); (503) 873-8681; oregonstateparks.org/park_211. As one of the most scenic places in a scenic state, Silver Falls State Park is not to be missed. The temperate rain forest here in the

mt. angel moonshine

There was a time that Silverton was dry and Mt. Angel was wet. No, they weren't subjected to strangely alternating weather patterns. Before Prohibition, Mt. Angel could legally sell alcohol and Silverton couldn't. Commerce working the way it does, those with managed to make an industry out of providing to those without. One point of transfer was the Gallon House Bridge, the last of Marion County's original covered bridges. Located over Abiqua Creek on Gallon House Road a little more than a mile northwest of Silverton, the bridge was constructed in 1917. Soon after, the north end of the bridge became a pigeon drop, or place to exchange "white lightning" whiskey for cash. The illegal trade is long gone, but the bridge remains. It's worth seeing, and you can still make a toast while you are here—even if it's just with a swig from your water bottle.

lower elevation of Oregon's Cascade Mountains is lush and gorgeous, and in this park 10 waterfalls can be found. Ranging from the grand South Falls (177 feet) to the delicate Drake Falls (27 feet), the Trail of Ten Falls/Canyon Trail takes them all in with a moderate hike of 6.9 miles. If you aren't feeling up to it or are traveling with folks who aren't, there are several shortcut options, so don't be afraid to venture out on the trail if just for a short distance. Keep in mind, though, that because the Canyon Trail is narrow and bordered by sharp drop-offs in spots, bicycles, skateboards, in-line skates, and pets are not allowed. It's all about the waterfalls, some of which are more than 100 feet high. The trail in several places leads through mossy caverns behind the water's shimmering descent, where you can feel the mist and the damp spray. The Canyon Trail and the falls lead to a forest floor covered with ferns, mosses, and wildflowers, as well as stands of Douglas fir, hemlock, and cedar. While thousands visit the park every year, it is large enough for solitude, too. Open all year; the park is usually snow-free even in mid-winter, but the falls and wildflowers peak from late March to May. Oregon State Parks charges a fee per car to park anywhere in the state park. Silver Falls State Park also offers RV, cabin, and tent camping in the overnight campground.

Silverton Murals. Downtown Silverton (pick up a map of mural locations at the site of the Four Freedoms mural at S 2nd and E Main Streets or download one at silvertonor.com/murals). In the early 1990s, local artist David McDonald painted Norman Rockwell's famous "Four Freedoms" on a wall in downtown Silverton. The idea caught on. Today there are nearly a dozen murals to be discovered in downtown Silverton, each with a historic story to tell. Make it a point to see them all or stumble upon them—they are hard to miss.

where to eat

O'Brien's Cafe. 105 N Water St.; (503) 873-7554. Traditional small-town diner offering breakfast and lunch items like omelets, buttermilk pancakes, chicken strips, burgers, and Philly sandwiches. A back deck overlooks Silver Creek, and O'Brien's is known for the antiques and collectibles that can be found throughout the building, including Santa's mailbox by the front door. This cafe is also a popular destination for the bus tours that come to Silverton to see the murals. $.

Seven Brides Brewing. 990 N 1st St.; (503) 874-4677; sevenbridesbrewing.com. Several years ago, three dads and two uncles would gather on a Saturday in one of their garages to master the art of home brew. Before long, they decided it was good enough to sell. Today, they serve lunch and dinner 7 days a week to happy patrons, and brew up a bunch of beers including an imperial IPA called Bridezilla—look out. $–$$.

Silver Grille. 206 E Main; (503) 873-8000; silvergrille.com. This restaurant has been described as not only the best in Silverton but one of the best in the Willamette Valley. Handmade pastas, a salad called the Naughty Librarian, dishes like shrimp scampi and rockfish piccata, and tasty desserts are prepared by a high-end chef in a small town in a lovely, elegant space. Open for dinner Wed through Sun 4 to 9:30 p.m. $$.

where to stay

Birdwood Inn. 511 S Water St.; (503) 873-3247; birdwoodbandb.com. A charming vintage home near downtown Silverton. All rooms have queen-size beds and are beautifully decorated in a classic style. Each room has a private bath with a clawfoot tub; splurge and stay in the private suite with a fireplace. Morning coffee is served to your room and a full breakfast is served in the dining room. $–$$.

Edward Adams House B&B. 729 S. Water St.; (503) 873-8868; edwardadamshouse bandb.com. A warm, romantic, turn-of-the-century feel dominates at this Queen Anne Victorian house, designed and built in 1890. Choose from three beautifully furnished rooms. The house is listed on the National Registry of Historic Places and is also a Silverton Heritage Landmark. Breakfast includes juice, fresh fruit, homemade baked goods, granola, oatmeal, and an entree using local organic eggs. $$.

Oregon Garden Resort. 879 W Main St.; (503) 874-2500; oregongardenresort.com. This lovely new hotel, restaurant, and resort not only has great views of the Oregon Garden, it has a full spa, lounge with nightly entertainment, fireplaces, private landscaped patios and balconies, a heated outdoor swimming pool, and a hot tub. Rooms come with a buffet breakfast. The restaurant offers fine Northwest cuisine and is open for breakfast, lunch, and dinner 7 days a week. $$–$$$.

worth more time

Willamette Valley Pie Company. After your Silverton visit, you may decide to return to I-5 via Silverton Road SE, which heads west into Salem. If so, don't miss the chance to stop at the Willamette Valley Pie Company. These folks process around 12 million pounds of fruit a year to make your life a little sweeter. The creator and purveyor of freezer jam, raw honey, natural syrup, fruit snack bars, packaged vegetables and fruits, and (most especially) divine premade cobblers and pies uses all homegrown Willamette Valley fruits. The facility is located at 2994 82nd Ave. NE in Salem, and tours are available upon request. Just call (503) 362-8678 or see wvpie.com.

day trip 05

south

rivers & trees:
mill city, detroit

mill city

The North Santiam Canyon encompasses several small towns that sit along the North Santiam River, one of Oregon's loveliest rivers. Paralleling the river is OR 22, a primary east-west highway through the Cascade Range, which summits at the Santiam Pass at 4,817 feet. Travelers are treated to many views of the North Santiam River as it falls through the canyon, its waters crisp and vibrant, the forest around it lush and beautiful.

At the time of Lewis and Clark, there were Douglas fir trees in Oregon that were more massive than the giant sequoias of California. Logging and lumbering supported entire generations of North Santiam Canyon residents. Mill City was named in 1886, when four entrepreneurs set up a mill that they named the Santiam Lumbering Company. Tucked away in the forests off of this highway are pockets of remaining old growth.

By Mill City, 30 miles east of Salem, travelers east are just beginning to leave behind the rich flats of the Willamette Valley and to get a sense of the mountainous terrain ahead. There isn't a whole lot going on in this quiet Oregon town, except for lovely scenery and plenty of recreational activities. Stop here to grab a bite to eat before you head into the mountains.

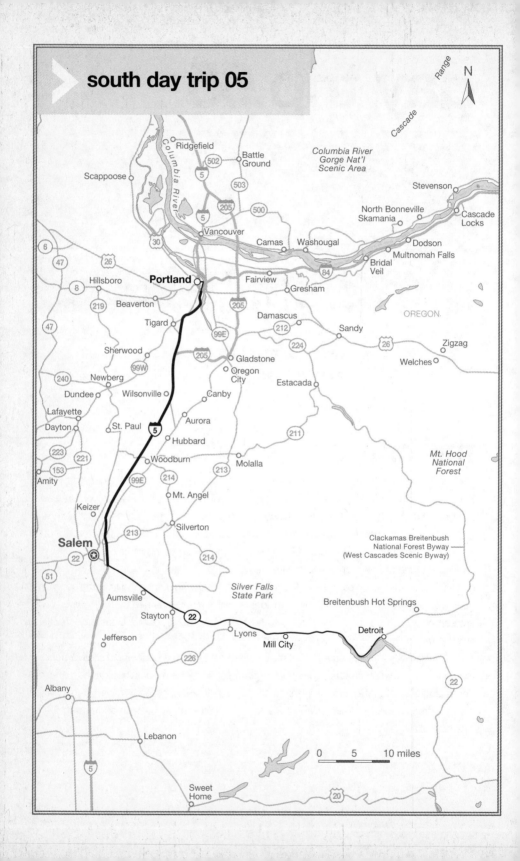

south day trip 05

N

Cascade Range

Columbia River

Ridgefield

Battle Ground

502

Scappoose

5

503

Stevenson

205

500

North Bonneville
Skamania

Cascade Locks

30

Vancouver

Camas

Washougal

Columbia River Gorge Nat'l Scenic Area

6

Dodson

Multnomah Falls

47

26

Bridal Veil

84

Hillsboro

Portland

Fairview

Gresham

219

Beaverton

205

Damascus

OREGON.

8

Tigard

99E

212

Sandy

26

Zigzag

Sherwood

205

224

Welches

47

99W

Gladstone

240

Newberg

Wilsonville

Oregon City

Estacada

Dundee

Canby

211

Lafayette

Dayton

St. Paul

5

Aurora

223

221

Hubbard

Mt. Hood National Forest

153

Woodburn

213

Molalla

Amity

99E

214

Keizer

Mt. Angel

213

Silverton

Salem

214

Clackamas Breitenbush National Forest Byway (West Cascades Scenic Byway)

22

51

Silver Falls State Park

Aumsville

22

Breitenbush Hot Springs

Stayton

Jefferson

Lyons

Mill City

Detroit

226

22

Albany

Lebanon

0   5   10 miles

5

Sweet Home

20

getting there

From Portland, take I-5 south to Salem, 46 miles. Pass through several Salem exits to exit 253, which indicates Detroit Lake/Bend. Take a left to turn east onto OR 22/US 22. Mill City is another 29 miles east.

where to go

Camp Dakota. Crooked Finger Road, Scotts Mills; (503) 873-7432; campdakota.com. This 45-acre forested campground and adventure park invites guests to stay in a deluxe yurt, do a zipline course or a high ropes course, play paintball, pan for gold, and much more. Open year-round, but some activities are weather-dependent.

Kimmel Park. 330 Santiam Pointe Loop NE. This lovely park sits on the North Santiam River and is a great spot for a picnic or family gathering. But Kimmel's primary attraction is its boat launch, and many people flock here during the warmer months to find water access for their kayaks, canoes, and whitewater rafts. It's also a great place to fish and observe nature and wildlife.

Opal Creek Ancient Forest Center. Twenty miles north of Gates on North Fork Road; (503) 892-2782; opalcreek.org. The Opal Creek Wilderness and neighboring Bull of the Woods Wilderness is the largest contiguous area of low-elevation old growth Douglas fir left in Oregon. The Opal Creek Ancient Forest Center exists to interpret, protect, and share this forest with the public. Many school programs and family workshops are offered during the programming season, which runs from mid-April to mid-November. You can even take a class on lichens or fungi. Or head out on an exploration of your own on the many available hiking trails—you'll likely see a great menagerie of wildlife, birds, fish, and insects (as well as those big majestic trees). Opal Creek also offers some lodging in rustic cabins. All visitors to Opal Creek need a Trail Park permit to park at the trailhead. The permits cost $5 per car for a one-day pass or $30 for a full-year pass. Full-year passes are available at most Forest Service offices and at the Santiam Sports Center in Mill City, (503) 897-2881, or you can pay per day from a self-serve pay station (cash or check only) at the trailhead.

The Oregon Experience. Headquartered in Mill City; (503) 897-3291; oregon-experience .com. If you are itching to get out onto the waters of the North Santiam River but don't have the gear or the know-how, the Oregon Experience is the outfitter to call. Licensed guide Arden Corey shares the extensive knowledge of forestry, wildlife, and fisheries that he has acquired during 30 years with the US Forest Service and 27 years spent on the North Santiam River on guided fishing and rafting trips. Drift boat fishing for spring Chinook salmon and summer and winter steelhead is a challenge in a beautiful place; rafting can be leisurely or thrilling—sometimes both in one trip. Rafting $40 to $55; fishing $100 to $125.

Stayton Jordan Covered Bridge. On Marion Street off the Stayton/Sublimity turnoff from OR 22. This covered bridge has been rebuilt twice—first in 1988 after years of disrepair, and again in 1998 after a devastating fire destroyed the first rebuild. Now connecting two parks, the bridge is a lovely destination just off the highway. Stop here for a lunchtime picnic.

where to shop

Gene's Meat Market. 21991 Fern Ridge Rd., Mehama; (503) 859-2252; genesmeat market.com. Day tripping and meat shopping may not immediately come to mind as companionable activities, but you might think twice once you know that every smoked meat category that Gene's carries has won at least one Grand Champion Award in the past 10 years, and that many popular varieties of sausage are made on-site. Bring a cooler and stock up.

Hardwood Components, Inc. 20573 OR 22, Mehama; (503) 859-2144; hardwoodcom ponents.com. Reminding us all that the North Santiam Canyon once made an honest living on the timber industry is this little sawmill and shop. For more than 40 years, the owners of Hardwood Components have milled native trees like big leaf maple, Oregon white oak, and wild cherry into lumber. You'll also find black walnut, alder, and ash, available in small or large amounts. Much of Hardwood Component's lumber is air dried for up to two years before kiln drying. Pick up some of Oregon's best woods for your next remodel project or woodcraft work.

where to eat

Giovanni Mountain Pizza. 146 NW Santiam Blvd.; (503) 897-2614. Hand-tossed dough and fresh ingredients make this a local's favorite for pizza. Try the spinners—made from pizza dough and stuffed with Italian sausage and ricotta cheese, served with a side of warm marinara sauce. This is a great, casual place to take the whole family, including the kids. Open 7 days a week for lunch and dinner. $.

Rosie's Mountain Coffee House. 647 Santiam Blvd.; (503) 897-2378; rosiesscones .com. When traveling through the more remote areas of the beautiful Pacific Northwest, sojourners are often left disappointed after a search for a good meal (not to mention a clean restroom). Rosie's Mountain Coffee House aims to change that. Here real food is served in fresh, delightful abundance. Savory quiche, veggie and meat wraps, fruit smoothies, and fresh scones are just some of the treats you'll find at Rosie's. If you're yearning for soy milk in your Allan Brothers latte while communing with the natural world of the North Santiam Canyon, Rosie's is the place for you. $.

Sierra Mexican Restaurant and Market. 302 W North Santiam Hwy., Gates; (503) 897-2210. The skinny on this place is that the exterior is deceiving. Don't be fooled—inside you'll find fabulous authentic Mexican food. The tortillas and salsa are great, and the rice has bits of carrots and peas, giving it an almost Asian twist. $.

Trexler Farm Cafe. 20146 Ferry Rd. SE, Stayton; (503) 859-4488; trexlerfarm.com. A secret hot spot of the North Santiam, this little-known farm store/cafe serves high-quality, farm-fresh, nutritious lunches 6 days a week on a farm that was home to the old Mehama Fish Hatchery. Try the BBQ tri-tip beef sandwich, artichoke wrap, or the Greek Isle wrap. Wine tasting, organic foods, and great coffee are all here waiting to be discovered. The facility is also available for private and group events by appointment. Open for lunch Mon through Sat, 11 a.m. to 2 p.m. $–$$.

detroit

The original town of Detroit is under water. Born on the pursuits of logging and fishing, Detroit's fate changed when the Army Corps of Engineers selected the site for the Detroit Dam in the 1930s. Three thousand workers descended on the area to build the dam at the peak of construction in 1950. That was the good news. The bad news was that the proposed dam would put the town under 100 feet of water. Many businesses closed and relocated to the new town site—along with the residents, of course. Life reconvened on higher ground 1 mile north of the old town, just west of the confluence of the North Santiam River and Breitenbush River.

Today that dam makes Detroit a recreationalist's heaven. Detroit Lake is now the number one recreational lake in the state of Oregon. This is the spot for all types of water sports: fishing, boating, swimming, waterskiing, and personal watercraft. Camping, swimming, hiking, and the like are very popular, too.

getting there

Detroit is 20 miles east of Mill City directly on OR 22.

where to go

Boating. Whatever your craft of choice, Detroit Lake will float it. Folks come here to motor boat, sail, paddle, canoe, kayak, and water ski. For great water skiing or wakeboarding, get out on the lake early, as skiing is best when the water is calm. Sail boaters should direct their vessel toward the dam, where the wind is the windiest and most constant. For respite, tie up in the calm waters and sheltered coves of the Breitenbush Arm (near Detroit Lake Marina) or Blowout, located at the far southwest end of the lake, for a picnic or swim. Bon voyage!

Fishing. Detroit Lake is over 9 miles long with more than 32 miles of shoreline, and provides many accessible locations for fishermen. For good fishing from the shore, try areas where a creek enters the lake, like Tumble Creek, French Creek, and the Breitenbush River. Fishing from the Detroit Dam provides easy access with very good fishing action. There are also several high lakes around Detroit, many of which are stocked with fish. These lakes are open year round, but may be inaccessible in winter. To fish from a boat, find lake access at Detroit proper or Detroit Lake State Park, which has two boat moorage docks. Detroit Lake fishing is best April through October.

Hiking. There are many options for the hiker near Detroit, whether you'd enjoy scaling the steep hills of the Cascade Range or strolling around the flatter flanks of the lake. Try the Rocky Top Trail for the former or the Beachie Trail for the latter. To find more information on each, visit the Detroit Ranger Station, near Detroit Lake State Park on Highway 22.

where to eat

The Cedars Restaurant & Lounge. 200 Detroit Ave.; (503) 854-3636; thecedarsrestaurant .com. Marked by a tall, lit, blinking green and red tree on its roof, this family-oriented restaurant has been serving food to hungry Detroit Lake visitors for more than 50 years. Breakfast is available all day long, and a large full-service liquor lounge with lottery, adjacent to the restaurant, keeps tourists happy. Cedars, and Detroit in general, likes to advertise itself as "the friendliest place by a dam site"—but don't expect quick service. Things are a little slower in the woods. $–$$.

KC's Espresso and Deli. 210 Forest Ave.; (503) 854-3145. This little spot is tucked on a quiet lot off of the highway, with a big deck and yard for outdoor dining in the warm months. Indoors, funky decor is the backdrop to a feast of burgers, sandwiches, shakes, and the like, served by some very kind folks. $.

where to stay

Breitenbush Hot Springs. Ten miles north of Detroit on the Breitenbush River; (503) 854-3320; breitenbush.com. This lovely hot springs and retreat is tucked away in an amazing ecosystem. The landscape is 154 acres of wildlife sanctuary surrounded by national forest. The 3 meadow hot springs pools are lined with smooth rocks and overlook the river. The 4 tiled spiral tubs, with increasing temperatures, are aligned in the cardinal directions and adjoined by the cedar tub cold plunge. The sauna is a cedar cabin resting atop bubbling hot waters. Guests stay in simple, rustic cabins kept warm year-round with heat from Earth-heated waters. Some have a sink and toilet, and bathhouses are nearby. In summer and early fall, personal campsites are available. Bountiful vegetarian meals, mostly organic, are served buffet style 3 times daily. Day-use access available. Often closed for private gatherings—check website for availability and driving directions.

Detroit Lake State Park. 44000 North Santiam Hwy. SE; (503) 854-3346; oregonstate parks.org. What's a summer without camping? This large state park and campground offers many amenities including an amphitheater, boat launch ramp, playground, showers, evening interpretive programs, firewood, and more than 200 camping sites for RVs and tents. Day use $5; camping $19 to $24. $.

The Lodge at Detroit Lake. 175 N Detroit Ave.; (503) 854-3344; lodgeatdetroitlake .com. For those who'd rather not camp, try this lodge (built in 2010) with gorgeous, wooden rustic exterior. Inside you'll find spacious rooms with full kitchenettes, log beds, Western decor, 42-inch flat screen TVs, jetted tubs, fireplaces, built-in air conditioning, on-demand hot water, and Wi-Fi. It's a great place to rest your head and still be near outdoor splendor. $$.

worth more time

The stunning Clackamas-Breitenbush National Forest Scenic Byway, part of the West Cascades Scenic Byway, only open seasonally, runs 70 miles between Detroit and Estacada past a sparkling river, thick forests, lovely bridges, and high rock formations. In the fall, beautiful foliage lines the route. A favorite for motorcycle tours. The mountain pass, which offers great views of Mt. Jefferson, snows over in the winter and this road closes.

day trip 06

south

be a duck:
eugene

eugene

The city of Eugene anchors the southern tip of the Willamette Valley. As the second largest city in Oregon and home to the University of Oregon, Eugene draws thousands of visitors each year. In addition to sports fans and students' families, the city also attracts recreationalists to its natural beauty and outdoor opportunities.

Sometimes called "Track Town USA," Eugene may be best known nationally for its famous running tradition. It's said that the tradition of jogging was born here, and the university has turned out many Olympic track stars, including Steve Prefontaine and Alberto Salazar. In 1964, the international sports company Nike was founded in Eugene by Phil Knight and Bill Bowerman, the University of Oregon track coach.

Eugene is also known as the hippie capital of Oregon. This is said with the utmost kindness and respect. In the 1960s and 1970s, Eugene and the university were central to left-wing political activities like war protests, and folks with "alternative" lifestyles were likewise attracted to the area. In the 1970s, Eugene became an innovator in grass-roots community projects and more earth-focused ways of living. Small natural food stores, student cooperatives, and alternative schools cropped up here long before they did other places in the state or nation.

Though the city has migrated toward the mainstream since those tumultuous times, Eugene is still a great place to buy tie-dye and homemade candles, stage a political activism

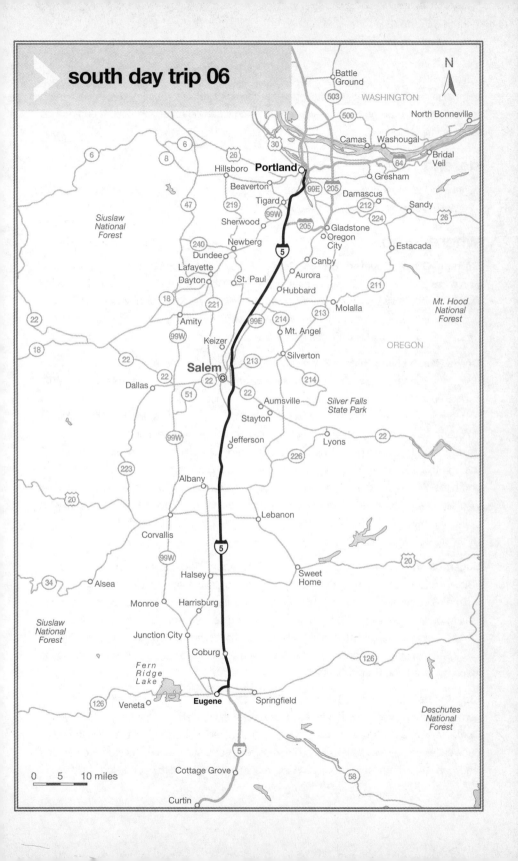

campaign, and participate in cutting-edge "green" projects. Eugene's residents trend toward the laid-back and happy—traits with which it can be refreshing to surround oneself for a day trip or longer.

getting there

Eugene is 110 miles due south of Portland on I-5. Take exit 194B off I-5 to merge onto OR 126 W. Travel west and follow signs for downtown.

where to go

Cottage Grove Covered Bridge Route. eugenecascadescoast.org/covered-bridges. Known as the "Covered Bridge Capital of Oregon," Cottage Grove is home to this state's scenic byway. Drawing visitors from across the nation every year, this seven-bridge route also takes you on a journey past Dorena Lake, several swimming holes, the historical Bohemia mining district, and filming locations made famous by the movie *Stand By Me*.

Dorris Ranch Living History Farm. Two miles east of I-5 at the intersection of South 2nd and Dorris Streets, Springfield; willamalane.org/pages/parks/dorris. Established in 1892, this 250-acre farm is Oregon's oldest working filbert (hazelnut) farm and the nation's oldest commercial filbert farm still in continuous operation. George Dorris and his wife, Lulu, set up a farm here in 1892, ultimately creating a hazelnut legacy. More than half of all the commercial filbert trees now growing in the US originated from Dorris Ranch nursery stock. Walk through this 250-acre historic site and natural area, admiring a variety of plants, flowers, and birds. At the Masterson homestead, step back in time to the year 1852 and discover what life was like for a newly arrived pioneer immigrant family. Brochures with a map of area paths are available at the entrance kiosk. Open weekdays and weekends from 6 a.m. until dusk for self-guided tours.

Eugene Saturday Market. 8th and Oak Streets (Apr to Nov); Lane Events Center, 796 W 13th Ave. (Nov to Dec); (541) 686-8885; eugenesaturdaymarket.org. Saturday markets are a dime a dozen these days, but that wasn't the case in 1970 when the Eugene Saturday Market began operations. Now it's known as the oldest weekly, open-air crafts festival in the US. Come and enjoy more than 200 craft booths, delicious food, and live entertainment every Sat, rain or shine, Apr through Oct. For the months of Nov and Dec, the market moves indoors to the Lane Events Center.

King Estate Winery. 80854 Territorial Rd.; (541) 942-9874; kingestate.com. One of the gems of Oregon wine, King Estate has been pleasing wine aficionados for nearly 20 years. Come here to taste the pinot noir, pinot gris, and limited amounts of chardonnay they produce each year, as well as take in the impressive Tuscan-style estate and stunning pastoral landscape. Also home to an award-winning restaurant dedicated to pairing Northwest wines with regional food products. Check out the pear garden installed over the underground cellar—it's a lovely little retreat.

Mount Pisgah Arboretum. 34901 Frank Parrish Rd.; (541) 747-3817; mountpisgah arboretum.org. Don't miss this 209-acre living museum. Riverside trails, evergreen forests, a water garden, bright wildflower meadows, and open views across oak savannas delight all ages. Seven miles of all-weather trails and 23 bridges make for great exploring and hiking. Open daily from dawn to dusk; $2 parking fee per vehicle.

Olive Grand. 35 E 8th St.; (541) 685-1000; olivegrand.com. Eugene's first and only olive oil tasting bar offers unique blends of fine olive oils, vinegars, herbs, and much more. Savor rich and aromatic flavors and learn to appreciate the distinctions that result from olive varieties, regional climates, and unique harvesting methods. What flavors do you most enjoy? You might be surprised to learn it's something radically different, like chocolate scones dipped in blood orange-flavored olive oil. Delicious! Open daily Mon through Sat from 10 a.m. to 6 p.m. or by special arrangement for groups and organizations.

Pacific Tree Climbing Institute. (866) OLD-TREE; pacifictreeclimbing.com. Everyone who ever climbed a tree as a kid and loved it will thrill at this opportunity. Pacific Tree Climbing Institute guides tree climbing expeditions in the legendary trees found in the Pacific Northwest. Their purpose is to demonstrate that remaining old growth groves have greater

the oregon country fair

Some events just have to be experienced at least once in a lifetime, and the Oregon Country Fair is one of them. Since 1969, organizers have been putting on this groovy gathering in the woods outside of Veneta, 13 miles west of Eugene. In some ways, the Oregon Country Fair is just another summer celebration, with loads of entertainment, handmade crafts, and delectable foods. In other ways, the fair is a mind-blowing adventure with magical surprises at every turn. Creativity, costumes (or—ahem—lack thereof), and the nourishment of the spirit in every way imaginable are enthusiastically encouraged. The last time I visited, I saw a woman with a typewriter in her lap selling made-to-order poems, a man painted from head to toe as a butterfly (and wearing nothing but the paint), a pirate on stilts, and a gigantic bicycle-powered, papier-mâché vehicle called a "hippypotamus." The Oregon Country Fair epitomizes Oregon's free spirit and, if nothing else, is an entirely welcome alternative to your average summer festival. Held the second weekend in July every year. Visit oregoncountryfair.org.

value as intact forests than as lumber. This message hits home as a guide takes you safely and expertly into the marvelous ecosystem that is a tree canopy. Day trips and overnighters available—yes, you get to sleep in the tree.

Ruth Bascom Bike Path. See eugene-or.gov for a downloadable map. This popular 12-mile bike path follows the Willamette River through many of Eugene and Springfield's favorite parks and attractions. Let your kids play at the Skinner Butte River Play playground, or search for wildlife at the Delta Ponds. Here's where you'll see all of those Eugene joggers, too—though it's mostly called running now. Easy access to and from downtown Eugene, and connects with a larger trail system, the Ridgeline Trail, should you desire a longer or more challenging hike, ride, or run.

Silvan Ridge Winery. 27012 Briggs Hill Rd.; (541) 345-1945; silvanridge.com. Founded in 1979, today Silvan Ridge makes distinctive Willamette Valley pinot noir and pinot gris as well as an effervescent early muscat. Tastings are complimentary; no food available on-site but bring-your-own picnics are welcome. Open daily noon to 5 p.m.

Spencer Butte Trail. 85385 Willamette St.; (541) 682-4800. This moderate to difficult 1.7-mile loop trail climbs 784 feet before reaching the summit of Spencer Butte. The 360-degree view from the summit gives a great overview of the Eugene area and beyond, including views of the Three Sisters and Fern Ridge Reservoir.

Studio West Glassblowing Studio. 245 W 8th Ave.; (541) 683-WEST; visitstudiowest .com. Studio West is a full production glass studio and gallery. Resident artists put on a show in the viewable studio for visitors every Fri and Sat night from 6 to 9 p.m. This studio also offers "blow your own" mini-workshops, allowing you to create your own keepsake to take home. Open Tues through Thurs 11 a.m. to 5 p.m.; Fri and Sat 11 a.m. to 9 p.m.

Sweet Cheeks Winery. 27007 Briggs Hill Rd.; (541) 349-9463; sweetcheekswinery.com. The 65-acre Sweet Cheeks Estate Vineyard sits on 140 acres of prime sloping hillside located in the heart of the Willamette Valley. Come for the view and the wine—pinot gris and Riesling. Open daily.

University of Oregon. Agate and East 13th Streets; (541) 346-1000; uoregon.edu. The university has been Eugene's centerpiece since its inception in 1876. The campus is a beautiful spot to take a walk, see interesting architecture, and enjoy flora and fauna, as well as witness the youth and exuberance of the student body. Keep an eye out for buildings that appeared in the 1978 film *Animal House,* which was filmed on campus. Here are a few other highlights:

Deady Hall. UO's first building was completed in 1876, when university enroll-ment was 177 students, and faculty numbered 5. It was designated a national historic landmark in 1977.

Hayward Field. Historic Hayward Field is one of the most famous track and field facilities in the world. The field was home to Bill Bowerman's famous "Men of Oregon" from 1948 to 1973—track teams that finished in the top 10 at the NCAA championships 16 times, including taking four team titles (1962, '64, '65, '70) and two second-place trophies. Hayward Field hosts many track and field events per year, including the Oregon State High School Championships, the annual Prefontaine Classic, and the Eugene Marathon. The 2008 and 2012 Olympic Team Trials for Track and Field were also held here.

Jordan Schnitzer Museum of Art. 1430 Johnson Lane.; (541) 346-3027; jsma .uoregon.edu. This premier Pacific Northwest visual arts center features Chinese, Japanese, Korean, and American art from its historic and contemporary collections in engaging exhibitions. Open Tues, Thurs, Fri, Sat, and Sun 11 a.m. to 5 p.m.; Wed 11 a.m. to 8 p.m. Free admission for children and University of Oregon students. The museum also includes a cafe, Marche Museum Cafe, open 7 days a week.

Living Arboretum. Wander through more than 500 different species of trees on campus. Especially in the fall, when the colors change, the campus is gorgeous.

Museum of Natural and Cultural History. 1680 E 15th Ave.; (541) 346-3024; natural-history.uoregon.edu. As Oregon's primary repository for anthropological and paleontological collections, the Museum of Natural and Cultural History houses nearly one million ethnographic and archaeological objects and almost 100,000 fossils and biological specimens from Oregon, the Pacific Northwest, and around the world. Open Wed through Sun, 11 a.m. to 5 p.m.

Sporting Events. (541) 346-4481; goducks.com. The mascot is the duck, and the supporters are willing to quack at the top of their lungs! Football and basketball are the primary fan-pleasers, but the University of Oregon offers the chance to see lacrosse, golf, cross-country, soccer, and even ultimate Frisbee matches. The impressive Matthew Knight Arena opened in 2011 to house UO's basketball games; Autzen Stadium has hosted football games since 1967. Get your tailgate on and be a duck!

where to shop

Fifth Street Market and International Cafes. 296 E Fifth Ave.; (541) 484-0383; 5st market.com. A Eugene icon, the Fifth Street Market opened in 1976 in an old poultry warehouse. Originally, local craftspeople and farmers rented booth space for two dollars a day, selling their wares and foodstuffs to a local crowd in this unique reclaimed space. Several remodels and decades later, the historic downtown Eugene marketplace comprises some of the Northwest's finest cafes, shops, and restaurants. Locally owned stores offer everything from shoes to suitcases to candy to cards, and local craftspeople are still able to lease a small sales space for their handcrafted wares. Many stand-alone restaurants, as well as a bustling upscale food court area with 5 or 6 small cafes to choose from and well-lit comfortable seating, feed hungry visitors. The international cafes are a great destination if you are with a group with diverse tastes. Live music is often on hand, and the sprawling multi-level marketplace with balconies and water fountains is almost always a feast for the senses, with the smell of fresh food, fresh flowers, and fresh baked goods wafting in the air. Retail shops open Mon through Sat 10 a.m. to 7 p.m., Sun 11 a.m. to 5 p.m. International cafes open Mon through Sat 8:30 a.m. to 7 p.m., Sun 9 a.m. to 6 p.m.

where to eat

Ambrosia. 174 E Broadway; (541) 342-4141; ambrosiarestaurant.com. Italian fare is served up in this upscale environment anchored by a lovely, antique bar. A second-floor balcony gives a bird's-eye view of the bar and main restaurant. Open Mon through Fri 11:30 a.m. to close, Sat and Sun 5 p.m. to close. $$–$$$.

Beppe and Gianni's Trattoria. 1646 E 19th Ave.; (541) 683-6661; beppeandgiannis.net. Just off campus, this Italian restaurant is consistently voted "best" by weekly newspaper *Eugene Weekly*. It is a must! Try the spaghetti, homemade fettuccine, or penne pasta with choice of sauces—puttanesca, pomodoro, pesto, and carbonara. Open for dinner nightly. $$–$$$.

Cafe Lucky Noodle. 207 E 5th Ave.; (541) 484-4777; luckynoodle.com. Serving a dynamic menu of Italian and Southeast Asian cuisine, Lucky Noodle offers everything from organic yam tempura to glass noodle stir fry to chicken Marsala. Open Mon through Fri 11 a.m. to midnight, Sat and Sun 9 a.m. to midnight. $$–$$$.

Creswell Bakery. 182 S 2nd St., Creswell; (541) 895-5885; creswellbakery.com. An off-shoot of Heidi Tunnell Catering, Creswell Bakery offers from-scratch breads, pastries, breakfast, and lunch 5 days a week. Try the chicken and chips, made from chickens raised just down the road at the bakery's farm. Open Tues through Fri 7 a.m. to 6 p.m.; Sat 8 a.m. to 2 p.m. $$.

The Glenwood. Two locations: 1340 Alder St.; (541) 687-0355; and 2588 Willamette St.; (541) 687-8201; glenwoodrestaurants.com. The Glenwood is a Eugene tradition. I think I had my first meal at the Glenwood at about the age of 5, and every time I get back to Eugene, it's one of the places I must visit. A huge menu covers fabulous, hearty, home-cooked meals extensively, from eggs Benedict to tempeh stir fry. Big portions, reasonable prices, and a casual, comfortable atmosphere make these restaurants a favorite for everyone from college students to retirees. Alder Street location is open 7 a.m. to 9 p.m. daily. Willamette Street location open weekdays 6:30 a.m. to 9 p.m., Sat and Sun 7 a.m. to 9 p.m. $–$$.

Keystone Cafe. 395 W 5th Ave.; (541) 342-2075; keystonecafe.net. Another classic Eugene restaurant that's been around since the 1970s, Keystone provides nourishing food in generous portions at reasonable prices in a warm and friendly atmosphere. The menu pleases carnivores, vegetarians, and vegans alike. The heated outdoor patio is the best choice for getting a table during the busy breakfast rush. Open 7 a.m. to 3 p.m. every day. $.

Marché. 296 E 5th Ave.; (541) 342-3612; marcherestaurant.com. Marché has been a Eugene institution for years, but they expanded operations several years ago to serve the Inn at the 5th when it opened. Delicious, French-inspired, farm-to-table cuisine is delivered in a warm and charming space. The exhibition kitchen features a beautiful wood-fired oven, and an expanded bar area allows for more casual dining. Open for breakfast, lunch, and dinner 7 days a week. $$-$$$.

Ox and Fin. 105 Oakway Center; (541) 302-3000; oxandfin.com. Dishes made from the best of the Northwest with an Italian flair are served at this elegant urban dining restaurant, reminiscent of the finest steak houses. Dishes include ling cod risotto, grilled octopus, and oxtail pappardelle. Open 7 nights a week for dinner, Tue through Sat for lunch. $$–$$$.

Sweet Basil Thai. 941 Pearl St.; (541) 284-2944; sweetbasileug.com. Serving elegant Thai food in the heart of downtown Eugene, Sweet Basil won the prestigious Chef's Night Out Overall Best Bite Award for 2010. Open for lunch Mon through Sat 11:30 a.m. to 3 p.m., dinner Sun through Thurs 5 to 9 p.m., dinner Fri and Sat 5 p.m. to 10 p.m. $$–$$$.

Sweet Life Patisserie. 755 Monroe St.; (541) 683-5676; sweetlifedesserts.com. Desserts, desserts, and only desserts. Cakes, cheesecakes, tortes, pies, tarts, cupcakes, pastries, and gelato all come out of this popular patisserie. All-day hours soothe the needy sweet tooth almost any time of day. Open Mon through Fri 7 a.m. to 11 p.m., Sat and Sun 8 a.m. to 11 p.m. $.

where to stay

Augusta House. 2585 Bowmont Dr.; (541) 342-8615; augustahouse.net. The Augusta House only has 2 rooms, but each is 700 square feet of well-appointed glory. A king-size bed and queen sofa sleeper, each with luxurious soft bed linens and pillow menu, gives you lots of room to spread out. Contemporary, luxurious accommodations with beautiful views of the city. $$–$$$.

The Campbell House. 252 Pearl St.; (541) 343-1119; campbellhouse.com. Built in 1892 and fully restored as a grand historic inn, the Campbell House is within walking distance of Fifth Street Market, the Hult Center, and downtown, and offers personalized service, comfortable surroundings, and all the amenities one would expect from a fine hotel. Voted one of the top 25 inns in America. $$–$$$.

Inn at the 5th. 205 E 6th Ave.; (541) 743-4099; innat5th.com. This boutique hotel opened in downtown Eugene a couple of years ago, adjacent to the 5th Street Market. It's super-classy, with unique art on the walls in every room, room service provided by Marché Restaurant, an on-site spa, and plenty of charm. The lobby is very elegant without being stuffy and is home to an amazing table made from a maple tree that used to stand on the site. $$–$$$.

Valley River Inn. 1000 Valley River Way; (800) 543-8266; valleyriverinn.com. Beautiful views of the Willamette River and nice rooms with Northwest charm, modern convenience, and luxurious comfort make this a Eugene mainstay. Valley River Shopping Center is right next door and offers lots of shopping, dining, and entertainment opportunities. $$–$$$.

worth more time

The McKenzie River, which runs from Clear Lake in the Cascade Range west into Springfield and Eugene, is one of the loveliest rivers in the state. Many small communities can be found along US 26 and the river, including Walterville, Vida, and McKenzie Bridge. Fly-fishing, rafting, and relaxing at one of many lovely lodgings are all wonderful outings within an hour out of Eugene. In fact, this river was the birthplace of the famed McKenzie River driftboat, and you'll see many if you don't actually choose to catch a float in one. Hike or mountain bike the spectacular **McKenzie River Trail,** or take a dip at **Belknap Hotsprings,** a developed hot springs, campground, and resort. Whatever you do, you'll be surrounded by incredible beauty and a fabulous example of the lush ecosystem of the western Cascade Range.

southwest

day trip 01

southwest

pioneer country:
newberg, dundee

newberg

Like many of its surrounding communities, the great allure of Newberg lies in its bucolic small-town charm and scenic beauty, all so near the big city. Newberg is a lovely town surrounded by forests and farmlands less than 30 miles from the Portland Metro Area. The Chehalem Mountains and the Willamette River buffer Newberg, providing a peaceful sense of place. Tourists flock here to taste the region's world-famous wine, but the rural countryside offers up opportunities beyond wine tasting—boating, fishing, hunting, and golf are popular activities. The beach is an hour west, the snowy Cascades an hour east. These advantages haven't gone unnoticed, and Newberg has grown in population in recent years. Still, it remains a relaxed and rewarding place to spend a day or a lifetime.

The Newberg area is also steeped in Oregon history. Hudson Bay Company trappers created the first European settlement in the area in a place called Champoeg, which is located approximately 7 miles southeast of Newberg. Pioneers followed, clearing the rich land for farming. Ultimately, Champoeg earned the distinction of serving as the site where Oregon's provisional government was established in 1843. Newberg has presidential roots, too. Herbert Hoover and his family lived in a home here, which you can visit.

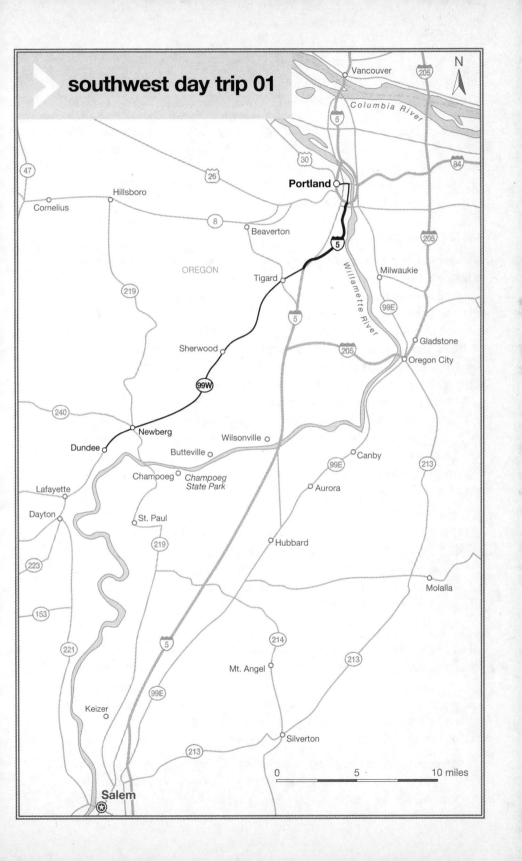

southwest day trip 01

getting there

Take I-5 south out of Portland to the OR 99 W exit, exit 294, to Tigard/Newberg. OR 99 W will merge with Pacific Highway W; continue to follow OR 99 W/Pacific Highway W to the southwest for a total of 24 miles from the Portland City Center.

Be aware that because OR 99W travels through many suburbs of Portland, it's slow going. The 24-mile trip could easily take you an hour to drive.

where to go

Champoeg State Heritage Area. Champoeg is located south and east of Newberg. Take a left onto Champoeg Road off the St. Paul Highway.

You could spend an entire day at the Champoeg State Heritage Area, and come away with a real sense of Oregon's history as well as that of this beautiful countryside. The Champoeg prairie has been settled longer than just about anywhere in this state. Originally home to the Kalapuya Indians, this rich landscape's abundant game lured British and French Canadian fur trappers; later, its fertile farmland attracted American settlers. On May 2, 1843, Oregon's first provisional government was established here.

Champoeg may have gone on to become the state capital if not for a huge flood of the Willamette River in December 1861, which essentially destroyed the town. Settlers eventually rebuilt, but by that time the headquarters for the fledgling state of Oregon had moved to Oregon City.

There is much to do here on the banks of the Willamette at this location today. Here are a few ideas:

The Butteville Store. 10767 Butte St. NE; (503) 678-1605; buttevillestore.com. The oldest continuously operating retail store in Oregon sits here on the banks of the Willamette River at the end of the Champoeg walking path. This little store serves delicious homemade soups, sandwiches, salads, and desserts, including Tillamook ice cream and fresh fruit pie, with a big dose of local history. Open daily May through Oct: Sun through Fri 9 a.m. to 6 p.m. and Sat 9 a.m. to 9 p.m. Live music plays on Saturday nights.

The Champoeg Interpretive Center. 8239 Champoeg Rd. NE; (503) 678-1251; champoeg.org. This big red barn-like structure includes a museum that was updated for Oregon's 150th anniversary in 2009. The exhibits bring alive the ways of the Kalapuya Indians, fur trappers, explorers, and settlers. Living history events take place all summer long, and there is a really nice gift shop and book store on-site, too. Open year-round, 7 days a week.

Champoeg State Park. The park features two main day-use areas, the Oak Grove and Riverside. Riverside features the old town site, an outdoor amphitheater, river access, and the Pioneer Mother's Cabin. Oak Grove has room for large groups, plus space for disc golf. Both are connected by a paved trail perfect for running, strolling, and biking. The trail snakes through dense woodland, offering peek-a-boo views of the Willamette River. More than 130 bird species have been identified in the park; ask for a Champoeg bird checklist at the visitor center. There's a campground on the east side of the park.

Hoover-Minthorn House. 115 S River St.; (503) 538-6629. The boyhood home of Herbert Hoover, 31st president of the United States, was built in 1881 by Jesse Edwards and is the first residence built and still standing in Newberg. The furniture in President Hoover's bedroom, which he inhabited from 1885 to 1889, is the actual set he used as a boy. Other furnishings in the house were gathered from homes in the countryside around Newberg. Open Mar through Nov, Wed through Sun 1 to 4 p.m.

The 99W Drive-in Theatre. 3110 Portland Rd.; (503) 538-2738; 99W.com. Thank goodness for the family that has kept this old-fashioned drive-in theater in Newberg open since August 1953, when it opened with *Sea Devils* and *Under the Sahara* as its first features. Twice the screen has been destroyed by Oregon storms, but the owners rebuilt. Today the 99 W. is one of only four drive-ins left in operation in Oregon and is on the National Register of Historic Places. Open late Apr or early May until late Oct.

Vista Balloon Adventures, Inc. (800) 622-2309; vistaballoon.com. Here's one fabulous and scenic way to see the countryside. Hot-air balloon flights are offered by this company from Newberg at dawn in Oregon's beautiful wine country. Flights take about an hour, and a lovely catered brunch is included after the flight. Flights are offered Mon, Wed, Fri, weekends, and holidays. Flight season is April 1 through the first weekend in Oct. All flights are weather permitting.

Wineries. So many wineries, so little time. You, day tripper, will need more than one day trip as well as a designated driver to hit all of the wineries in this area (which is why we've included tour company listings). We've only listed a handful of the wineries that exist around here. There are over 200 in the entire Willamette Valley region. See oregonwinecountry.org for a longer list. Choose wisely and call ahead to make sure your selections are indeed open. Most wineries are up in the hills out of town—bring a good map or electronic mapping system and pay close attention to addresses.

   Alexana. 12001 NE Worden Hill Rd.; (503) 537-3100; alexanawinery.com. Dr. Madaiah Revana lives in Texas, but that didn't stop him from opening a winery in Oregon. In the spring of 2005, Revana began a search for both the ideal region and an experienced winemaker with the goal of producing pinot noirs that could rival those from Burgundy. He chose this site in the Red Hills American Viticultural Area (AVA). The winery and tasting room overlooks the 80-acre vineyard and features warm wood, floor-to-ceiling windows, and an expansive 20-foot bar with a layered soil display. In addition to pinot noir, Alexana is making some lovely chardonnay, Riesling, and pinot gris. Open daily.

Adelshiem. 16800 NE Calkins Lane; (503) 538-3652; adelsheim.com. Adelshiem was established in 1971 and is one of the oldest vineyards in the valley. Today the winery uses sustainable farming practices to bring out the best in each of their unique vineyard sites. In the winery, traditional and modern techniques are combined to craft wines in a style that centers on elegance, complexity, and richness in flavor and texture. The winery is located at the base of the scenic Chehalem Mountains, and the tasting room is open 7 days a week from 11 a.m. to 4 p.m.

Bergstrom Wines. 18215 NE Calkins Lane; (503) 554-0468; bergstromwines .com. The Bergstrom philosophy is that winemaking is an agricultural pursuit— that the wine that you enjoy in your glass depends on a vineyard's and a farmer's performance in any given year, matched with the challenges put forth by Mother Nature. The very best Oregon pinot noir can only be achieved through non-industrial, artisan winemaking. The tasting room and patio here offer a beautiful view and are open from 10 a.m. to 4 p.m. daily.

Chehalem Wines. 106 S Center St.; chehalemwines.com. Well known for quality red and white wines, Chehalem focuses on cool-climate wine varieties that reflect both site and climate in complex, structured, and intensely fruited wines. Chehalem is a local Calapooia Indian word best translated as "gentle land" or "valley of flow-ers," phrases that capture a long-standing, almost religious reverence for the land— a philosophy Chehalem Wines tries to emulate. Varietals include pinot noir, pinot gris, chardonnay, Riesling, pinot blanc, Grüner Veltliner, and Gamay noir. Tasting fees are refundable with purchase of two bottles. Open daily from 11 a.m. to 5 p.m.

Fox Farm. 602 E 1st St.; (503) 538-8466; foxfarmvineyards.com. This very small production winery makes finely crafted, food-friendly, sensibly priced wines. In addition to their own delicious vintages, Fox Farm offers the wines of eight other local boutique wineries at their tasting room, which is open daily from noon to 8 p.m. Check out the web site for events listings.

Penner Ash. 15771 NE Ribbon Ridge Rd.; (503) 554-5545; pennerash.com. This is a truly lovely winery in a very scenic spot. On 80 acres, the winery sits on a hillside overlooking breathtaking and expansive views of the Chehalem Valley. Fif-teen acres of pinot noir grapes produce great wine annually, which you can taste right here, with a view. The tasting room is open Wed through Sun from 11 a.m. to 5 p.m. Winery tours are available Sat and Sun at 10 a.m.—call for reservations.

Rex Hill Vineyards and Winery. 30835 N OR 99 W; (503) 538-0666; rexhill .com. Located in an old fruit and nut drying facility, this winery sits on a hill and boasts a spectacular view. Visitors can see the original tunnels into which the carts of drying racks were rolled. The winery produces chardonnay, pinot gris, and pinot noir. Rex Hill also offers harvest tours and a variety of "exploring wine essentials" seminars—call for reservations. Tasting room open daily 10 a.m. to 5 p.m.

Roco Winery. 13260 NE Red Hills Rd.; (503) 538-7625; rocowinery.com. Rollin Soles began his career crafting wine in Switzerland, Australia, California, and Washington. In 1986, he sunk his roots into the Willamette Valley. Since then, he's produced some of Oregon's top pinot noirs, chardonnays, and sparkling wines, first for Argyle Winery and more recently for Roco, his private winery. This estate vineyard in the Chehalem Mountains is the birthplace of wines served in the White House, praised by Robert Parker, the *Wine Enthusiast,* and most recently received a 95 score from the *Wine Spectator.* The comfortable tasting room is a pleasant place to while away an hour, and don't be surprised if you find Rollin himself pouring wine. Open: June through Oct: Thurs to Mon 11 a.m. to 5 p.m.; Nov to May: Thurs to Sun 11 a.m. to 5 p.m.

Wine Tours. Wine country and guided tours go together like a horse and carriage, for many reasons. It's easier to take in views of the lush vineyard landscape when you aren't driving, a guide knows the often-winding country routes exactly, and you can feel a little freer to enjoy the wine itself if you don't have to operate a vehicle after consumption. Here are a few tour options in this region:

Black Tie Tours. (971) 832-0436; blacktietours.com. Black Tie can accommodate up to 6 guests per tour, and can choose a handful of favorites for you or tailor the tour to personal wine preferences, bottle price point, or specific winery requests. Minimum of 3 hours; lunch and some tasting fees are not included. Primarily serving the Newberg/Dundee/McMinnville area.

Embrace Oregon Tours. (503) 474-0762; embraceoregon.com. This company goes big with tours of all sorts offered all over the state, including wine and beer tours. Give them a call to customize the trip of your choosing, or jump on one of their prepackaged tours, which often include an overnight stay at a local B&B.

My Chauffeur Wine Tours. (503) 969-4370; winetouroregon.com. This company offers 4-hour, 6-hour, and 8-hour tours of Yamhill County wineries. They will pick you up in Portland or in wine country, wherever you prefer. Travel in groups of 2 or 52. Prices begin at $50 per person and go up depending on length of tour and services (a pre-packed picnic lunch is an option).

where to eat

JACS Deli. 111 E First St.; (503) 538-1113; jacsdeli.com. This place looks like a roadside diner, and technically is. But the flavors are much fresher and tastier than you might expect

could it be any prettier around here?

Wine grapes have only really been grown in the Willamette Valley since the 1970s. Before that, people didn't think the feat could be done. And anyway they were busy growing lots of other things in the valley's renowned rich and productive soils, like prunes, pears, apples, walnuts, and hazelnuts. Today, pinot noir grapes grow exceptionally well around here, and Oregon pinot noirs are widely favored. Some say they are the best in the world. Yamhill County is home today to dozens of wineries of all sizes and production levels. But if it's fruits and nuts you're after, you can still find those trees 'round these parts, as well as signs of the old homesteads that surrounded themselves with such pretty trees. In fact, these hardwoods interspersed with Oregon's famous evergreens dotted with the occasional grand old barn are part of what makes the hillsides and views around here so very beautiful. The wine grape vineyards are extremely lovely, themselves.

to be served in a place that used to be a gas station. Soups, sandwiches, hot case items, and, most famously, frozen custard please the palate here. Open Mon to Sat 11 a.m. to 7 p.m., Sun noon to 7 p.m. $–$$.

The Painted Lady. 201 S College St.; (503) 538-3850; thepaintedladyrestaurant.com. The painted lady movement restores Victorian homes using contrasting colors that bring out a building's decorative flourishes. This restaurant is located within a beautiful example of a painted lady Victorian home, and serves fabulous Pacific Northwest cuisine sourced locally. The menu is prix fixe, 5 courses for $70; wine pairing an additional $65. Open Wed through Sun for dinner from 5 to 10 p.m. $$$.

Recipe, A Neighborhood Kitchen. 115 N Washington St.; (503) 487-6853; recipenewberg or.com. This classic Victorian home in the heart of old town Newberg defines fine dining with French flavor in a setting reminiscent of the home dining room, while showcasing the excellent foods of the Willamette Valley and an outstanding list of wines both local and foreign. The farmhouse atmosphere features reclaimed barn wood tables, refinished wood chairs, a hand-built copper top bar, and warm earth tones throughout. A true locals' favorite for excellent food and a comfortable atmosphere. ***Note:*** Look for a new three-themed restaurant, named KAOS, by the same owners to open on 3rd Street in McMinnville in 2015. $$$.

Ruddick/Wood. 720 E First St.; (503) 487-6133; ruddickwood.com. One of the coolest spaces I've seen in awhile, Ruddick/Wood serves locally focused, seasonal, new-American fare alongside craft beer, wine, and cocktails in a renovated 1920s garage in downtown

Newberg. Dark wood, lots of reclaimed features like huge sliding barn doors, and interesting accents (like a map of local vineyard American Viticultural Areas [AVAs] painted on the wall) make this place super hip and cozy. Open Tues through Sat 11:30 a.m. to 3 p.m. and 5 to 9 p.m.; Sunday 9:30 a.m. to 3 p.m. and 5 to 9 p.m. $$$.

Subterra. 1505 Portland Rd., Suite 120; (503) 437-4984; subterrarestaurant.com. Subterra serves white tablecloth dining without prices quite as high as they can go around here. The menu includes baked brie with bourbon maple figs, duck confit, and grilled lamb kebabs. Open for lunch Wed through Sat from 11:30 a.m. to 2 p.m., for dinner Wed through Sat 5 p.m. to close, and for Sunday brunch from 10 a.m. to 2 p.m. The wine bar offers small plates and affordable wines by the glass. $$–$$$.

where to stay

The Allison Inn and Spa. 2525 Allison Lane; (503) 554-2525; theallison.com. The Allison is the result of one woman's vision for a destination resort in Oregon's wine country. This elaborate, full-service lodging boasts over 80 luxurious and incredibly comfortable rooms, with fireplaces, soaking tubs, and views of the estate vineyard. There is also a huge spa and fitness center on-site, worthy of a day trip all its own. The indoor pool and hot tub are surrounded by windows, the landscape is exacting and representative of Oregon's natural beauty, and the entire resort is outfitted with hundreds of works from regional artists. The restaurant, Jory, pays tribute to Oregon's acclaimed wines, microbrews, handcrafted distilled spirits, and agricultural bounty—some of which are grown right outside in the restaurant's half-acre garden. Indulge by trying several of the offered one-ounce tasting pours. The grounds are beautiful and boast a mile-long trail around the property. Both room and board are very expensive here, but the Allison's service, attention to detail, and ambience are world-class. $$$.

Le Puy Wine Valley Inn. 20300 NE Hwy. 240; (503) 554-9528; lepuy-inn.com. Owners Lea and Andy brought their backgrounds as professional architects to what was a (massive) single-family structure with an outstanding wine country view and transformed it into an 8-room bed-and-breakfast retreat. Desiring to be an authentic eco-inn, Le Puy exemplifies sustainability from the food offered, to the products used, to the care shown for the environment from the exterior to the interior. But it's the owners' understanding of the use of space, feng shui, and guest comfort that make this place truly special. $$–$$$.

Wine Country Farm. 6855 NE Breyman Orchards Rd.; (800) 261-3446; winecountryfarm .com. This historic home, built in 1910, today offers a quiet, peaceful respite with fantastic views of the Willamette Valley and Cascade Range. Still a working farm, raising grapes and Arabian horses, Wine Country Farm has a vineyard and tasting room on-site and is near many wine-tasting destinations. $$–$$$.

dundee

At a distance of only 30 miles from Portland, Dundee wears multiple hats: bedroom community, close-in day trip, dinner destination, road bike route. Despite the encroaching city (development along OR 99 from Portland to Dundee has become essentially seamless), Dundee remains relatively rural and small, with a population of just over 3,000 and a restful atmosphere. And yet, little Dundee offers a level of culture and style associated with a big city. Many highly rated restaurants are here, not to mention award-winning wineries.

Dundee's proximity to Portland also makes it a popular destination via bicycle. OR 99 W provides a protected bike lane, but cyclists often find the scenery and experience better on side streets and country roads. Grab a map and choose to cruise the side of the city with the meandering Willamette River and Dundee's Ash Island, or the other side, where acres of vineyards are found.

getting there

Continue on OR 99 W out of Newberg, heading southwest. Dundee is 2.5 miles southwest from Newberg on OR 99 W.

where to go

Oregon Olive Mill at Red Ridge Farms. 5510 NE Breyman Orchards Rd., Dayton; (503) 864-2200; oregonolivemill.com. In 2005 the Durant family planted a small olive orchard at Red Ridge Farms. They've been adding trees to it every year since. Today there are more than 17 acres and 13,000 trees on this site, as well as a new structure housing a state-of-the-art Italian olive press and a boutique bottling line. Taste and buy their unique olive oils at the Red Ridge Farms store, open Wed through Sun 9 a.m. to 5 p.m.

Wineries. The Dundee area, specifically the Dundee Hills American Viticultural Area (AVA), encompasses 6,490 acres of pristine wine growing country. It is home to Oregon's earliest pinot noir plantings, and considered by most to be the heart of Oregon wine country. The Dundee Hills AVA extends to the west, southwest, and northwest of Dundee, and most of the wineries are actually in these hills, not in Dundee proper. Bring a good map or electronic mapping system and pay close attention to addresses.

Archery Summit Winery. 18599 NE Archery Summit Rd., Dayton; (503) 864-4300; archerysummit.com. Archery Summit only makes pinot noir, and makes it very well. Visit their tasting room to sample their excellent wine, sit on the terrace, take in views of the Willamette Valley and breathtaking Mt. Jefferson, and learn more about Oregon pinot noir. A $15 fee includes tastes of four highly rated pinot noirs. Guided tours are given at 10:30 a.m. and 2 p.m. daily, by appointment only. Tours begin in the vineyard and continue through the winery, from the sorting tables to the aging caves and bottling room. Archery Summit guides will teach you more than you ever imagined there was to know about pinot noir, whether you are a fan or a novice. The tasting room is open every day from 10 a.m. to 4 p.m.

Argyle Winery. 691 OR 99 W; (888) 427-4953; argylewinery.com. Housed in a former hazelnut processing plant are the modern winery operations for Argyle Winery, a popular and accessible winery. Argyle produces pinot noir, dry Riesling, chardonnay, and pinot gris, as well as 3 types of vintage Oregon sparkling wines made in the méthode Champenoise: brut, blanc de Blaney, and rosé. They are delicious, and many Oregon wineries have followed in Argyle's footsteps by producing sparkling wines today. The tasting room is a wonderful place to taste Argyle wines, hear live music, see local art displays, and experience some of the Oregon winemaking culture. Open daily 11 a.m. to 5 p.m. except major holidays.

Domaine Drouhin. 6750 Breyman Orchards Rd., Dayton; (503) 864-2700; domainedrouhin.com. Domaine Drouhin was established in the 1980s and was one of the forerunners in the Oregon pinot noir phenomenon. The Drouhin family has been making wine in Burgundy, France, since 1880, and specifically sought out a Willamette Valley estate after tasting some of the early pinot noir produced from Oregon in the 1960s and 1970s. Fourth generation Drouhin family members still make the wine and run the Oregon business. Their pinot noir bottlings are frequently awarded "Outstanding" scores from *Wine Spectator* and *Wine Advocate* critics, and the Domaine Drouhin chardonnay has been named "Best New World White Wine." The winery itself has been described as "palatial," occupying the top of a hill with panoramic and amazing views. The tasting room is open Wed through Sun from 11 a.m. to 4 p.m.; there is a tasting fee of $10 for a flight of 3 wines. No appointment is necessary for groups of 7 or fewer. Domaine Drouhin does not allow picnics on their property, but the view of 90 acres of hillside vineyards on a 225-acre estate might just be enough to satisfy you.

Sokol Blosser Winery. 5000 NE Sokol Blosser Lane, Dayton; (800) 582-6668; sokolblosser.com. The outstanding architecture of Sokol Blosser's tasting room, completed in 2013, offers guests a multitude of tasting "experiences". Indoor, outdoor, small and intimate, spacious and airy, take your pick. The many spaces all share this modern, streamlined cedar-paneled structure and the wines of Sokol Blosser. Mostly pinot noir but also including pinot gris and the Evolution line in red and white, these wines are very drinkable. Open 10 a.m. to 4 p.m. daily.

Stoller Vineyards. 16161 NE McDougall Rd., Dayton; (503) 864-3404; stoller vineyards.com. Stoller Vineyards offers excellent wines and friendly hospitality in a stunning setting, but their true claim to fame is their eco-friendly practices. Bill and Cathy Stoller's vision of blending vineyard stewardship with environmental sustainability was recognized in 2006 when Stoller became the first LEED certified winemaking facility in the US. Today, the winery continues to operate sustainably and provide delicious pinot noir, chardonnay, and pinot noir rosé as well as panoramic views including Mt. Hood. The tasting room is open daily from 11 a.m. to 5 p.m.

White Rose Wines. 6250 Northeast Hilltop Lane; Dayton; (503) 864-2328; whiterosewines.com. Planted in 1980 at the top of a hill near Dayton, the White Rose pinot noir vines consistently produce fruit of great character and complexity. This small winery makes some very delicious pinot noir and offers it in its adorable tasting room, open 11 a.m. to 5 p.m. daily, except in Dec, when it is only open by appointment. There is a $15 tasting fee.

Winderlea Vineyard. 8905 NE Worden Hill Rd.; (503) 554-5900; winderlea.com. The owners of this incredibly scenic spot spent 14 months walking thousands of acres of vineyards and tasting hundreds of wines from those vineyards to find the perfect site to produce elegant, sensuous, and balanced wines. The Dundee Hills are renowned for their soil—the red volcanic, clay loam soil known as Jory—and its scenery, which is very elegantly captured from Winderlea's modern, many-windowed tasting room. Open daily from 11 a.m. to 4 p.m.

where to eat

The Barlow Room. 306 Ferry St., Dayton; (503) 714-4328; thebarlowroom.com. As is true of the best saloons, guests feel comfortable the minute they walk into the Barlow Room. Belly up to the massive wooden bar and order a fresh cocktail or item off of the low-key but excellent menu and feel even more at home. This place is owned by the Czarnecki clan of the famous Joel Palmer House, and retains that level of quality in a much more casual and affordable environment. Sam Barlow was a fellow pioneer to Palmer, and the pair worked together to create the Barlow Road passage to Oregon. This old building maintains the Oregon pioneer spirit with exposed brick walls showcasing historic photos of Dayton and the Willamette Valley. Open Wed through Sun, 11 a.m. to close. $–$$.

Dundee Bistro. 100-A SW 7th St.; (503) 554-1650; dundeebistro.com. This bistro with full bar and fireside, courtyard, and private party seating is as comfortable as it is satisfying. Created by the Ponzi family, who have owned and operated world-acclaimed vineyards in the Yamhill Valley for 35 years, the Dundee Bistro prepares and presents dishes that reflect culinary sophistication while also catering to winemakers who want to have lunch in overalls and field boots. The menu changes daily and features locally grown organic, sustainable products—visitors might choose baby arugula with Italian plums and chèvre or halibut fish and chips. Open daily 11:30 a.m. to close. $$–$$$.

Joel Palmer House. 600 Ferry St.; (503) 864-2995; joelpalmerhouse.com. Joel Palmer founded the town of Dayton and built this spectacular home in 1857. Today the Joel Palmer House is a renowned restaurant that features wild mushrooms and other local ingredients in excellent dishes that match the glorious wines of the local region. Founding chef Jack Czarnecki is world-renowned; today, the next generation of the family has taken the reins, with Jack's son Chris Czarnecki as the executive chef at the Joel Palmer House. The prices are very high, but many believe this is the best place to eat in wine country, and the Joel Palmer House remains a well-known, classic fine-dining destination. Open Tues through Sat for dinner. $$$.

Red Hills Market. 155 SW Seventh St.; (971) 832-8414; redhillsmarket.com. Chef Jody Kropf grew up in Brownsville, helping his family to run the local restaurant they owned. Today, he is at the helm of Red Hills Market, a highly pleasant shop, deli, and restaurant in Dundee. Whether it's soup, salads, sandwiches, coffee, wine, dessert, or a selection from the foodie-friendly shelves of product, everything here is excellent. The new building has the old-fashioned air of the best gathering places—crowded, boisterous, cozy, and filled with friends. $–$$.

Tina's Restaurant. 760 OR 99 W; (503) 538-8880; tinasdundee.com. Opened in 1991, this restaurant is a bit of a flagship for the Dundee area wining and dining scene. An understated exterior shrouds a cozy and intimate interior, with a comfortable bar and 2 dining rooms divided by a fireplace. The owners know everyone and even if they don't know you, they'll treat you like they do. The menu offers some fabulous unique items like soufflé, braised rabbit, and steamed salmon. The wine list, as you'd expect, is amazing. Desserts include fruit cobblers in season and crème brûlée. Open for dinner nightly from 5 p.m. to close, and for lunch Tues through Fri from 11:30 a.m. to 2 p.m. $$$.

where to stay

Black Walnut Inn and Vineyard. 9600 NE Worden Hill Rd.; (503) 429-4114; blackwalnut -inn.com. If you are feeling extravagant, book an overnight stay at the Black Walnut Inn. Newly constructed and reminiscent of an old Tuscan villa, this inn sits in the hills outside Dundee and is filled with modern art and amenities blended expertly with beautiful antiques, old world details, and the works of local artisans. The European elegance extends from the incredible architecture to luxurious linens, soaking tubs, king and queen size beds, and breathtaking views. The rooms run as much as $495 per night, but you'll be comforted to know that they come with a full gourmet breakfast and afternoon refreshments. $$$.

Franziskas Haus. 10305 NE Fox Farm Rd.; (503) 887-0879; franziskahaus.com. This newly constructed log lodge structure has a 29-foot stone-crafted fireplace in the great room, and that's just for starters. The place has 3 rooms, each cozy and distinct, with elegant, Old World accents, and is graced with views of surrounding filbert orchards, grazing sheep, nearby vineyards, and the distant Chehalem Hills. Breakfast is delicious and German-inspired. $$–$$$.

The Inn at Red Hills, Babica Hen Restaurant, and Wine Tasting Rooms. 1410 N OR 99 W; (503) 538-7666; innatredhills.com. The Inn at Red Hills offers lodging, dining, and wine tasting right in one place in lovely downtown Dundee. The inn is composed of two free-standing buildings with a charming stone courtyard in between, and is easily accessed off of the highway. There are 20 rooms boasting large windows with views of the countryside and small relaxation areas with either a sofa or oversized chairs. Kick back, read a book, and gaze at those vineyards. The restaurant, Babica Hen (babicahencafe.com), is the second location of the popular Lake Oswego eatery. Focusing on breakfast and lunch (but also serving dinner) from farm fresh, locally sourced ingredients, Babica Hen excels at waffles and even makes some that are gluten-free. Definitely try the chicken and waffles. Also on-site are four wine-tasting rooms: Le Cadeau (lecadeauvineyard.com/visit/tasting -room); Evening Land Vineyards (eveninglandvineyards.com); Angela Estate (angelaestate .com); and Tertulia Cellars (tertuliacellars.com/tasting-room). Convenience and a great location make this place popular. Lodging: $$$. Dining: $–$$.

day trip 02

southwest

wine country:
mcminnville, carlton

mcminnville

McMinnville is the county seat and the largest of Yamhill County's cities. Located at the confluence of the North and South Forks of the Yamhill River, McMinnville has a charming and thriving downtown and is surrounded by rolling and lovely pastoral hills. Also lovely is the campus of Linfield College, a four-year undergraduate liberal arts college: Pioneer Hall, built in 1882, and Melrose Hall, built in 1929, are both exquisite examples of architecture, and the campus also boasts many old and lovely trees.

McMinnville had its 15 minutes of national fame back in 1950, when photographs of a reported unidentified flying object were taken from a local farm and published in the city's newspaper. Within a month, the photos had made it into *LIFE* magazine. A debate has raged ever since about the validity of the photos, and more than once photographic experts were hired to prove or disprove the case, to no avail. McMinnville residents took the whole affair lightly, however, and to this day, each year in May, stage a UFO Festival, the second-biggest in the nation.

If you don't make your day trip around UFO season, definitely shoot for wine tasting and shopping season (which, luckily, is all year). McMinnville is full of both opportunities, as well as some truly fabulous restaurants.

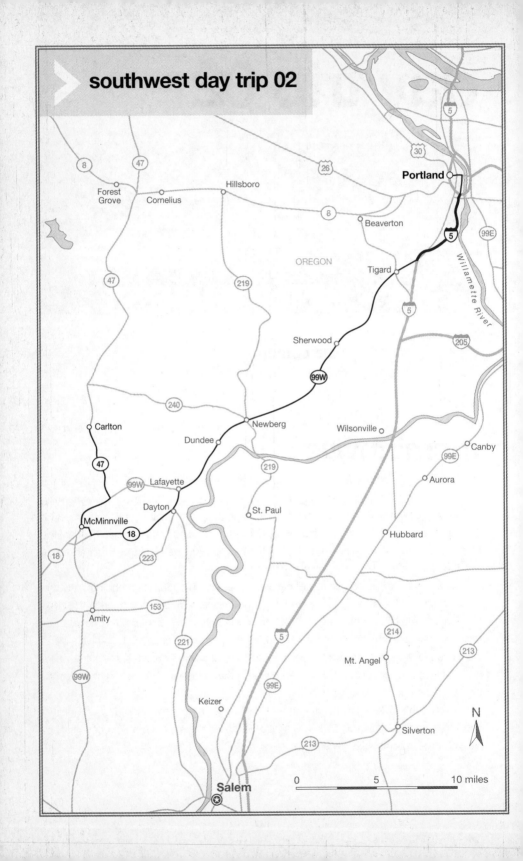

getting there

Take I-5 out of Portland to exit 294, heading southwest on OR 99 W, Travel through Tigard, Sherwood, Newberg, and Dundee. Turn left onto OR 18 W/SE Dayton Bypass. After 6 miles, take the Salmon River Spur ramp to make a slight right onto NE Three Mile Lane/OR 18 Spur, which will immediately turn into McMinnville's 3rd Street.

Be aware that because OR 99 W travels through many suburbs of Portland, it's slow going. It will likely take you more than an hour to drive 35 miles.

where to go

Evergreen Aviation and Space Museum. 500 NE Captain Michael King Smith Way; (503) 434-4180; sprucegoose.org. This massive facility has an aviation museum, a space museum, an IMAX theater, and an estimated 5-hour tour time! Even if you don't have that much time, consider popping in to see the famous *Spruce Goose.* The single hull flying boat capable of carrying 750 troops was designed by Howard Hughes and flown only once before being stored for years. Finally, it was donated to this museum, where it is treated as the crown jewel. This living museum celebrates aviation's rich history, honors the patriotic service of our veterans, and offers enlightening educational programs in aviation. As if that isn't enough, the site also includes a water park, with 3 water slides that descend from a real 747 airplane parked on the roof, plus smaller pools and water play areas appropriate for kids from toddlers on up. Open every day, including weekends, from 9 a.m. to 5 p.m. Tickets vary in price from $23 to $25 depending on age and whether or not the visitor chooses to include an IMAX movie; water park is $12 to $32.

Farms: You-Pick, Produce, and Christmas Tree. It's not all about wine around here. Some farms do what they've always done in the rich, organic Willamette Valley soil and grow vegetables, raise sheep and cows, and even grow Christmas trees.

Draper Farms. 11105 SW Baker Creek Rd.; (503) 472-2358; facebook.com/DraperFarms/info. You-pick raspberries and tomatoes when posted or advertised. Farm stand season is May 1 through October 31 from 9 a.m. to dusk daily. Call for availability.

Farmer John's Produce and Nursery. 15000 SW Oldsville Rd.; (503) 474-3514; farmerjohnsproduce.com. This family farm has been growing wonderful things since 1882. Today, the farm follows organic practices but without the organic certification. Farmer John's is open to the public mid-May through October 31 and offers a wide array of products depending on the season including bedding plants, hanging baskets, strawberries, pumpkins, kiwi, Indian corn, artichokes, tomatoes, and potatoes.

Foxridge Tree Farm. 2960 NW Hill Rd. N; (503) 835-9606; foxridgechristmas treefarm.com. This you-cut Christmas tree farm offers noble, Douglas fir, and grand trees to take home. Open weekends only between November 26 and December 19.

Ramsby's Tree Farm. 16460 SW Oldsville Rd.; (503) 843-3149; nwtrees.com. Between Thanksgiving and Christmas, cut a Christmas tree at this lovely farm south of McMinnville. Choose from noble, Douglas fir, grand, Turkish, and Nordmann fir, all grown here in the rich soil of Yamhill County. Open daily 9 a.m. to 5 p.m. November 26 through December 20.

Wheatland Ferry. Wheatland Ferry Road; (503) 588-5304; wheatlandferry.com. Located 1 mile north of the Yamhill–Polk county border in Oregon, the Wheatland Ferry shuttles passengers across the Willamette River, linking Marion with Yamhill and Polk Counties. It's a little old-fashioned blast from the past, a fun ride and an honest commuting solution for many locals. Hours of operation: daily 5:30 a.m. to 9:45 p.m. year-round. Closed Thanksgiving and Christmas. Cost is $2 for passenger cars.

Wineries. The Oregon wine country bounty continues in McMinnville. If you aren't in the mood to drive to surrounding wineries, visit 3rd Street, downtown, and simply begin wandering. There are several wine bars on this street, and more seem to appear all the time. If you prefer to go to the source, here's a partial list, some in town, some out. See downtown mcminnville.com for a longer list.

Coehlo Winery. 111 5th St., Amity; (503) 835-9305; coelhowinery.com. Portuguese wine has long been considered a well-kept secret of Europe. Coehlo means "rabbit" in Portuguese, and is also the family name of the folks who created this winery, which presents a tasting room in a spacious old hardware store in downtown Amity. Don't miss a chance to try the two kinds of port, in addition to pinots and the like. Open daily 11 a.m. to 5 p.m.

Elizabeth Chambers Cellar. 455 NE Irvine St.; (503) 412-9765;elizabethchambers cellar.com. McMinnville's former power plant, just off the main street in downtown, was once Panther Creek Winery, owned by the Chambers family. When they sold Panther Creek to investors, Elizabeth Chambers stayed in this cool location and started her own label. This enormous brick building built in 1923 makes a lovely tasting room for her pinot gris and pinot noir, and is open noon to 5 p.m. There is a $5 tasting fee, which is refundable with wine purchase.

J Wrigley Vineyards. 19390 SW Cherry Hill Rd., Sheridan; (503) 857-8287; wrigley wines.com. This estate vineyard located in the McMinnville American Viticultural Area (AVA) is 200 acres of prime vineyard land, planted in 2008 by the Wrigley family. The property and the wine are both lovely and highly recommended by locals, who make this welcoming place a destination for soup nights on Friday in the winter as well as other events year-round.

R. Stuart and Co. Wine Bar. 528 NE 3rd St.; (503) 472-4477; rstuartandco .com. This little downtown tasting room is done up in warm colors, big street-front windows, and chandeliers. Their wines—primarily a pinot noir and pinot gris—are delicious. The wine bar is the perfect setting to linger over a glass of something and a snack with friends, or purchase wine to take home. For a little variety, R. Stuart also offers a couple of local microbrews and Portland Roasting Company organic espresso. Open Sun through Wed noon to 6 p.m. and Thurs through Sat noon to 8 p.m.

Terra Vina Wines. 585 NE 3rd St.; (503) 474 6777; terravinawines.com. The small family-owned Terra Vina Wines makes wines grown on their vineyard on Parrett Mountain in the Chehalem Mountains American Viticultural Area (AVA), as well as from grapes sourced from Eastern Oregon and Washington. The warm and friendly tasting rooming in McMinnville offers tastings, wine by the glass, small plates, and a friendly space with a view of the street in which to relax. Open Thurs through Sun.

where to shop

Brigittine Monks' Gourmet Confections. 23300 Walker Lane, Amity; (503) 835-8080; brigittine.org. This Roman Catholic monastery manufactures quality gourmet fudge and truffles as its means of self-support. It's great candy that receives accolades from candy experts and customers alike. The store, at the monastery, is open Mon through Sat from 9 a.m. to 5 p.m. and Sun from 1 to 5 p.m.

Currents Gallery. 532 NE 3rd St.; (503) 435-1316; currentsgallery.com. This artists' collective and cooperative is an excellent place to find treasures and gifts of all kinds. Discover arts and crafts from woodworking to clay to jewelry to clothing to handmade soaps in this light and airy space. Open Mon through Sat 10 a.m. to 6 p.m., Sun 10 a.m. to 2 p.m.

Third Street Books. 334 NE 3rd St.; (503) 472-7786; thirdstreetbooks.com. Every small-town downtown needs a really great book store, and this is McMinnville's resident book lover's dream. Third Street Books is a general interest bookstore with mostly new books, but some used books are on the shelves as well. There is also a great selection of magazines, cards, and other unique gift items here to discover. Open Mon through Sun 10 a.m. to 6 p.m.

Yamhill Valley Dry Goods. 416 NE 3rd St.; (503) 883-0019; yamhillvalleydrygoods.com. A lovely collection of high-quality clothing, shoes, jewelry, and small gifts in a cute street-level storefront. Oregon-made products and more for men and women. Open Mon through Sat 10 a.m. to 6 p.m. and Sun 11 a.m. to 4 p.m.

where to eat

Bistro Maison. 729 NE 3rd St.; (503) 474-1888; bistromaison.com. Authentic French food including coq au vin, steak au poivre, cassoulet, mussels, and fondue is offered at this lovely little bistro in an old house in historical downtown McMinnville. Bistro Maison makes an incredible brunch, and in the summer, the gardens and patio are delightful places to spend a mealtime. Open for lunch and dinner Wed through Sun. $$$.

Crescent Cafe. 526 NE 3rd St.; (503) 435-2655. More refined than your average breakfast cafe, Crescent Cafe puts out phenomenal, well-put-together local foods, including home-made breads that are to die for. Daily specials are truly special, assembled by a chef with as much love as would be lavished on the finest fine-dining dinner. Try the Carlton Farms pork biscuits and gravy (the biscuits are enormous and divine) or the blood orange juice. Open until about 1:30 p.m. Wed through Sun—expect a wait on weekends. $.

Golden Valley Brewery and Pub. 980 NE 4th St.; (503) 472-2739; goldenvalleybrewery .com. This downtown building was a working warehouse in the 1920s and now houses a brewery, brewpub, and restaurant. This small craft brewery, founded to revive a traditional style of brewing, is dedicated to producing ales and lagers of rare complexity and great balance. But their menu is pretty great, too. Golden Valley has always had a kitchen garden and sources produce and meats locally. And guess what? They even serve Oregon wines. Open every day for lunch and dinner. $$–$$$.

La Rambla Restaurant and Bar. 238 NE 3rd St.; (503) 435 2126; laramblaonthird.com. You can't miss this beautiful bright red and orange stucco building in McMinnville's down-town. The interior is vibrant and richly detailed, too, but the main attraction is the food. La Rambla creates Northwest inspired cuisine from Spain by blending classics with Spanish influences and the best food the Pacific Northwest has to offer. Hot and cold tapas plus larger plates are available to pair with a selection from the incredible wine list, which includes more than 400 local and Spanish wines. Open for lunch and dinner 7 days a week. $$–$$$.

Nick's Italian Cafe. 521 NE 3rd St.; (503) 434-4471; nicksitaliancafe.com. Since 1977, Nick's has served multi-course fixed meals and a la carte dishes that helped to put McMinnville on the gastronomic map. The menu features local foods made with true Italian style, including Dungeness crab and pine nut lasagna, Cornish game hen, and lamb. Open for lunch and dinner Tues through Sat (closed from 2:30 to 5 p.m.). A small lounge in back is a cozy hangout. $$–$$$.

Red Fox Bakery and Cafe. 328 NE Evans St.; (503) 434-5098; redfoxbakery.com. McMinnville's first independent artisan bakery in the heart of downtown features true

'tis the season

Summer is Oregon's glory time, when the weather is perfect, the flowers are in bloom, the air is fresh and glorious, and the landscape a rich delight for the senses. Touring Oregon's wine country is definitely a pleasure in summer (but you won't be alone in that thinking or endeavor). For a quieter experience, consider a trip off-season. I was in McMinnville and Carlton last winter, just before Christmas, and it was a great trip. Fewer humans, more intimate service at destinations, buildings lit up for the holidays, and a peaceful, dormant landscape made for a fantastic, if simpler, experience. The wine, by the way, tastes delicious in all seasons.

handcrafted breads and pastries. A light lunch of sandwiches and soups is served daily, as well. Your sweet tooth will not be neglected—Red Fox makes some delightful brownies and rather addictive macaroons. Try the sbrisolona (almond butter cookie). Open Mon through Sat 7 a.m. to 4 p.m., Sun 8 a.m. to 2 p.m. $.

Thistle Restaurant. 228 NE Evans St.; (503) 472-9623; thistlerestaurant.com. This hip little restaurant off of 3rd Street is a not-to-be missed experience. The small menu changes daily, is written up on a chalkboard, and usually lists about 12 items of "playful American cuisine," followed by a list of the local farmers, fishers, and purveyors who provided the ingredients—most sourced within 45 miles. The space is simple but classy and fun, and also includes a cozy bar overseen by a master bartender mixing up top-notch cocktails served in vintage glassware. Open for dinner Tues through Sat. $$$.

Wildwood. 319 NE Baker St.; (503) 435-1454. This is a classic breakfast joint offering up big fat traditional breakfasts, good prices, and big portions. Egg beaters and old memorabilia cover the walls, giving the place a retro chic. A word of warning—Wildwood is popular and the wait can be lengthy, especially on weekends. Open for breakfast and lunch. $.

where to stay

Hotel Oregon. 310 NE Evans St.; (503) 472-8427; mcmenamins.com. Hotel Oregon anchors the heart of downtown McMinnville, just as it has since 1905. Once home to a restaurant and lounge, banquet hall, Greyhound bus depot, Western Union, soda fountain, and beauty parlor, this handsome 4-story building, renovated by the McMenamin brothers, is a delightful destination in the heart of Oregon's wine country. Take a trip to the subterranean bistro-style Cellar Bar or magnificent Rooftop Bar, which boasts a breathtaking 360-degree view of city lights, vineyard-laden hills, and the Coast Range. (Also perched atop the building is a flying saucer—a nod to the annual UFO festival that happens here.) New is the Carter the Great bar, focused on craft cocktails. Stay overnight in one of 42 European-style guest rooms, or hit the restaurant for omelets, burgers, pastas, salads, or one of McMenamins 200 signature ales. $$.

Third Street Flats. Historic McMinnville Bank, 219 NE Cowls St.; Odd Fellows Lodge, 555 NE 3rd St.; (503) 857-6248; thirdstreetflats.com. Take two old downtown buildings, renovate their second floors into a total of 11 unique, stylish urban-style flats, and you have this wonderful lodging option in McMinnville. The owners wanted guests to have the amenities and convenience of their own pied-à-terre coupled with the luxury of a quality hotel. They succeeded—the flats are fun, right near the action, quiet, and very comfortable. $$–$$$.

carlton

Carlton puts the "I" in idyllic. This little town brims over with charm, from the quaint and appealing downtown to the sweeping vistas and rolling hills that surround it. Rich soil covers those hills, and settlers began farming this land 150 years ago. Eventually a railroad went in and Carlton grew a little—but not much. Today it's still a tiny hamlet, albeit a tiny hamlet sprinkled with riches, both metaphorical and actual. Investors and retirees have scooped up ranches and vineyards around this small town, and the growth of the wine industry has beckoned a smattering of top-notch restaurants and shops. Park and walk the entire downtown—there are several wine bars and tasting rooms as well as a few attractive shops.

At the same time, there are still plenty of people living simple lives around here, and doing so with a lot of hometown spirit. Residents take seriously the city's motto—"A great little town."

getting there

Head north out of McMinnville on OR 99 W. After just a couple of miles, turn left onto OR 47 N/Tualatin Valley Highway. Continue 4 miles into Carlton.

where to go

Wineries and Tasting Rooms. "Where to Go" translates to "where to go to taste some wine" here in Carlton. You can park your car and walk to all of these destinations:

Barking Frog. 128 W Main St.; (503) 702-5029; barkingfrogwinery.com. According-ing to Native American lore, the barking frog is a symbol of prosperity, considered friendly as it is said he signals to mankind that all is well with the environment. At Barking Frog winery, the winemaking style is to utilize fully ripe fruit and to maximize and build complexity with structure in all wines. The winemakers want to allow the uniqueness of each wine's terroir to be expressed. Open Fri through Sun 1 to 5 p.m. or by appointment.

Cana's Feast Winery. 750 W Lincoln St.; (503) 852-0002; canasfeastwinery .com. Located in a Tuscan-inspired building just north of historic downtown Carlton, Cana's Feast Winery has a rich history of combining the tradition of bold, Northwest red wines with good food, hospitality, and celebration. They produce Burgundy, Bordeaux, and Rhone-style red wines, and host lunch and dinner for guests on occasion, usually in the summer on the weekends, pairing great foods with great wines. The west terrace offers spectacular views of the Coast Range and is the perfect place to relax. Two bocce ball courts host lively games on the lawn. The tasting room is open daily, 11 a.m. to 5 p.m.

Carlton Winemakers Studio. 801 N Scott St; (503) 852-6100; winemakers studio.com. This place is as revolutionary as it is a fabulous destination. The idea behind the studio was to create a space where artisanal wine producers could come together under one roof in a state-of-the-art facility to produce and promote their ultra-premium wines. In that way, the Carlton Winemakers Studio became an incubator for small boutique winemakers. As many as 10 vintners can oper-ate within the studio walls at one time, and each showcases his or her current releases in the shared Tasting Room, itself a totally cool modern room with a concrete bar, high ceilings, and large windows. This place epitomizes the cama-raderie and innovation that is Oregon wine country and gives visitors a chance to taste many boutique wines. Not to be missed. Open daily from 11 a.m. to 5 p.m.

The Horse Radish. 211 W Main St.; (503) 852-6656; thehorseradish.com. A hip little wine and cheese bar that also has live music every Friday night. With amazing sandwiches and great cheese plates prepared and served by a multigenerational family, this place is a little gem in wine country. $$.

Scott Paul Wines. 128 S Pine St.; (503) 852-7300; scottpaul.com. Scott Paul Wines is a bit of an anomaly in that not only do they produce their own Oregon pinot noir, they also import champagnes and burgundies from over 20 small family artisanal producers in Burgundy and Champagne, France. At this tasting room, you can try all of these wines. There is a $10 tasting fee, which is waived with a 3-bottle purchase. Tasting room open Dec through Mar on Sat only from 1 to 5 p.m. From Apr to Nov, Scott Paul is open Fri through Sun from 1 to 5 p.m.

The Tasting Room. 105 W Main St.; (503) 852-6733; pinot-noir.com. This tast-ing room, one of Carlton's original wine tasting establishments, offers dozens and dozens of yummy wines in a lovely space downtown. Specializing in showcas-ing the fruits of the labors of smaller wineries that don't have their own tasting rooms, the Tasting Room is a great opportunity to try a wide variety of the valley's wines. Open noon to 5 p.m. Thurs through Mon (but call ahead, as hours vary seasonally).

Ken Wright Cellars Tasting Room. 120 N Pine St.; (503) 852-7010; tyrusevan .com. Ken Wright, known for his highly rated, single-vineyard pinot noir, introduced a new label in 2003, Tyrus Evan, which crafts expressive warm-climate varietals from southern Oregon and Washington State, including claret, syrah, malbec, and cabernet franc. His original label continues to produce outstanding Oregon pinot noir. Except for a few days a year, the Ken Wright/Tyrus Evan winery isn't open to the public so Wright created this tasting room and shop in a beautifully restored train station in historic downtown Carlton to offer tastes of his creations to the world. Tasting fee refundable with full case purchase. Open 7 days a week from 11 a.m. to 5 p.m.

where to eat

Cuvee. 214 W Main St.; (503) 852-6555; cuveedining.com. French country cuisine is elevated at this local's favorite restaurant to elegant comfort food. Fresh seafood, select meats, seasonal vegetables, and house-made breads are served with the very best Oregon wines. Cuvee is as comfortable for quiet romantic dinners for two as it is for energetic celebrations. Hours vary seasonally—call ahead. $$$.

Filling Station Deli. 305 W Main St; (503) 852-6687; fillingstationdeli.com. Enjoy breakfast, lunch, ice cream, and a full espresso bar on the deck at this old gas station in downtown Carlton. The building isn't as appealing as the food, which is delicious. Try the breakfast and lunch sandwiches (on a fresh baguette) or the soup of the day. Open 7 a.m. to 3:30 p.m. daily except Wed; closed January 1 through February 15. $.

where to stay

Abbey Road Farms Bed and Breakfast. 10501 NE Abbey Rd.; (503) 852-6278; abbey roadfarm.com. Ever slept in a silo? Most folks surely have not. This unique lodging consists of 3 renovated silos, converted into lovely modern suites. They sit on an 82-acre working farm that cultivates 3 unique crops—maraschino cherries, grass seed, and dairy goats. The farm and gardens are beautiful, the silo suites comfortable. Get used to farm living—coffee is available at 7:30 a.m. and the breakfast bell rings at 8:30 a.m. $$$.

The Winery Lofts. (503) 852-7010. This is a bit of a best-kept secret. These 1-bedroom studio fully furnished lofts sit right in downtown Carlton over the tops of the storefronts and are available to rent for a weekend or week away. Each unit is beautifully appointed and has a kitchenette with complimentary breakfast items and light snacks. Wireless Internet access, cable TV, and DVD are provided. Staying right downtown in Carlton means you can hit all of the wine tasting spots and restaurants without having to step into your car. $$.

day trip 03

southwest

>>> **history & community:**
albany

albany

Albany has a bit of an underdog mentality compared to Corvallis, its more familiar college-town cousin to the southwest. But in fact many of those who teach and work in Corvallis live in Albany, for several good reasons. Albany is similar in layout and feel to Corvallis, with the downtown grid set upon the Willamette River. But Albany is quieter, with a strong sense of community and connection to history and the land.

Albany is home to four historic districts, more than 700 historic buildings, and the most varied collection of architectural styles in the state. These historic buildings are the pride and joy of Albany residents, who bring tremendous community spirit to their old-fashioned small-town atmosphere. More history is to be discovered in the outlying areas, including several preserved covered bridges.

Like many small Oregon towns recovering from the economic changes of the last several decades, Albany is working to renovate its downtown. A paved path runs along the Willamette riverfront, allowing for walking, biking, and the like. Downtown also holds a few gems in the way of food and wine—some of Oregon's best farm-to-table eats and award-winning wines can be enjoyed in this lovely small town.

getting there

Albany is about an hour south of Portland, on I-5. Take I-5 south for 69 miles to exit 234A.

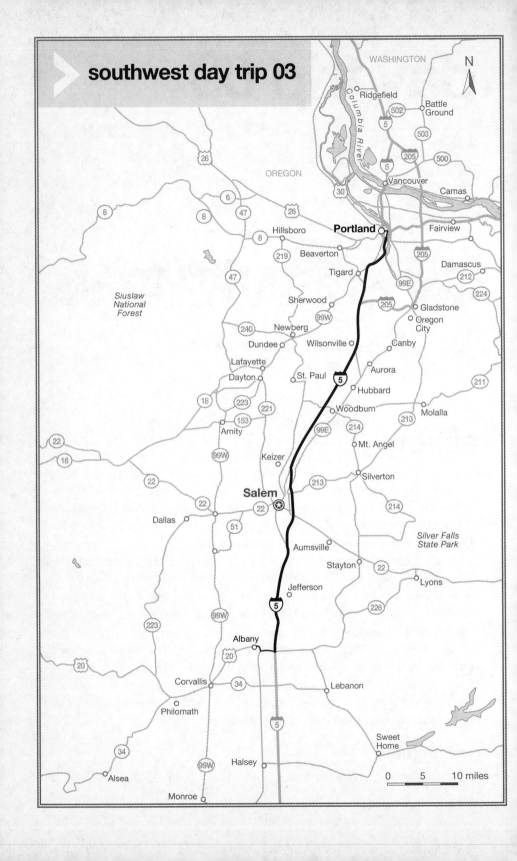

southwest day trip 03

where to go

Albany Antique Mall. 145 SW 2nd Ave.; (541) 704-0109; albanyantiquemall.com. This two-story antiques extravaganza is fun to explore even if you're not into doilies and china—the displays here are wildly varied, with everything from collections of antique woodworking tools to rainbow-colored Fiestaware to beautiful furniture to retro toys from the 1960s and 70s. The second floor houses one of the largest collections of vintage clothes in the Willamette Valley—you can find gorgeous dresses from the 1950s, funky pantsuits from the 1970s, and even a rack labeled "Hippie Dresses." This is a great place to wander and explore on a rainy afternoon.

Albany Carousel Mechanism. 503 1st Ave. W; (541) 791-3340; albanycarousel.com. There's a new component to the historic carousel museum experience in Albany (below). Now guests can also visit the historic Dentzel carousel mechanism. Dating from 1909 and originally used in Point Pleasant Beach, New Jersey, the mechanism was donated to Albany by the great-grandson of master carver Gustaf Dentzel. Today it's been fully restored and is housed in a warehouse on private property until the new carousel building is complete. Visitors can climb on the finished animals that have been mounted on the mechanism, and watch as volunteers flip a switch and the carousel swirls to life, with lights, music, and motion. Open for tours; call for details.

The Albany Historic Carousel & Museum. 503 1st Ave. W; (541) 791-3340; albany carousel.com. One part museum, one part artists' studio, 100 percent magical, the Albany carousel project is an attraction like no other. Volunteers have been at work for a dozen years to create a carousel from scratch, by carving and painting by hand 52 animals to eventually be mounted on an antique carousel mechanism, on-site. Guests are invited to chat with the volunteer wood-carvers and witness up close the incredible detail that goes into these carousel creatures. Each creature is adopted by a different local family, and each animal has a story behind the whimsical details included in the artistry. The museum also includes historic carousel animals dating from the 1800s, and will eventually house the completed carousel with a historic mechanism dating from 1909 as its centerpiece. Open Mon through Sat.

Albany Historic Districts. Throughout Albany; albanyvisitors.com. Albany's four historic districts, packed with more than 700 eye-catching historic buildings, draw visitors from far and wide who take self-guided walking tours all year long and enjoy annual interior tours each July and December. Albany's collection of historic buildings is the most varied in the Northwest, with everything from fanciful Queen Anne Victorians to cozy Craftsman bungalows.

> **The Monteith District.** This district is named after Thomas and Walter Monteith, two Scotsmen who traveled west from Albany, New York, in the 1840s and built the first frame house in the city in 1849—still existing as the Monteith House Museum.

The Hackleman District. Named after Abner Hackleman, a settler from Iowa who crossed the continent with oxen in 1845, the Hackleman district covers 28 square blocks and contains more than a dozen architectural styles. It contains Albany's oldest existing church and some of Albany's largest and most ornate homes.

The Downtown Commercial District. Albany's commercial history began with the Monteith brothers, who opened a general store in their house downtown in 1848. Today, downtown is still home to a collection of buildings dating from that time up through the early 1900s, with a variety of architectural styles.

The Airport District. Albany's Municipal Airport is the oldest airport in the Northwest and the second-oldest airport in the world. It was established in the fall of 1909, just six years after the Wright Brothers' first powered airplane flight at Kitty Hawk, North Carolina. The only airport older than Albany's is the College Park, Maryland, airport established in August 1909 by the US military for the Wright brothers' aviation research. It's the oldest airport in continuous service on its original site in western Oregon, and the only airport in Oregon to be on the National Register of Historic places.

Albany Regional Museum. 136 Lyon Street S.; (541) 967-7122; armusuem.com. The Albany Regional Museum reveals some of the tastier tidbits of Albany's history in well-curated and kid-friendly exhibits. Did you know that Albany had a significant role in the

up in the air

Years ago, I covered the Albany Art & Air Festival for a travel magazine and was invited to take to the sky above Linn County with an experienced pilot named Bill in his giant balloon of many colors. I'll never forget the peaceful, surreal feeling of gliding over the earth on only the power of the wind and heated air. Albany's annual Art & Air Festival brings dozens of hot air balloon pilots and their balloons to Albany each year for three days of flights. Not everyone gets a ride, but all visitors can walk right up to the massive rainbow-hued balloons during morning lift-offs to witness the magic as the pilots fire up the burners and balloons take flight. Kids can get free airplane rides from local pilots at Albany's historic airport, and local artists fill Timber-Linn Park to show off their work. Free concerts and the eye-popping night glow, when tethered balloons light up the summer night at the park, cap off the free event.

women's suffrage movement, including the fact that women's rights leader Abigail Scott Duniway made her home in Albany? Or how about that Albany has the second-oldest airport in Oregon and was the site of Oregon's first airplane flight in 1910? Learn about these and more at this great regional museum.

Covered Bridges. Throughout Linn County; albanyvisitors.com/historic-albany/covered -bridges. Long ago, builders put roofs over their bridges to protect the timbers from Oregon's rainy climate. The life span of a wood bridge is about 10 years; however, by covering the bridge it could last 80 years or more. Today, many of these built-to-last structures remain, serving as a picturesque reminder of Oregon's past. Linn County is home to 9. Take a self-guided cycling or driving tour of peaceful country roads to see some or all of these treasures. Early covered bridge owners often financed construction by charging tolls: 3 cents for a sheep, 5 cents for a horse and rider. You, my friend, may now visit for free.

Monteith House. 518 2nd Ave., (541) 928-0911; monteithhouse.org. Built in 1849, the Monteith House was the first frame house in Albany—that is, the first house that was something more than just a log cabin. Saved from going to ruins in the 1970s by a group of local history lovers, the Monteith House has now been restored to period authenticity and serves as a revered house museum, said to be the most authentically restored pioneer-era home in the state. Many of the furnishings on display in the house actually belonged to the Monteith family and were brought west to Oregon on a long voyage via the Isthmus of Panama. During the summer time, the Monteith is open and staffed by docents in period dress: noon to 4 p.m. Wed through Sat, mid-June through mid-Sept. The rest of the year it's open for by appointment, for seasonal tours, and for special children's events like Pioneer Day Camp and Pioneer Storytime. No cost.

Thompson's Mill. 725 Summer NE St., Shedd; (800) 551-6949, (541) 491-3611; oregon stateparks.org. Thompson's Mill is the oldest water-powered mill in Oregon, still working, and now an official State Heritage Site. Visitors can watch the mill's massive gears in action and grind their own flour. In addition to the mill, park rangers raise a flock of heritage breed poultry. Open daily from 9 a.m. to 4 p.m. No cost.

Waverly Lake. SE Salem Ave. and SE Lake St.; (541) 917-7777; cityofalbany.net. Every summer, a fleet of pedal-powered paddleboats is available for rent on the small picturesque Waverly Lake. It's $5 to rent a boat for half an hour, which is plenty of time to paddle around the lake, startling the flocks of ducks and geese that live there year-round. It's a simple thing, but a family favorite. Waverly Park also boasts a few picnic tables and a paved path. A boat area is available late June through Aug, Thurs and Fri from noon until 6:30 p.m. and Sat and Sun from 10 a.m. until 4:30 p.m.

where to eat

Calapooia Brewing Co. 140 Hill St. NE; (541) 925-1931; calapooiabrewing.com. For years the cozy Calapooia brewpub was Albany's only microbrewery, and it's still a go-to pub for locals to hang out, sip a craft brew, eat tasty pub food, and listen to live music or play darts. They're known for their chili beer, a spicy brew accented with real chili peppers. The covered patio is a great place to hang out on summer nights—be sure to look up and see the assorted decor on the ceiling. $.

Deluxe Brewing. 635 NE Water Ave.; (541) 928-7699; sinisterdeluxe.com. Located in the Borden building, a historic industrial building along the Willamette riverfront, and opened in 2011, Deluxe Brewing specializes in smooth, German-style lagers. Their renovated brewery space has a funky, industrial vibe, and the Oregon Barbecue Company has a food truck in the parking lot serving up mouthwatering, smoky barbecue. Deluxe calls themselves Albany's first "Brewstillery"—their distilling operating, Sinister Distilling, currently has gin and whiskey in production that will be released in 2015. $.

First Burger. 210 1st Ave. W; (541) 704-1128; thefirstburger.com. Owned by Matt and Janel Bennett, the creative masterminds behind Sybaris, First Burger manifests Matt's obsession for truly great food into classic diner meals. House-made buns fresh every day, meats sourced from only local ranches, old-fashioned malts and milkshakes, plus creative special burgers that are different every time you go in. How about a PB&J burger, anyone? It's a buffalo patty topped with bacon, peanut butter, and jelly—served with sweet potato fries. Surprisingly and memorably delicious. $.

Frankie's. 641 NW Hickory Drive, #160; (541) 248-3671; frankies-oregon.com. Frankie's is the perfect blend of comfortable neighborhood cafe and upscale bistro. Chef Cody Utzman takes fresh, locally sourced ingredients and creates farm-to-table versions of American classics: steaks, burgers, seafood, and pasta. Great specials, a killer happy hour, and a kids' menu featuring food that is both high quality and suited to a child's palate, Frankie's is a go-to spot for foodies and 5-year-olds alike. Utzman is a native of Albany who gained culinary experience in New York, twice competed (and won!) on the Food Network's *Chopped* cooking competition show, and then decided to return to his hometown to run a restaurant with his sister. Frankie's is named after their late father. $$–$$$.

Novak's Hungarian. 2306 Heritage Way SE; (541) 967-9488; novakshungarian.com. The only authentic Hungarian restaurant in the state and one of only a handful in the nation, Novak's serves up house-made sausage, schnitzel, breads, and amazing European-style pastries, all using original family recipes passed down through generations of the Novak family. $$.

Sweet Red Wine Bistro. 208 1st Ave. W; (541) 704-0510; sweetredbistro.com. This great little wine and espresso bar has an upscale atmosphere, a good wine list, and the

a walk through time

Interested in Albany's historic architecture but short on time or unsure where to begin? An easy walking tour, beginning on Washington Street in downtown, takes you past some favorites. Begin at the The Monteith House (518 2nd Ave., near 2nd Avenue and Washington Street), which dates from 1849 and is the oldest house in Albany. It's now in use as a house museum, open in the summer and by appointment, and one of the most authentically restored pioneer-era houses still standing in Oregon. Pass by the Whitespires Church at 5th Avenue and Washington Street, with a soaring gothic tower, and rare still-intact stained glass windows by the Povey Bros. Glass company of Portland. On your right will be the Cathey House at 730 Washington St. (known locally as the "The White House")—the front features a beautiful two-story portico accented with dramatic white columns. Take a left on Ninth. You'll go past Central School, which dates from 1915 and was one of the remaining buildings designed by Oregon architect Charles Burggraf. It's a classic brick schoolhouse and still in use as a public school today. Take another left at Broadalbin Street. You'll see many gorgeous historic homes in varied styles on this street, from Italianate to French Second Empire to Queen Anne, all dating from the 1880s to 1910s. The Dawson House at 731 Broadalbin St. recently underwent renovations to become a bed-and-breakfast, and at press time was set to open in the spring of 2015. The original owners ran the Owl Drugstore; in honor of their store, "owl eyes" are incorporated into the architectural details under the gable of the house. On the corner of Fifth and Broadalbin is the United Presbyterian Church, built in 1913 and based on an English Gothic Cathedral. Circle back to where you started, with a spring in your step and a slice of Albany's history on your mind.

best cheese plate in the mid-valley. They have a good selection of light lunch items (tomato gorgonzola soup is reliably delicious), a solid dinner menu, and decadent desserts. $$.

Sybaris Bistro. 442 1st Ave. W; (541) 928-8157; sybarisbistro.com. Chef Matt Bennett's creativity and attention to detail shine in this eclectic Northwest bistro, where the menus vary with the seasons, the crops, and the whims of the chef. His collaborations with the Grande Ronde tribe have made him known as an expert in the native foods of the Kalapuyan people, and he's twice been invited to cook native Northwest cuisine at the James Beard House in New York. Expect a small but incredible menu, with notes from the chef on the back for some dishes, plus excellent service, and many amazing accompanying Oregon wine options in an intimate, comfortable space. $$–$$$.

where to stay

Edelweiss Manor. 1708 Springhill Dr. NW; (541) 928-0747; edelweissmanor.com. Edelweiss Manor is located on 2.86 acres of what was once a 300-acre farm devoted to production of walnuts, prunes, and grapes. Today it's a historic farmhouse B&B surrounded by serene gardens, featuring an on-site art studio as well as a day spa. Mineral soaks or sauna visits are complimentary for B&B guests, as is breakfast made from locally grown ingredients. $$.

worth more time

There's a penny embedded in the center of Main Street in Brownsville, Oregon, and every year visitors from around the world stop and try to pick it up. It's just one of many tiny details that are remnants of the 1985 filming of the movie *Stand by Me*, a movie by Rob Reiner that featured stars like Wil Wheaton, Jerry O'Connell, and River Phoenix well before they were household names. The movie became a cult classic and today fans from Japan, Denmark, and many other parts of the world make pilgrimages to see filming spots in Brownsville. Some of the "old-fashioned" details in Brownsville, such as a 1950s-style advertisement for Coca-Cola on the side of a building and a sign advertising the Blue Point Diner, aren't historic remnants at all but were created specifically for the movie and still remain today. Each year on July 23 the town hosts *Stand by Me* Day in the movie's honor. See historic brownsville.com for a walking tour and map of filming locations.

day trip 04

southwest

be a beaver:
corvallis

corvallis

Corvallis is the kind of place that sneaks up on you. At first glance, the small city located at the confluence of the Willamette and Mary's Rivers can come off as sleepy, old-fashioned, and dripping wet. Catch Corvallis on a bad day and all you'll see are shuttered storefronts and the arc of your umbrella.

On a good day, however, the sun lights up the lovely old neighborhoods, hundreds of leafy hardwood trees in over a dozen parks, and a classy college campus that define this town. Add to that Corvallis's educated, cultured population—by some accounts this city has a higher education rate per capita than any other city in the state of Oregon, surely something to do with the presence of Oregon State University. It may be subdued here, but things are definitely smart and interesting.

Joseph C. Avery first laid claim to the land here in 1845. He's the one credited with coining the word "Corvallis"—an amalgam of the Latin words for "heart of the valley." The plateau upon which the city is built extends into the foothills of the Coast Range, which offer great opportunities for hiking and wildlife spotting. The forest and fields here can be soaking wet, it's true. But all of that rain only makes things greener and more beautiful come summer, when Corvallis has its chance to shine.

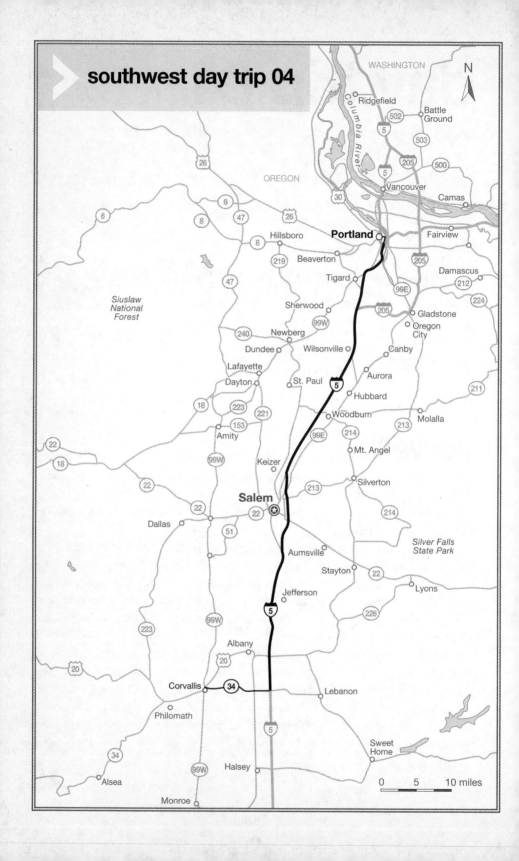

getting there

Take I-5 south out of Portland. Drive 72 miles to the OR 34 W exit, exit 228. Take this exit and turn right (west). Continue to follow OR 34 W for 10 miles to Corvallis.

where to go

Alley Art. visitcorvallis.com. Tour more than 25 sculptures and enamel-on-metal reproductions of poems, photographs, silkscreen prints, and more on this self-guided tour of public art along Madison Avenue from the riverfront to Central Park. The tour begins on the north side of Madison Avenue at 8th Street (adjacent to Central Park); art pieces are numbered consecutively to the riverfront and back. See website for more information and a downloadable tour brochure.

The Corvallis Arts Center. 700 SW Madison Ave.; (541) 754-1551; theartscenter.net. Located in the heart of downtown Corvallis on the edge of a rose-filled park, the Arts Center showcases local art by well-known and emerging artists from all around Oregon. Housed in a historic church, the Arts Center also hosts classes and workshops year-round, and is home to a fun gift shop filled with local goods. The Main Gallery features solo, small group, and juried exhibitions that change monthly. See the website for current show information. Open noon to 5 p.m. Tues through Fri.

Oregon State University. (541) 737-1000; oregonstate.edu. Founded in 1868 and originally an agricultural college, Oregon State University is one of Oregon's oldest public institutions. The campus was designed by the Olmsted Brothers in 1909, emphasizing trees and an architectural harmony anchored by basic classical forms in brick. Though the campus has grown considerably since then, the current design is laid on a grid of wide, tree-lined streets, has a classic old-American feel, and is lovely to stroll through, particularly in the fall when the trees change color.

> **Athletic Events.** osubeavers.com. Oh yes, you can bet your bottom dollar that Oregon State University fans come out in droves regularly to root for their mascot, the Beavers, and their athletes. Men's crew on the Willamette River, football in Reser's Stadium, women's basketball, swimming, soccer, track—you name it, you can see it at Oregon State University.

> **Irish Bend Covered Bridge.** The west side of campus is dedicated primarily to agricultural research. This covered bridge and historic landmark is on a path through the research farm. Moved from its original location here in 1988, the bridge is between 35th and 53rd Streets on the west side of the OSU campus, spanning Oak Creek.

Tyee Century Farm and Wine Cellars. 26335 Greenberry Rd.; (541) 753-8754; tyeewine .com. Located on a Century Farm just south of downtown Corvallis, Tyee Wine Cellars is a family-owned and -operated vineyard and winery. The vintage milking barn still stands today on this former dairy farm. Visit the on-site art gallery adjoining the tasting room, which offers pinot noirs, chardonnays, pinot gris, and more. It's worth noting that Tyee's 2012 pinot noir was ranked #1 in *Portland Monthly*'s blind tasting of the 50 best wines in Oregon. Open Apr through Dec, Sat and Sun, noon to 5 p.m.

where to shop

Beekman Place. 601 SW Western Blvd.; (541) 753-8250. Feel like poking around in the past? This is a great little antiques mall full of vintage clothing, furniture, and oddities. The fun thing about an antiques shop is that you just never know what will turn up. Come and see if you'll find a treasure or two to carry back home as a day trip souvenir.

Corvallis Brewing Supply. 119 SW 4th St.; (541) 758-1674; lickspigot.com. It may not occur to you to shop for home brewing equipment on a day trip—or maybe it will, as there is nothing like a relaxing day out of town to make one ponder picking up a leisure activity. In any case, this place is worth a stop for its wide range of rather exciting and exceptionally brilliant commercial beer, wines, hard ciders, sake, mead, and craft sodas. Open Tues through Fri 11 a.m. to 6 p.m., Sat 10 a.m. to 5 p.m.

Irene's Boutique. 201 SW 2nd St.; (541) 286-4040; irenesdowntown.com. Women's clothing and accessories as well as little gift items make up the contents of this cute little shop. They are very selective about the products they feature, focusing on American-made, sustainable, and handcrafted items. You'll never walk out of here with a shirt or a necklace that you'll wind up seeing on half a dozen other people. Open Mon through Sat 10 a.m. to 5:30 p.m.

Oregon Coffee and Tea. 215 NW Monroe Ave.; (541) 752-2421; oregoncoffeeandtea .com. We here in the Pacific Northwest do worship our coffees. Teas, too, have recently earned a rather hyper level of fanaticism. Here's the place to come and indulge your beverage fancies. This beautiful and newly expanded shop stocks more than 400 teas and dozens of coffee varieties to choose from. If that just sounds overwhelming, rely on the very helpful staff. Open Tues through Fri, 10 a.m. to 6 p.m., Sat 9 a.m. to 5 p.m.

Sibling Revelry. 145 NW 2nd St.; (541) 754-1424; siblingrevelry.com. Find pottery, garden art, jewelry, socks, hats, and more at this clothing and gift shop that operates with just a touch of whimsy. This is a great place to pick up a gift or something for you. Open every day: Mon through Sat 10 a.m. to 6 p.m. and Sun noon to 5 p.m.

Soft Star Shoes. 521 SW 2nd St., #201; (866) 763-2525; softstarshoes.com. These soft and flexible shoes are crafted on the premise that barefoot is best. If one must wear a shoe, than choose a Soft Star, which mimics barefoot conditions. Customers have the option of customizing shoes down to the very last detail, or choosing from a variety of pre-made shoes. Visitors can also take a tour at this unique shoe factory located in downtown Corvallis.

where to eat

Aqua. 151 NW Monroe Ave.; (541) 752-0262; aquacorvallis.com. Aqua's beautiful riverfront location is not to be missed, but the proof of the place is in the food. Showcasing Hawaiian regional cuisine and delicious Pacific Rim fare exquisitely, Aqua offers dishes like fish tacos and lobster rolls. The menu can be fairly expensive, but the food is prepared impeccably. Don't miss the hibiscus-infused butter. Open for dinner 7 days a week. $$$.

Big River. 101 NW Jackson; (541) 757-0694; bigriverrest.com. A Corvallis classic, this restaurant offers fine dining in a cool old building on the riverfront. Big River never disappoints with a consistently marvelous Pacific Northwest menu offering local organic produce, natural meats, sustainable seafood, and mouthwatering desserts. A wide range of pizzas, seafood and meat dishes, salads, and yummy starters pleases a diverse crowd, and the bread bakery, located on-site, crafts artisan loaves daily. Big River's bar features local and regional wines, single malts, seasonal martinis, and jazz on weekends. Open for lunch Mon through Fri and dinner Mon through Sat. Call for reservations. $$–$$$.

Block 15 Brewery and Restaurant. 300 SW Jefferson; (541) 758-2077; block15.com. These folks are willing to push the envelope continually to put forth fabulous beers. Be sure to try one of their stone-fruit ales. The kitchen produces honest casual food, much sourced from Oregon, including Painted Hills Natural beef burgers, slow smoked Carlton Farms pork, pastas, crisp salads, beer-battered fries, and vegetarian options. Stop in for a quick snack, an extended meal, or "hoppy hour" from 3 to 6 p.m. Open Sun through Wed 11 a.m. to 11 p.m. and Thurs through Sat 11 a.m. to 1 a.m. $–$$.

Gathering Together Farm. 25159 Grange Hall Rd., Philomath; (541) 929-4270; gatheringtogetherfarm.com. Gathering Together Farm is both a restaurant and a farm that specializes in certified organic vegetable and fruit production. Shop their farm stand for the best seasonal organic vegetables in the valley or visit the restaurant for a truly unbelievable meal. The store is open 9 a.m. to 5 p.m. Tues through Sat, seasonally. Lunch is served at the restaurant Tues through Fri, breakfast is served on Sat, and dinner is served Thur and Fri nights, though hours vary seasonally and you should definitely check ahead of time and make a reservation. The menu might include leg of lamb with fingerling potatoes, carrot ginger soup, and cherry crème brûlée to finish. $$.

LUC. 134 SW 4th; (541) 753-4171; i-love-luc.com. An intimate setting with an ever-changing menu that showcases the best of what Corvallis and Benton County have to offer in wines and food. Any given evenings' offerings are limited and subject to change, but are also guaranteed to be delicious. Duck leg confit, parsnip mash, mustard crème fraîche, braised pork shoulder, sunchokes, black kale, gastrique and Kumamoto oysters (served raw), or rice wine mignonette might just hit the spot. $$–$$$.

Nearly Normals. 109 NW 15th St.; (541) 753-0791; nearlynormals.com. For a casual meal, Nearly Normals is my favorite Corvallis restaurant. There is nothing you can't get here, and all of it is fabulous. The menu focuses on vegan and vegetarian foods, but proteins of all varieties are happily added to the food. The huge selection offers everything from curry to burritos to pasta to pad thai. Nearly Normals emphasizes fresh ingredients (organic when available), original recipes (born from creative chaos), and thoughtfulness in preparation—a combination of ethics they call "gonzo cuisine." The building and design are as eclectic and wild as the food, and the outdoor patio is a marvelous garden with shading trellises. If you are craving a tofu stir fry or Tijuana tempeh enchiladas, this is the place for you. Open Mon through Sat for breakfast, lunch, and dinner. $$.

New Morning Bakery. 219 SW 2nd St.; (541) 754-0181; members.peak.org. This downtown bakery is roomy, cheery, accessible for all, and is the perfect stop for breakfast or brunch. Muffins, scones, bagels, croissants, Danishes, coffee cakes, cinnamon rolls, pecan sticky buns, pies, cookies, brownies and bars, pastries, soups, stews, calzones, wraps, lasagna, polenta, spanikopita, ravioli, panini, and chowders . . . are you hungry yet? Open Sun 8 a.m. to 8 p.m., Mon through Thurs 7 a.m. to 9 p.m., and Fri and Sat 7 a.m. to 10 p.m. $.

where to stay

Alder Creek Guest House. 7920 NW Skillings Dr.; (541) 719-8525; aldercreekcottage .com. This cute converted barn has easy access to biking and walking trails and is the perfect location for a little relaxation. Kick back in this newly renovated, stand-alone vacation lodging with a luxurious bed, fireplace, kitchenette, deck, and bath. Prices are reduced the longer you stay. $–$$.

Donovan Place Guest Houses. 5720 SW Donovan Place; (541) 758-6237; donovanplace .com. Stay in an 1880s farmhouse or an adjacent flat on a working Christmas tree farm of Douglas, grand, and Nordmann fir; Norwegian spruce; and blue spruce. Also on-site is owner Dale Donovan's pottery studio. A beautiful, charming little property 2 miles from downtown. $$.

Hanson Country Inn. 795 SW Hanson St.; (541) 752-2919; hcinn.com. This charming country home holds a treasure trove of antiques, museum quality art, and splendid architectural details. As an inn, it embodies an atmosphere brimming with beautiful gardens, balconies, cozy warmth, unique charm, and elegant ambience. Rooms are spacious, beautifully decorated with antiques, and feature original built-in cabinetry and sitting rooms. Come morning, enjoy a full gourmet breakfast in the sun-filled dining room. Close to downtown. $$.

tree tour

It's little known to even those who know me well that I have a master's degree in Forestry, earned at Oregon State University—which is how I can say with certainty that if one is to study trees, Oregon is the place to do it. While you are in Corvallis, get a glimpse of the variety and beauty of Oregon's forests on the Oregon State University campus. The college has won many awards for its tree diversity and forestry program, and offers a self-guided tour of the historic campus and its trees with the help of a brochure available at the Corvallis Tourism Visitor's Center at 553 NW Harrison (541-757-1544). I'll send you off on your tour with this factoid—Pseudotsuga menziesii, aka Douglas fir, is the Oregon state tree. Learn to spot it and you'll see hundreds on the day trips in this book.

Leaping Lamb Farm. 20368 Honey Grove Rd., Alsea; (541) 487-4966; leapinglambfarm .com. This is a pretty cool option for those of us who wanted to live on a farm when we were kids. A self-contained cabin on this property, which was homesteaded in 1896 and has been farmed ever since, is rented to guests. Formerly known as Honey Grove Farm, it has been a working farm since the fields were first cleared, growing hay, raspberries and blueberries, garlic, apples, pears, plums, and grapes, and raising turkeys, cattle, and sheep. The lodging includes 2 bedrooms with queen-size beds, a full bath, a complete kitchen and eating area, a large, airy living room with a double-futon couch, and a multi-level deck with views overlooking orchards and pastures. The kitchen comes with a do-it-yourself breakfast, with cereals, fruits, bread, juice, coffee, teas, waffles, and anything else you can think to whip up from the provisions in the cupboard and fridge. Guests can buy eggs and other produce from the farm. It's a great family-friendly farm stay where you can learn as much as you want about farming or just sit back and just relax. Two-night minimum on weekends. $$.

day trip 05

southwest

all the fish in the sea:
newport

newport

Newport lies on the Central Oregon Coast, about halfway between California and Washington. The city strikes a balance between the artsy coastal towns of the northern Oregon coast and the working coastal towns of the southern Oregon coast. Many Newport folks work hard at traditional hands-on jobs in the forest or sea—fishing, logging, or tending to oyster beds—but there's also a big contingent of artistic types residing in Newport, from painters to writers. These diverse communities come together and blend their lives just fine, which is part of why Newport is known as "the friendliest town on the Oregon Coast."

Newport got its start on oysters. A whole batch of them was discovered in Yaquina Bay in 1862, and the delicious sea delicacies began to be exported to San Francisco and beyond. Soon after that the area opened for settlement, and a thriving tourism industry popped up immediately—an especially amazing fact given that there wasn't even a road to Newport until 1927.

From the get-go, development in Newport centered around two distinct areas: the Bayfront and Nye Beach. These remain the city's primary gathering places, each with its own character. Recently rejuvenated Nye Beach is an artsy village, home to many fine dining establishments—it's also the primary access to a world-class sandy beach. The Bayfront is a traditional coastal vacationer's dream—galleries, saltwater taffy and ice cream vendors,

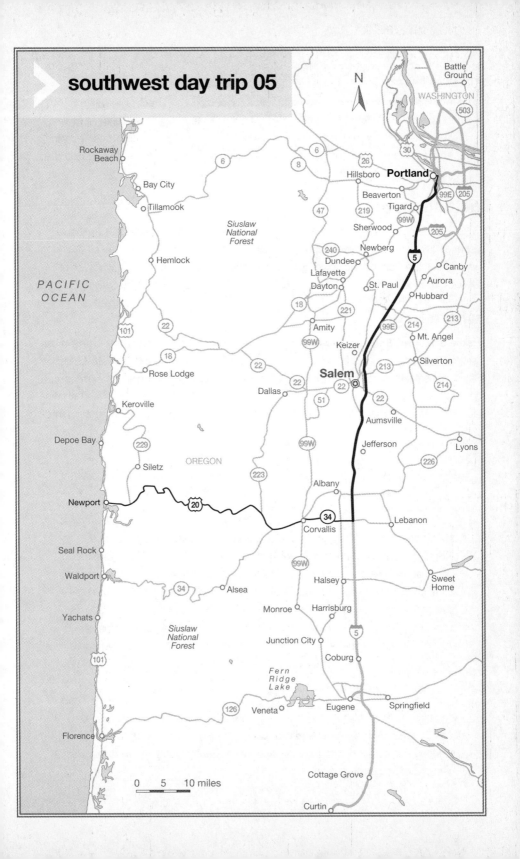

southwest day trip 05

beer, fish and chips, and carnival-type attractions abound. Don't overlook the Highway 101 Corridor and South Beach, the location of the Oregon Coast Aquarium and Rogue Brewery.

No matter where you go, take a jacket—like all of the Oregon Coast, it can be windy here. And don't forget your appetite! Newport is home to more than 80 restaurants, ranging from four-star dining to small, cozy cafes.

getting there

Take I-5 south out of Portland for 72 miles to exit 228. Turn right onto OR 34/Corvallis-Lebanon Highway. When you reach the outskirts of Corvallis, turn left to stay on OR 34 (it will become the Corvallis-Newport Highway). Continue west for 21 miles, at which point OR 24 will turn into US 20. Continue west for another 30 miles until you reach Newport.

where to go

Hatfield Marine Science Center. 2030 S Marine Science Dr.; (541) 867-0126; hmsc .oregonstate.edu. The public wing of Oregon State University's Mark O. Hatfield Marine Science Center showcases live marine animals, interactive marine science puzzles and games, and other aspects of our amazing ocean planet. Trained volunteers and a fabulous bookstore are major perks. Last time I was there, the lobby was home to a gigantic,

nye beach

One of my favorite walks anywhere is on Nye Beach. Park in the Nye Beach turn-around off of Coast Street and hit the sand. One can walk either direction, but I like to head north first, toward Yaquina Head. As the waves roll in to your left, admire shore pine-and-salal cliffs to your right. It's about 2 miles all the way north to the beach's terminus to the base of Yaquina Head, and to get there you may have to traverse a stream running across the sand to the ocean. If you do make it to the north end of Nye Beach, you'll likely see some surfers braving the waves. Then check out the tide pools at the base of the rocky cliff. Starfish, anemones, tiny fish, barnacles, and urchins are visible at low tide. Birds nest above. Waves crash against the rocks. If you're feeling truly ambitious, climb the trail to Yaquina Head and walk the length of the natural outcropping to the lighthouse. That'll add at least another hour to your journey. The best part—you still have the long walk back, but this time, the wind is at your back, your legs are wearing out, the smile is lodged on your face, and all of this activity has earned you your evening's allotment of fish and chips.

touchable octopus. Open year-round: 7 days a week in summer, Thurs through Mon fall through spring. Free admission, but a suggested donation of $5 per person or $20 per family is gratefully accepted.

Mariner Square. 250 SW Bay Blvd.; (541) 265-2206; marinersquare.com. Two attractions in one in this Bayfront establishment, priced at a bargain if you catch them both. Hours vary seasonally.

> **Ripley's Believe it or Not.** Robert Ripley captured the bizarre, which is definitely what can be found here, from shrunken heads to the magic harp. Don't get lost for all eternity in the deep-space hall of mirrors.

> **The Wax Works.** Hundreds of sculptures, each elaborately molded and detailed from wax, in the form of Hollywood legends to sci-fi creatures. Creepy, but cool.

Newport Visual Arts Center. 777 NW Beach Dr.; (541) 265-6540; coastarts.org. The Newport Visual Arts Center, located at the historic Nye Beach Turnaround, is a municipal public art exhibition and programmatic space for art education programs. Two shows every month feature Northwest artists. Open Tues through Sun, 11 a.m. to 6 p.m. Free admission.

The Oregon Coast Aquarium. 2820 SE Ferry Slip Rd.; (541) 867-3474; aquarium.org. A truly worthy destination, the Oregon Coast Aquarium is home to more than 15,000 marine animals in a beautiful setting. Resident species include sea otters, sea lions, octopuses, sharks, tufted puffins, and an array of tropical fish, and the grounds are gorgeously, natively landscaped with salal, boxwood, shore pine, and wildflowers. The ocean and bay are both nearby, and exhibits offer a close-up view of what lies at their depths. Don't miss the jellyfish—they are magical. Open every day except December 25. Open in winter 10 a.m. to 5 p.m. daily, summer 9 a.m. to 6 p.m. daily.

The Rogue Brewery "Brewers on the Bay." 2320 OSU Dr.; (541) 867-3664; rogue.com. This big grey warehouse with a red silo out front is where Rogue makes its famous, award-winning microbrews. Visit for brewery tours, lunch or dinner at the upstairs pub, and a taste from—count 'em—50 taps. There is also plenty of logo wear for sale and a panoramic view of Yaquina Bay and the marina. Open Sun through Thurs 11 a.m. to 8 p.m., Fri and Sat 11 a.m. to 9 p.m. Brewery tour at 3 p.m. daily.

Yaquina Head. 750 NW Lighthouse Dr.; (541) 574-3100. This 100-acre Outstanding Natural Area is an absolute don't-miss. There's no better view of the ocean, wildlife, and the Yaquina Head Lighthouse than from this natural peninsula just north of Newport. Harbor seals, brown pelicans, auklets, and up to 300,000 common murres inhabit the rocks off the point. Whale-watching is a winter and spring seasonal delight. Several trails allow for small hikes with killer views. There is a great Interpretive Center on-site that sheds light on the natural and human history of Yaquina Head. The wind blows powerfully here and storm-watching can be excellent. But the pièce de résistance is Cobble Beach. Over millennia, chunks of basalt have fallen from the hillside, tossed and bashed in the surf, and morphed into hundreds of gorgeous black round rocks known as cobbles. These make up the small beach nestled out of the north wind at the base of the head. As soon as you hear the satisfying crunch of your feet working their way through thousands of lovely spherical stones, as soon as you see the way the black stones illuminate the ocean water in an entirely unique way, you'll know you are someplace special. But the real thrill is to come. Waves arrive on the beach as they do on any beach anywhere—large or small, high or low—but as the waves recede through the basalt cobbles, the most wonderful and unusual sound results— a watery tinkling, a musical waterfall. You've never heard anything like it. Yaquina Head is open daily; hours vary per season. $7 per vehicle.

where to shop

The Kite Company. 407 SW Coast Hwy.; (541) 265-2004; thekitecompany.com. This enormous retail space houses the largest kite store on the Pacific Coast. Every kind of kite you could dream of can be found here, including delta kites, dragon kites, box kites, diamond kites, stunt kites, and parafoil kites. Catch the wind!

Peerless Puffin. 742 NW Beach Dr.; (541) 265-3153. Find fun gifts, cards, and bath and body care items in this cute little shop with all the windows, right by the beach.

Toujours Boutique. 704 NW Beach Dr.; (541) 574-6404; toujoursboutique.com. Lovely clothes for women. Separates in beautiful color combinations, bags, hats and shoes, scarves, and jewelry all coordinate to create a look that is comfortable and natural, yet sharp and sophisticated. Some great jewelry, too.

where to eat

April's at Nye Beach. 749 NW 3rd St.; (541) 265-6855. Fine Northwest cuisine served with a view of the ocean. The interior is cheery with watercolor paintings and white linens. The food is delicious seafood and pastas. Don't pass up anything with saffron as an ingredient, or the decadent house-made desserts. Open Wed through Sun, 5 p.m. to close. Reservations recommended. $$–$$$.

Cafe Mundo. 711 NW 2nd Ct.; (541) 574-8134; cafemundo.us. This place is a groovy, hidden treasure. On what was not so long ago a vacant lot with a small kitchen/trailer on it now sits one of the coolest restaurants around. Behind a row of hedges is a 2-story structure, the inside of which is painted plywood and Sitka spruce, hung with eclectic local art and a massive kite, and interspersed with skylights. Redwood driftwood salvaged from the beach was used to create the barn-style doors that open the ground floor to the outdoor garden seating area. Mundo hosts an open mic night weekly, frequent live music, and even some theater productions. The menu boasts sushi to omelets to bento. Tourist or not, you'll feel like a local here. Open Tues through Sat 11 a.m. to 10 p.m., Fri and Sat 11 a.m. to midnight. $–$$.

arr place

There's a great little restaurant in Nye Beach that you'd never know about if you didn't stumble upon it or get sent there by a loyal convert. It's called ARR Place— the A, R, and R being the first initials of the first names of the family of three who run the place and live above it. This trio doesn't take kindly to the norms of restaurant management, including a set menu and regular hours, but also eschews serving less than unquestionably superb food. In fact, their motto is "actual food touched by human hands." You might find teriyaki albacore, mushroom and leek quiche, or bread pudding on that day's menu—always, there's some sort of scramble/hash option that's a mix of whatever is fresh, available, and yummy. Whatever you choose, it will be cooked and served by the owners, and will taste delicious. Call (541) 265-4240 or see arrplace.com for more information—though like the building, the website won't tell you much. Best just to wander by 143 SW Cliff St. and check the chalkboard in the window for this week's hours.

The Chowder Bowl. 728 NW Beach Dr.; (541) 265-7477. This Nye Beach tradition is a simple traditional beach cafe with award-winning clam chowder, seafood, burgers, beer, wine, and lots of other goodies, like bread pudding with hard sauce. You'll often find a line outside. $–$$.

Kam Meng. 4424 N Coast Hwy.; (541) 574-9450; kammeng.com. Genuine Hong Kong–style cooking in a big green and yellow building on US 101. The exterior is deceiving, but the food speaks for itself. The black bean sauce, seafood hot pot, and green bean chicken are all excellent. $–$$.

Local Ocean. 213 SE Bay Blvd.; (541) 574-7959; localocean.net. A casually sophisticated fish market and grill unlike any other, and quite possibly the source of the very best seafood on the Oregon Coast. Market-style dining is accented with a central open kitchen where chefs prepare fresh grilled seafood dishes. Diners sit near floor-to-ceiling windows with roll-up glass doors, which overlook fishing boats in the harbor and the Yaquina Bay Bridge in the distance. A new upstairs addition offers more seating in a classy space with even more jaw-dropping views. The fish and chips are heavenly, and the crab po' boy sandwich is completely refreshing. I never visit Newport without eating at Local Ocean at least once, even if I'm not hungry. Open 7 days a week for lunch and dinner. $$–$$$.

Mo's. 657 SW Bay Blvd.; (541) 265-7512; moschowder.com. Mo's has been an Oregon Coast mainstay for nearly 60 years. With a unique, informal, and friendly style, traditional beach fare is served at long wooden tables. You can't go wrong with the chowder. $–$$.

Nana's Irish Pub. 613 NW 3rd St.; (541) 574-8787; nanasirishpub.com. Outdoors it's light and airy, indoors dark and moody. Nana's is a quintessential Irish pub with surprisingly excellent food. Homemade and hearty pot pies, fish and chips made with house beer batter, savory Reuben sandwiches, and homemade soups and salad dressings are all freshly prepared and wonderful. Naturally, there's plenty of beer on tap, and, very frequently, live music. Open Sun through Thurs 11 a.m. to midnight, Fri and Sat 11 a.m. to 1 a.m. $–$$.

Panini Bakery. 232 NW Coast St.; (541) 265-5033. Great pizza, excellent scones, and pastries that aren't overly sweet. The lunchtime sandwiches change daily, are excellent, and sell out quickly. Very limited seating; cash only. $.

The Rogue Ales Public House. 748 SW Bay Blvd.; (541) 265-3188; rogue.com. If you don't make it to the brewing facility (above in Where to Go), at least hit the brewpub on the Bayfront. Rogue Ales are made with the finest hops and barley malt, free range coastal water, and proprietary yeast. The menu is huge and varied—but with all of those beers on tap, who needs food? And anyway, with all of those beers on tap, who needs food? Open Sun through Thurs 11 a.m. to 1 a.m., Fri and Sat 11 a.m. to 2 a.m. $–$$.

where to stay

Elizabeth Street Inn. 232 SW Elizabeth St.; (541) 265-9400; elizabethstreetinn.com. The rooms here are fairly standard, but the view and location can't be beat. Located on a bluff overlooking the magnificent Oregon Coast in the heart of Nye Beach, it's the perfect place to stay to take in all of Newport. $$–$$$.

Fairhaven Vacation Rentals. Coast Avenue; (888) 523-4179; fairhavenvacationrentals .com. If you are traveling with a group or extended family, rent one of these gorgeous Victorian and cottage-style homes in Nye Beach. Just a few blocks from the beach, shopping, and great restaurants; several have views, hot tubs, and more. $$$.

Inn at Nye Beach. 729 NW Coast St.; (800) 480-2477; innatnyebeach.com. One of the newer properties in the area, the Inn at Nye Beach consists of 20 beautiful units, all with ocean views, balconies, and fireplaces. The inn benefits from solar-generated electricity and waste-water heat recycling. Choose from studios or 1- and 2-bedroom units, some with kitchenettes. Many units have sundecks with chairs, and stairs out front lead directly to the beach. $$–$$$.

Sylvia Beach Hotel. 267 NW Cliff St.; (541) 265-5428; sylviabeachhotel.com. Not for everyone, but those who love this place love it with both arms open and a ravishingly loyal happiness. The funky old 4-story hotel could be described as ramshackle, or full of awesome character, depending on your point of view. It's a hotel with a theme, and the theme is books. Each room is decorated to reflect a single author. Sleep with Mark Twain, Agatha Christie, Dr. Seuss, and many more. There is no TV, no Wi-Fi, no telephones, no radio.

Relax, read, visit quietly in front of the fireplace in the common library with a spectacular ocean view. Come for romance, come for solitude, come to make new friends. A fabulous breakfast is served each morning with a view of the ocean. Tip: If you're traveling with family or close friends, and have a solid sense of humor, reserve the Cuckoo's Nest, named after Ken Kesey's famous book, *One Flew Over the Cuckoo's Nest*. This top-floor room has four single beds and decor reminiscent of the dorms in the state mental hospital featured in the book. $–$$$.

west

day trip 01

west

farm country:
forest grove

forest grove

Forest Grove was born a small farming town, and once produced a significant amount of Oregon's strawberries. Over the years, the city has evolved to a bedroom community for Portland, and the bucolic countryside and small-town quiet has changed significantly. This small city is still a farming town of sorts, but these days the land that surrounds it is more likely to produce Oregon's famous pinot noir than strawberries, corn, and beans.

But especially since the small-farm renaissance of the last decade, a freshly picked, homegrown strawberry can still be found around here, as well as a fresh zucchini, carrots, and apples. The city has encroached on this section of Washington County, but there is still open farmland to be discovered. Wildlife, especially birds, continues to frequent the area, probably hoping for a bite of the same vittles we crave. Visit the surrounding countryside for fresh produce, good old-fashioned pumpkin patches, and a taste of the way things used to be.

Settled in the 1840s, the town was the first established in Washington County and is home to the oldest chartered university in the West, Pacific University. Ten of Forest Grove's buildings are on the National Register of Historic Places and an entire 18-block district represents history with homes dating as far back as 1854. Wandering downtown, visitors can still get a sense of what life was like 100 years ago, when Portland—only 25 miles away—was a true destination. Now Forest Grove is the best of both worlds—rural charm with a few big city accoutrements thrown in.

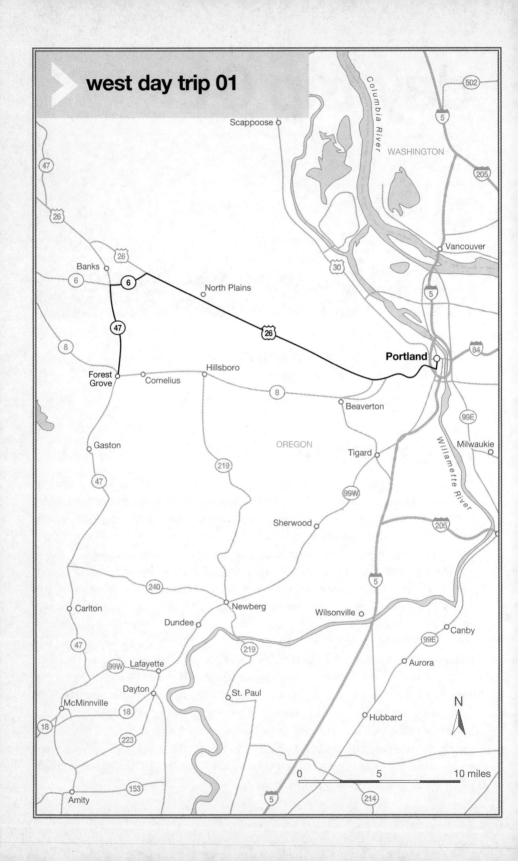

west day trip 01

getting there

Forest Grove is 25 miles west of Portland. Take US 26 W west out of Portland to merge with OR 6 W. Travel southwest another 2.6 miles and take the OR 47 (Banks, Forest Grove) ramp. Head south on OR 47 and follow signs into Forest Grove.

where to go

Killin Wetland. NW Killin and NW Cedar Canyon Roads, outside of Banks. Killin Wetlands is one of the largest remaining peat soil wetlands in the Willamette Valley and is a haven to wildlife. Its 373 acres harbor an uncommon willow species, Geyer's willow, as well as a breeding population of the state-sensitive red-legged frog. Birding enthusiasts are given the opportunity to see a nice population of breeding American bittern, sora, and Virginia rail. Many species of waterfowl are frequently spotted, too. Breeding plumage and courtship behavior are on stage as early as mid-February through mid-May. The area also attracts many species of migrating shorebirds looking for a rest.

Old Town. historicforestgrove.org. The 18-block Clark District is peppered with homes dating as far back as 1854, and several dozen pre-1900. Wander from downtown and soak up the atmosphere—it's pretty hard to get truly lost in a sweet little town like this.

Pacific University. 2043 College Way; (503) 352-6151; pacificu.edu. Forest Grove's Pacific University is the oldest chartered university in the West. Originally Tualatin Academy, the school was granted its original charter on September 26, 1849—predating statehood by 10 years, and serving as the first formal act of the territorial government. Pacific's Old College Hall, built in 1850, housed the original academy and is the oldest educational building in the West. Today, Pacific is a comprehensive liberal arts and health care university with 3,200 students. The campus is beautiful and a great opportunity to see some lovely old architecture and trees. Forest Grove itself was named for a grove of oak trees that still stands on campus. See the website for a guide to trees and more information.

Pumpkin Ridge Golf Course. 12930 NW Old Pumpkin Ridge Rd., North Plains; (503) 647-9977; pumpkinridge.com. En route to Banks on US 26 is North Plains, home to Pumpkin Ridge Golf Course, which has repeatedly been named one of the top courses in the state of Oregon. The course opened in the spring of 1992 to rave reviews and quickly became host facility to some of the game's best championships. There are 2 courses: the public course, Witch Hollow, and the private club, Ghost Creek. The course is known for stillness and quiet; just you, your clubs, and 36 holes of championship golf in a truly great setting.

Pumpkin Ridge Zip Tour. 15995 SW 74th Ave., Suite 200; (971) 371-3895; pumpkin ridgeziptour.com. Eight zip lines take you whizzing through a beautiful forest of Douglas fir and Western red cedars, with a bird's-eye view of the natural landscape. Travel from

strawberry fields forever

My mother grew up in Forest Grove. For 40 years, my grandparents ran a hardware store downtown. Some of my mother's fondest childhood memories are of walking directly from school to the store each day, where she would do her homework and help her parents until it was closing time. She also recalls being released from school early, in May instead of June, to go pick Oregon's famous strawberries. The rich soil of the northern Willamette Valley produced oodles of the delicious fruit beginning around mid-May, and the region's schoolchildren temporarily became day-laborers. They were paid by the flat, and went home with sticky fingers. During the 1950s and 1960s, Oregon farmers grew 90 to 100 million pounds of strawberries. Today, that number is closer to 20 million, and Oregon ranks third in the nation in strawberry production—a distant third to Florida and California. Still, many Oregonians—including my mother—would argue that ours are the best.

platform to platform, across majestic suspension bridges, and over breathtaking Brunswick Canyon. $65 to $75 for a 2-hour tour.

Tree to Tree. 2975 SW Nelson Rd., Gaston; (503) 357-0109; treetotreeadventurepark .com. Another Washington County zip line option, and more, southwest of Forest Grove on Hagg Lake in Scoggins Valley Park, is a "playground in the trees" that features aerial ropes courses, zip lines, and tree-top obstacles. Visitors move from platform to platform (tree to tree) via wobbly bridges, tightropes, zip lines, and more. Warning: not for the acrophobic (those fearful of heights). $48 and up.

You-Pick Farms. Grocery stores are great, but sometimes you want to do the work of gathering food from the ground it grew in yourself. Washington County is a great place to find farms of many varieties, several of which allow visitors to pick the fruits and vegetables of their labors. Teach the kids where their food comes from and what it takes to harvest it while enjoying some family time in the great outdoors at these farms.

Bays Farms. 14550 NW Bays Dr., Banks; (503) 324-0261. Bays Farms offers many varieties of produce to hungry Portlanders every summer season, including peaches, plums, nectarines, apples, pears, and kiwis. This is a destination in the winter, too, when you can come and choose a Christmas tree here. Open mid-July to December 23.

Gordon's Acres. 48360 NW Narup Rd., 3 miles west of Banks (Take OR 6 to milepost 46, turn north on Cedar Canyon Road, and follow signs 0.7 mile); (503) 901-7971. You-pick, ready-picked, or picked to order blueberries, raspberries, and kotatas. Open 7 a.m. to 6 p.m. daily July through Aug.

Jim Dandy Farm Market. 45770 NW Sunset Hwy.; (503) 324-3954. Jim Dandy's greenhouse opens in early May and features hanging baskets and vegetable plants. The fruit stand opens around June 1 when local strawberries ripen; other crops include blueberries, blackberries, raspberries, cherries, peaches, apples, pears, and assorted vegetables, including pumpkins, in season.

Wineries (and one Sakery). Some of the Pacific Northwest's best wineries are in the lush hills of Washington County. Try to include at least one in your day trip—not only do these vineyards offer great wine for the taste buds, they are a feast for the other senses, as well. Smell the rich soil, gaze upon the lovely vineyards, enjoy an afternoon at a winery.

Apolloni Vineyards. 14135 NW Timmerman Rd.; (503) 330-5946; apolloni.com. Apolloni Vineyards specializes in the production of traditional pinot noir and Italian-style wines. The tasting room is open Thurs through Mon, 11 a.m. to 5 p.m.

Cooper Mountain Vineyards. 20121 SW Leonardo Ln.; (503) 649-0027; coopermountainwine.com. In 1978, Robert and Corinne Gross planted their first vines, pinot noir and chardonnay. Today, Cooper Mountain is 100 acres and 5 varietals, with a commitment to sustainability through organic and biodynamic farming and winemaking. During the summer, visit for Neighbors Night, which hosts live music. Open from noon to 5 p.m. daily.

David Hill Winery and Vineyards. 46350 NW David Hill Rd.; (877) 992-8545; davidhillwinery.com. David Hill Vineyards offers sweeping views of Oregon's Coast Range and tastes of excellent pinot noir, pinot gris, Riesling, chardonnay, and Gewürztraminer from some of the oldest vines in the state. The tasting room is located in a farmhouse that was built in 1883, and the grounds are open for impromptu picnics.

Montinore Estate. 3663 SW Dilley Rd.; (888) 359-5012; montinore.com. A family-run winery, Montinore Estate holds high standards in sustainable agriculture and careful craftsmanship. Here you'll find estate-grown and -bottled, balanced pinot noir, pinot gris, Riesling, Gewürztraminer, and Muller-Thurgau wines. The tasting room and gift shop are open daily.

SakéOne. 820 Elm St.; (800) 550-SAKE; sakeone.com. How did the first American-owned and -operated saké (or sake) brewery in the world end up in a little farming town in Oregon? It's all about the water. Pure water is crucial to saké, and the Pacific Northwest has it. SakéOne's founders set up shop in Forest Grove, Oregon, at the edge of a rain forest, in 1997. SakéOne brews premium Junmai Ginjo styles in a range of distinct saké profiles for their Momokawa and Moonstone lines. Tours and tastings daily.

Shafer Vineyard Cellars. 6200 NW Gales Creek Rd.; (503) 357-6604; shafer vineyardcellars.com. Shafer Vineyard Cellars has been producing estate-grown and bottled wines since 1978. Pinot noir, pinot gris, chardonnay, Riesling, Muller-Thurgau, Gewürztraminer, sparkling wine, and dessert wines come out of this lovely winery, which boasts a picnic area with a spectacular view. The tasting room is open 11 a.m. to 5 p.m. daily.

Tualatin Estate Vineyard. 10850 NW Seavey Rd.; (503) 357-5005; tualatin estate.com. Wine grapes from Tualatin Estate's 145-acre vineyard have produced world-renowned wines for 28 years, and the winery is now a part of Willamette Valley Vineyards. The tasting room is open Sat and Sun from noon to 5 p.m..

where to eat

1910 Main. 1910 Main St., Suite A; (503) 430-7014; 1910main.com. "Comfort food: food that is simply prepared; food that comforts or affords solace; food that triggers childhood memories of home cooking and family gatherings." So say the owners of 1910 Main, who offer classic comfort food at its finest. This cute and classy place will bring a sense of nostalgia to diners, with local, updated twists. Open for lunch and dinner 7 days a week; brunch on Sat and Sun. $$.

Maggie's Buns. 2007 21st Ave.; (503) 992-2231; maggiesbuns.com. Maggie's Buns has been serving breakfast and lunch to happy people for a long time. From omelets or Maggie's McBagel at breakfast to fresh soups, chicken piccata, Greek orzo salad, and a handful of wraps, you can be sure that something at Maggie's will make your belly happy. Open Mon through Fri 6:30 a.m. to 5:30 p.m. and Sat 7 a.m. to 2 p.m. $–$$.

Pac Thai. 1923 Pacific Ave.; (503) 992-1800; pac-thai.com. Whether you like your Thai food spicy or sweet, you'll like Pac Thai. Vegetarian and vegan meals are available, and the portions are really good. The Thai ice tea is just right—not too sweet with a great tea flavor. Open for lunch and dinner—take out, too. $$.

Stecchino. 2014 Main St.; (503) 352-9921; stecchinobistro.com. This bistro serves a combination of French and Italian bistro–style cuisine, made from fresh local foods at good prices. Open for dinner Wed through Sat. $$.

where to stay

McMenamins Grand Lodge. 3505 Pacific Ave., (503) 992-9533; thegrandlodge.com. Built in 1922 as a Masonic and Eastern Star home, the Grand Lodge is an incredible building that was neglected until the amazing McMenamin brothers came along and renovated it. Reopened in 2000, the Grand Lodge now offers 77 European-style guest rooms, restaurants, small bars, an outdoor soaking pool, wine tasting, a 10-hole disc golf course, Ruby's Spa, and loads of the fantastic, eclectic artwork that McMenamins is known for. The stately columns, winding drive, and epic green lawn (it's truly enormous) beckon, drawing in visitors for what might turn out to be more than they bargained for ("Hotel California," anyone?). Dine in the Ironwork Grill or enjoy a casual meal at the Yardhouse Pub. The Doctor's Office Bar offers pool and a gorgeous antique back bar. Take in a movie in the Compass Room Theater. Get a room—you might be here a while. Restaurants and lodging: $–$$.

day trip 02

west

catch a wave:
tillamook, pacific city

tillamook

Tillamook is known for two things—cheese and fire.

In 1909, a farmer-owned dairy cooperative was established that would lay the groundwork for what would become a nationally recognized dairy products producer. Tillamook Cheese is distributed widely, and dairy farming continues to be a staple of the Tillamook County economy.

Between 1933 and 1951, a series of forest fires swept through the Northern Oregon Coast Range near Tillamook, ultimately destroying 355,000 acres of old-growth timber. The fires not only caused huge setbacks to the logging industry (during the Great Depression, no less), but also laid waste to large swathes of forest along the highway from Portland, making the devastation apparent to travelers and tourists who made trips to the county. The Tillamook Burn, as the series of fires is known, is still the stuff of legend to Oregonians.

Today, the forest has recovered, and Tillamook Cheese continues to flourish. Drivers pass through lovely trees to descend into the Tillamook Valley, where dairy farms dot the landscape. The city itself isn't considered one of the Oregon Coast's hotter destinations, but continues to thrive as a pleasant small town, bordered by the ocean on one side and hundreds of cows on the other.

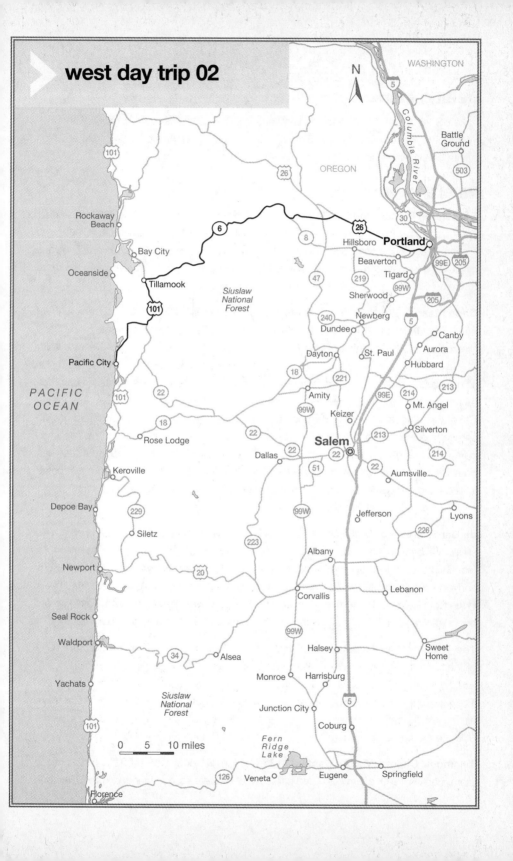

getting there

Take US 26 W/OR 26 W out of Portland and continue 20 miles to the junction with OR 6 W. Follow OR 6 W toward Banks/Forest Grove/Tillamook. Continue for 51 miles, at which point OR 6 W will dead-end into US 101, and the city of Tillamook.

where to go

Blue Heron French Cheese Company. 2001 Blue Heron Dr.; (503) 842-8281; blueheron oregon.com. Celebrating more than a quarter century on the Oregon Coast, the Blue Heron French Cheese Company is known for their famous brie. The shop includes a deli, unique gifts, and gourmet food. The kids will love the petting farm. Open 7 days a week: 8 a.m. to 8 p.m. in the summer; 8 a.m. to 6 p.m. in the winter.

Cape Meares Lighthouse and State Scenic Viewpoint. Off US 101 10 miles west of Tillamook; (800) 551-6949; capemeareslighthouse.org. Cape Meares is the site of the Cape Meares Lighthouse, an informational kiosk, viewpoints, the Three Arch Rocks National Wildlife Refuge, nature trails, and the Oregon Heritage Tree known as the Octopus Tree. From its headland, visitors get an excellent view of one of the largest colonies of nesting common murres on the continent. Bald eagles and a peregrine falcon have also been seen here. Cape Meares has more than 3 miles of hiking trails—one trail winds through old-growth spruce trees, including Oregon's largest Sitka spruce. In winter and spring, the cape can be a great place from which to spot whales. The park is open daily, throughout the year, from 7 a.m. to dusk with no day-use fee. The Cape Meares Lighthouse was constructed in 1889 and is the shortest lighthouse in Oregon. It is open daily Apr through Oct from 11 a.m. to 4 p.m. Free admission.

de Garde Brewing. 6000 Blimp Blvd., Unit A; (503) 815-1635; degardebrewing.com. This small rural brewery specializes in many diverse styles of ales, but focuses on spontaneous fermentations inspired by the European farmhouse traditions. Drawing on historic traditions and local experimentations, de Garde is making some of the most unique barrel-aged beers in the Northwest, and, in turn, has developed an impressive cult-like following. Tasting room open Thurs and Fri 3 to 7 p.m.; Sat noon to 7 p.m. and Sun 11 a.m. to 5 p.m.

The Tillamook Air Museum. 6030 Hangar Rd.; (503) 842-1130; tillamookair.com. One of the finest collections of World War II war birds, including a P-38 Lightning, F4U-Corsair, P51-Mustang, PBY Catalina, and SBD Dauntless dive bomber, is right here in Tillamook. The war planes and an exhibit hall featuring rare historical wartime and aviation artifacts are all housed in a rare World War II blimp hangar, the largest wooden structure in the world. Open to the public daily 9 a.m. to 5 p.m. except for Thanksgiving and Christmas.

Tillamook Cheese Visitor Center. 4175 US 101 N; (503) 815-1300; tillamookcheese .com. Back in 1909, a farmer-owned collective of dairy farms was founded in the Tillamook

Valley to ensure that locally produced cheese was the best it could be. The Tillamook County Creamery Association eventually expanded to include all of the small, independent cheese plants in the county, and, today, the association is made up of approximately 110 dairy families. They collectively own Tillamook Cheese. At the visitor center, see cheesemakers at work, learn about the cheesemaking process, view exhibits, and, best of all, taste award-winning cheeses and 38 flavors of ice cream. Open daily 8 a.m. to 6 p.m. Labor Day through mid-June; 8 a.m. to 8 p.m. mid-June through Labor Day. Closed Thanksgiving and Christmas.

The Tillamook County Pioneer Museum. 2106 Second St.; (503) 842-4553; tcpm.org. From the Tillamook Indians to Captain Gray's 1788 voyage into Tillamook Bay, the Tillamook coast has a fascinating history. Open Tues through Sun from 10 a.m. to 4 p.m.

The Tillamook Forest Center. Located 20 minutes east of Tillamook on OR 6; (503) 815-6800; tillamookforestcenter.org. Located at the heart of the Tillamook State Forest, the region's newest interpretive and educational center showcases the legacy of the historic Tillamook Burn through a wealth of innovative exhibits, programs, and interactive displays. Free admission. Open Wed through Sun in spring and fall; 7 days a week during summer; closed Dec through Feb.

where to eat

Alice's Country House. 17345 Wilson River Hwy.; (503) 842-7927. This little homey place is quaint, cozy, and tucked away in the beautiful rural coastal woods. Home-cooked burgers, pie, milk shakes, Philly cheese steaks, and prime rib please guests. There's nothing fancy here, but the food will fill you up nicely on a rainy day. $.

The Farmhouse Cafe at the Tillamook Cheese Visitor Center. 4175 US 101 N; (503) 815-1300; tillamookcheese.com. The visitor center houses a cafeteria-style restaurant, the Farmhouse Cafe. What's on the menu? Grilled cheese sandwiches, omelets with cheese, and burgers with cheese, of course. Breakfast and lunch are served here to tourists and local regulars, both of whom leave full (of cheese). $.

Pelican Brewery and Tap Room. (503) 842-7007; 1708 1st St.; yourlittlebeachtown .com/pelican/taproom. In 2013, Pacific City's Pelican Brewery moved their main brewing facility to Tillamook. On-site, find brewery tours as well as a 40-seat casual dining area overlooking the brewery floor, which gives you a passive education about the glass in front of you. The menu is pub fare, with some unique items like fried cheese curds, an elk burger, and stout ice cream floats, as well as signature clam chowder and fish and chips. Open daily 11 a.m. until 9 p.m. $–$$.

Roseanna's Cafe. 1490 Pacific Ave., Oceanside; (503) 842-7351; roseannascafe.com. Roseanna's is one of the most delicious restaurants on the coast, in one of the most

> ### water, water everywhere
>
> *Tillamook is an Indian word meaning "land of many waters," and isn't that the truth. This place is locally famous for sogginess. The pastures just west of Tillamook become so waterlogged during particularly wet winter storms that OR 6 can sometimes be closed. If you see cows wading, keep your eyes on the road to avoid turning your car into an aquamobile. In truly wet weather, call ahead or check the Oregon Department of Transportation's tripcheck.com to access road condition information.*

gorgeous small communities. On the menu you'll find chowder, sandwiches, a variety of fishes, prawns, scallops, oysters, chicken, steak, pastas, quiche, wine, domestic beers, and microbrews. Last but not least, homemade desserts—pies, cakes, puddings, cobblers, ice cream, and more. Open 7 days a week for breakfast, lunch, and dinner. $–$$.

where to stay

Thyme and Tide Bed & Breakfast. 5015 Grand Ave., Oceanside; (503) 842-5527; thyme -and-tide.com. Only 2 bedrooms at this tiny bed-and-breakfast, but they are beautiful, and Oceanside is a lovely, small alternative to Tillamook. A hearty breakfast will get you going for your day spent walking the beach or hiking the hills. $$.

pacific city

Imagine this as you drive to Pacific City—early visitors came by buckboard and horseback from the Willamette Valley, so excited by the prospect of the beach that they were willing to travel two days over a mountain pass to achieve a glimpse of the sea and hold sand in their own hands. Many of these early travelers had come from the Midwest on the Oregon Trail, and had never seen the ocean. Imagine their reaction when they crested that last hill.

Campgrounds and lodgings to accommodate these vacationers were some of Pacific City's first business endeavors. The other primary economical focus was fish. Salmon used to swim thick as seaweed in Nestucca Bay, at Pacific City. A commercial cannery was built on the east side of the bay in 1886, where it thrived for many years, canning and shipping 12,000 cans of salmon a year. Fishing, logging, and eventually dairy farming became the primary occupations in the Nestucca Valley.

Today, the fishing is still pretty good, at least recreationally, and plenty of travelers come to visit—but, thankfully, the journey is much easier.

getting there

From Tillamook, head south on OR 101/US 101 S/Oregon Coast Highway for 11 miles. Turn right onto Sandlake Road and follow for 4.3 miles. Turn left at stop sign and stay on Sandlake Road for another 6.5 miles. Turn slight right at next stop sign onto McPhillips Drive for another 1.4 miles. Continue onto Cape Kiwanda Drive for another mile. Turn left onto Pacific Avenue into town.

where to go

Dory Fishing. Pacific City is the only place on the Oregon Coast that is home to a large dory fleet. Visitors to Pacific City's beach can't miss the flat-bottomed boats and their trademark manner of taking off and landing—right through the waves onto the sand. Commercial dory fishermen have been fishing for salmon out of Pacific City since the early 1900s, and were the area's primary fishermen in the 1960s and 70s. Today the fleet is more modest but still impressive to watch, the salmon still taste great, and all dory fish are still caught with a hook and line. Try out salmon fishing from a dory with one of these outfitters:

> **Eagle Charters.** (503) 801-3464. Captain Dave Stiles leads beach-launched dory fishing trips.

> **Haystack Fishing.** (503) 965-7555; haystackfishing.com. Haystack Fishing is a licensed, beach-launched, dory fishing charter that offers ocean fishing for salmon, bottom fish, halibut, and crab. Captain Joe Hay leads the way! From June through Sept only due to ocean conditions.

Green Acres Beach and Trail Rides. 5985 Pacific Ave.; (541) 921-6289; beach-rides .com. Bob Straub State Park is a popular destination for horse owners from all over the state, because of the steep dunes and spectacular views. This outfitter leads guests into the park, along the beach, and to views of Haystack Rock, on an adventure that has quickly become recognized as one of the area's top attractions. $75 and up.

Nestucca Adventures. 34579 Brooten Rd.; (503) 965-0060; nestuccaadventures.word press.com. Offering everything from kayak and stand-up paddle board rentals, to fishing gear, to guided tours on the Nestucca River, this outfitter is located on the Nestucca River with a marina with a dock, making it convenient to launch for all skill levels. It's just a short paddle to the mouth of the river and the ocean, should you be so brave.

Oregon Hang Gliding. (541) 913-1339; oregonhanggliding.com. Pacific City, Oregon, and Cape Kiwanda have been central to the development of the sport of hang gliding in Oregon. Consistent and smooth winds have brought enthusiasts to this beach for nearly 40 years. If you just can't stand the thought of keeping your feet on the ground, call Oregon Hang Gliding for a lesson and take to the skies.

Surfing. Pacific City is one of the best places to surf on the Oregon Coast, and is especially good for beginners (I surfed for the first time there, and was pummeled by the waves in only the gentlest fashion). The break off Cape Kiwanda, on good days, provides a nice rolling surf. On bad days, well, kick back and watch the storm instead. For rentals and lessons, visit the Kiwanda Surf Co. or Moment Surf Co. (see below, in Where to Shop).

Twist Wine Co. 6424 Pacific Ave., Unit B; (503) 932-1744; twistwine.com. Twist Wine Co. serves Basket Case Wines, created by Chenin and Sean Carlton in 2006 in an effort to radically change the wine business, or at least one tiny corner of it. Here, it's not about exclusivity, arrogance, elitism, or pomposity—it's about having fun. Offering a cabernet sauvignon and a syrah, Twist also is known for great beers on tap, a small beer bottle shop, and a nice little gift shop called Reversal Apparel and Gifts (RAGS).

where to shop

Kiwanda Surf Co. 6305 Pacific Ave.; (503) 965-3627. Kiwanda Surf Co. is the Pacific City surfer's hub. This funky little shop looks just like a North Shore surfing joint, and offers a line of quality surfboards, surf apparel, and rental equipment including surfboards, body boards, skim boards, wetsuits, hoodies, booties, and fins. You can also rent a kayak here and set forth on the Nestucca River.

Moment Surf Co. 33260 Cape Kiwanda Dr.; (503) 483-1025; momentsurfco.com. Recently opened at the cape, Moment offers consistent open hours, fantastic surfing products and equipment, and outstanding service, including lessons. Moment pairs with various local hotels to create packages and has become the place to go around here for purchase, rental, and lessons. Open Sun to Thur 10 a.m. to 6 p.m.; Fri and Sat 10 a.m. to 7 p.m.

where to eat

Ben & Jeff's Burgers and Tacos. 33260 Cape Kiwanda Dr.; (503) 483-1026; benandjeffs .com. Attached to Moment Surf Co., this delicious destination serves burgers, tacos, burritos, fish and chips, beer, wine, soda, and a delicious margarita. Limited seating, or carry your meal out to the beach. Sun through Thurs: 11 a.m. to 5 p.m.; Fri and Sat: 11 a.m. to 7 p.m. $.

Delicate Palate. 35280 Brooten Rd.; (503) 965-6464; delicatepalate.com. Fine dining, Pacific City style. This bistro offers a tasty bar menu as well as fine dining. Feast on Dungeness crab cakes, braised baby back ribs, tomato soup in puff pastry, Fuji apple and gorgonzola salad, pan seared wild salmon, herb-crusted halibut, and grilled natural New York steak. Open Wed to Sun for dinner. $$$.

Grateful Bread Restaurant Bakery. 34805 Brooten Rd.; (503) 965-7337. The stuff of legends. First known for their fresh bread and pastries, Grateful Bread is now long-famous for their great breakfasts, lunches, and pizzas. There might be a wait for a table, but you will leave this lovely, well-lit establishment stuffed and happy. Open Thurs through Mon 8 a.m. to 4 p.m. Bakery open until 5 p.m. $–$$.

Pelican Pub & Brewery. 33180 Cape Kiwanda Dr.; (503) 965-7007; pelicanbrewery.com. Situated practically right on the beach, Pelican Pub and Brewery is a great place to hang out and watch the surf, eat great food, and drink award-winning microbrews. Awarded Champion Small Brewery at the 2014 World Beer Cup and Large Brewpub of the Year at the Great American Beer Festival in 2013, Pelican Pub is often the center of the action in Pacific City. Open Sun through Thurs 8 a.m. to 10 p.m.; Fri and Sat 8 a.m. to 11 p.m. $$.

where to stay

Cape Kiwanda RV Resort. 33305 Cape Kiwanda Dr.; (503) 965-6230; capekiwandarv resort.com. In keeping with the casual, beachfront, surfer atmosphere, many visitors to Pacific City simply bring their RV, or even a tent. In this case, the Cape Kiwanda RV Resort is the place to be. Right across from the beach and the Pelican Pub, it offers not only easy access to the surf, but also an exercise room, heated pool and spa, and a full market stocking fresh seafood, clothing, souvenirs, espresso, and fresh-scooped Tillamook ice cream. How many RV parks can say that? The park is also an excellent place to set your kid loose on a bicycle to lap the campground, make new like-minded friends, and pick up some surfing tips. $.

The Cottages at Cape Kiwanda. 33000 Cape Kiwanda Dr.; (866) 571-0605; kiwanda cottages.com. Two- and three-bedroom luxury oceanfront suites with full kitchens and awesome views overlooking the beach and the cape. These units are available for sale, too, should you become so enamored you don't want to leave. $$$.

Inn at Cape Kiwanda. 33105 Cape Kiwanda Dr.; (503) 965-7001; innatcapekiwanda .com. Boasting an ocean view from every room and cozy gas fireplaces, the Inn at Cape Kiwanda is the perfect quiet, relaxing, and romantic getaway in Pacific City. Downstairs at

it's a secret

Still a bit of a hidden gem, Pacific City holds a special place in the hearts of many Oregonians. Folks who've been around Pacific City for a long time say it's changed significantly, but compared to other coastal towns, it remains relatively undeveloped—an unincorporated community with no mayor or city council, awesome beaches, great restaurants, and a very sociable attitude. Enjoy this friendly, beautiful town . . . but shhhh . . .

this multi-storied hotel you'll find restaurants and shops. From the room, views of Haystack Rock, cozy gas fireplaces, and plush pillow-top beds with feather pillows will leave you satisfied. $$–$$$.

The Inn at Pacific City. 35215 Brooten Rd.; (888) 722-2489; innatpacificcity.com. A self-described "mom and pop operation," this inn is a nice inexpensive alternative to the fancier resorts. The 16-unit motor lodge is conveniently located within walking distance to shopping and dining. It's comfortable, affordable, and close to the action. $.

Shorepine Vacation Rentals. 33105 Cape Kiwanda Dr.; (877) 549-2632; shorepine rentals.com. A huge variety of fully furnished vacation homes, up to 5 bedrooms in size, and located throughout Pacific City, are available through this business. Plenty of choices to accommodate the most discerning beach-goers. $$$.

day trip 03

west

life's a beach:
cannon beach, manzanita

cannon beach

Cannon Beach is Oregon's resident artist. Galleries abound, in each a plethora of eclectic artistic talent. Cannon Beach offers all of the other things a coastal town should, too—gorgeous beach walks, tasty fish and chips, kites for sale, and rooms with a view. But here, it all comes with a bit more class.

As for the cannons of Cannon Beach, you can catch a glimpse of them, too. In 1846, the US Naval schooner *Shark,* part of a surveying fleet under Lieutenant Neil M. Howison, arrived off the mouth of the Columbia River. The ship landed in Astoria and, after a month, disembarked again only to encounter troubled waters and run up against rocks. The captain ordered the jettison of all cannons, and ultimately several washed ashore south of Cannon Beach at Arch Cape. One is displayed at the Cannon Beach History Center.

Interestingly, two more cannons were uncovered; in February 2008 after an especially low tide, the sand had been washed away from the beach at Arch Cape to reveal two cannons, presumably also from the wreck of the *Shark.* History has a way of staking its claim on even the most modern and stylish city.

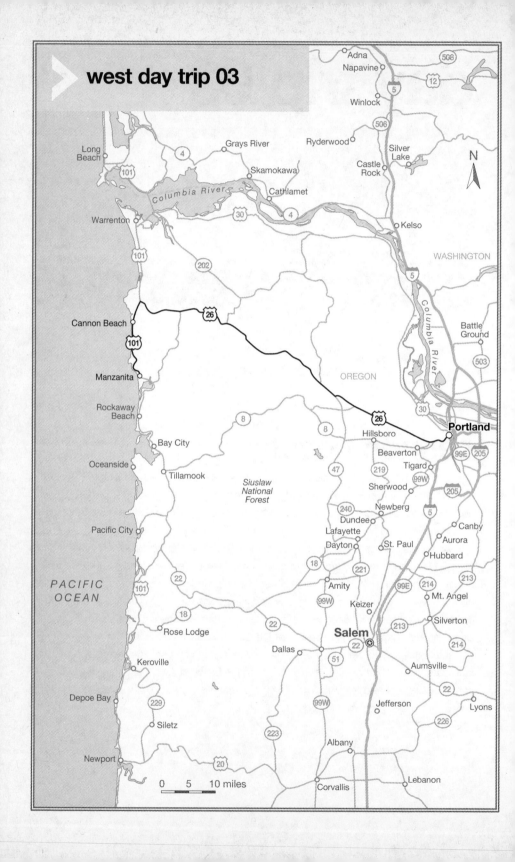

west day trip 03

getting there

From Portland, take OR 26/US 26 W west 73 miles until you reach OR 101/US 101 S/ Oregon Coast Highway. Turn south on US 101 and proceed 4.3 miles to the Cannon Beach exits. Follow signs into town.

where to go

Cannon Beach History Center. 1387 South Spruce St.; (503) 436-9301; cbhistory.org. Before and after the cannons, Cannon Beach has a very interesting history. This museum features a Native American longhouse, a rotating quilt show, concerts, lectures, and more. There's also information to be found here about the history center's fabulous, well-marked historical walking tour of Cannon Beach, which focuses on buildings in the downtown area. Open Tues through Mon, 1 to 5 p.m. Free admission.

Ecola State Park. Off US 101, 2 miles north of Cannon Beach; oregonstateparks.org/ park_188. Here's your "dramatic coastal views" destination. A paved road leads from Cannon Beach through the thick forest of this headland. After winding through Sitka spruce, visitors emerge to a gorgeous view of the Pacific Ocean. Hiking, picnicking, and exploration of the new Clatsop Loop Interpretive Trail are all fun things to do at Ecola State Park. Surfers enjoy Indian Beach and tide pool aficionados do, too. Migrating whales pass by in winter and spring, and wildlife and birds are here year-round. Daily use $5; annual pass $30.

Haystack Rock. cannon-beach.net/haystack. Haystack Rock is a 235-foot tall monolith (or sea stack) rock formation on the beach at Cannon Beach, the third-tallest such intertidal structure in the world. That means it can be reached by land on foot during low tides. Get a tide table to plan your trip to the popular tourist destination (minus or low tides are optimal). The tide pools here are home to many animals, including starfish, sea anemone, crabs, limpets, and sea slugs. The rock is also home to many sea birds, including terns and puffins. During the summer, volunteer interpreters are on the beach at low tide. Words of warning: The sea life that Haystack shelters is fragile. Treat it with care and do not step on sea life. Stay on sand and bare rocks only. And many people each year become temporarily trapped on Haystack Rock when high tide returns, making them unpopular with the local authorities. Pay attention to the tide.

Hug Point State Recreation Area. Four miles south of Cannon Beach on US 101. Before the highway was built, stagecoaches used to run along the beach here. North of the parking area at this site you can still walk along the original trail carved into the point. Look for the hidden waterfall around a small headland. The view north from Hug Point includes Silver Point Rock and Cannon Beach's famous offshore icon, Haystack Rock.

"Terrible Tilly" Tillamook Rock Lighthouse. Located 1 mile off shore of Tillamook Head, which is just a few miles north of Cannon Beach. You can't actually visit Terrible Tilly, but you can check her out from the shore—which might be preferable anyway. The lighthouse is nicknamed Terrible Tilly because of its location on a rock in the middle of the tumultuous Pacific Ocean. The now-decommissioned lighthouse was built in 1881 by the US Army Corps of Engineers, and lighthouse keepers actually had to be hoisted onto the rock with a derrick. The lighthouse was shut down in 1957 when it had become the most expensive US lighthouse to operate. Access today is by helicopter only. Enjoy Tilly from safe vantage points, Cannon Beach or Ecola State Park.

where to shop

Art Galleries. A visitor could make an entire day trip out of just Cannon Beach's art galleries. We couldn't list them all here, but this is a start. Bring your favorite art critic and your credit cards. Call for hours—many coastal establishments close up shop for a couple of mid-week days in the winter off-season.

Bronze Coast Gallery. 224 N Hemlock St., Suite 2; (503) 436-1055; bronze coastgallery.com. Specializing in limited edition bronze sculptures, the Bronze Coast Gallery has been in Cannon Beach for more than 17 years and has become one of the Oregon Coast's premier fine art galleries. The gallery also spotlights original painting, photography, and giclée reproductions, and features more than 30 award-winning regional, national, and international artists.

DragonFire Studio and Gallery. 123 S Hemlock St., Suite 106; (503) 436-1533; dragonfirestudio.com. DragonFire offers surprisingly affordable original art by local, regional, and national artists in media ranging from paint to fiber to metal. Seasonal 2- and 3-day workshops in everything from portrait composition to watercolors are offered, and live music occasionally accompanies the art.

George Vetter Foto Art. 231 N Hemlock St.; (503) 739-1415; georgevetterfoto art.com. George Vetter specializes in color and texture-rich photography that captures the essence and beauty of Cannon Beach. Giclée prints on canvas or paper.

IceFire Glassworks. 116 East Gower St.; (888) 423-3545; cbgallerygroup.com/ icefire. Glass art is a particular favorite of mine. It seems to fit even better at the beach, where the sparkle of the sea complements the beauty of blown and sculpted glass works, here by artists James Kingwell, Suzanne Kindland, Michelle Kaptur, and Mark Gordon.

Modern Villa. 224 N Hemlock St.; (503) 436-2428; modernvillagallery.com. Paintings by David Marshall, Sarah Goodnough, Ford Smith, Anne Packard, and others brighten the walls of this contemporary gallery, and maybe your house next.

beach art

For more than 50 years, Cannon Beach has hosted a sandcastle building contest in June. Everyone is invited to enter, from 6-years-and-under "Sand Fleas" to more experienced "Sand Masters." But given that Cannon Beach is repeatedly voted one of the best beaches in the US, it's worth coming on down to the sand and crafting a masterpiece out of sand any old time. See cannonbeach.org for more information.

Primary Elements Gallery. 232 N Spruce St.; (503) 436-0220; primaryelements gallery.com. Photography, wall art, sculpture, glass—the art at Primary Elements is inspired by nature and elemental forms.

White Bird Gallery. 251 N Hemlock St.; (503) 436-2681; whitebirdgallery.com. One of the first galleries to fully incorporate fine art with fine craft, White Bird has been making a mark on the Cannon Beach art scene since 1971.

Center Diamond. 1065 S Hemlock St.; (503) 436-0833; centerdiamond.com. A favorite with quilters and textile artists, Center Diamond offers special contemporary fabrics including a large selection of batiks, Asian, and seashore-related designs.

Dena's Shop on the Corner. 123 S Hemlock St., Suite 101; (503) 436-1275; denasshop .com. Higher-end contemporary women's clothing in a charming atmosphere. Open Mon through Sat 10 a.m. to 6 p.m. and Sun 10 a.m. to 5 p.m.

Found. 1287 S Hemlock St.; (503) 436-1812. A great mix of antiques, repurposed objects, cool artisan jewelry, artwork, stained glass, furniture, and table top finds. Found's finds run with a beachy theme—this is the place to find something to decorate your beach house or remind you of your beach vacation once you get back home.

La Luna Loca. 107 N Hemlock St.; (503) 436-0774; lalunaloca.com. The moon may or may not be crazy, but you'd be not to stop in and see La Luna Loca's handcrafts and fair trade items. Artisan-made clothing, sarongs, jewelry, and decor beat the rhythm of distant lands.

Maggie and Henry. 172 N Hemlock St.; (503) 436-1718;maggieandhenry.com. Henry's used to be a small imprinted sportswear store. Maggie's specialized in casual women's fashion. Then Maggie and Henry got married. Maggie and Henry is a blend of the two original stores, providing casual comfort for both women and men.

where to eat

Cannon Beach Hardware & Public House. 1235 S Hemlock St.; (503) 436-4086; cannon beachhardware.com. Nicknamed "Screw and Brew" by locals, this destination holds the unique distinction of being a place to grab hardware supplies and a pint of beer, simultaneously. The small menu features burgers, hot dogs, barbecue pulled pork, ahi tacos, and, most popularly, Cajun-flavored tater-tots. A full cocktail bar and wine are also available, and in-house TVs will generally feature top sporting events. $.

Driftwood Inn Restaurant and Lounge. 179 N Hemlock St.; (503) 436-2439; driftwood cannonbeach.com. Locals' favorite for seafood and steaks for over 60 years. The exterior has a Bavarian flavor, and a new outdoor patio has become prime real estate for happy diners, especially on sunny summer afternoons. Try the salmon, filet mignon, or steamed clams. $$–$$$.

EVOO Cooking School. 188 S Hemlock St.; (503) 436-8555; evoo.biz. Not your run-of-the-mill dinner experience, EVOO is like purchasing a ticket to a live show—one at which you learn something and are fed a delicious dinner. At EVOO (named for a frequently used ingredient, extra virgin olive oil), guests gather around the chef's kitchen-bar and watch him or her prepare three full meal courses paired with three wines, followed by a great dessert. A lively discussion about food and wine comes with the experience, too. This place is not to be missed and has become a full fledged destination! See website for class offerings and availability. $$$.

haystack rock trivia

Haystack Rock is a common name for geographical features of similar shape and size to the one in Cannon Beach, and there are several others even in Oregon. One is off the coast of Pacific City, next to Cape Kiwanda, and the other is in Coos County near Bandon.

Cannon Beach's Haystack Rock is accompanied by two smaller rocks. Most people call them the Needles, but I've also heard a rumor that to some others, the tall, elegant one will always be known as Sven, and the shorter, clumsy one as Lori.

Haystack Rock has been featured in many movies, including The Goonies, Kindergarten Cop, *and* Sometimes a Great Notion.

Newman's at 988. 988 S Hemlock St.; (503) 436-1151; newmansat988.com. Newman's at 988 serves classic French/Italian cuisine with a focus in the Piedmont and Genoa areas of Italy. Newman's at 988 serves an a la carte menu as well as a chef's prix fixe menu that changes nightly. Chef Newman uses the finest, freshest ingredients the North Coast has to offer and serves them in an intimate dining atmosphere enhanced by the music of legendary singers such as Frank Sinatra and Tony Bennett. Open daily in summer (beginning June 30), Tues through Sun after October 15, 5:30 to 9 p.m. $$$.

Sweet Basil's Cafe. 271 N Hemlock St.; (503) 436-1539; cafesweetbasils.com. Chef John Sowa conceived Sweet Basil's as a change in his own lifestyle and diet, after cooking Cajun food for years. We all get to benefit from his "fork in the road." Natural, organic, and wild ingredients go into healthy foods that still excite the palate. A nice selection of vegetarian and vegan choices as well as seafood, poultry, and pork dishes by way of salads, cold and hot sandwiches, wraps, panini, and fusion dishes all tickle the taste buds. Open for lunch; a wine bar is open evenings and serves tapas. $–$$.

where to stay

Blue Gull Inn. 487 S Hemlock St.; (503) 436-2714; haystacklodgings.com. Cannon Beach's hacienda by the sea, the Blue Gull brings a little Mexico to Cannon Beach. Each cottage has handcrafted wooded furniture made in the Blue Gull's own woodshop, and is located around a central courtyard with a Spanish-style fountain. $–$$.

The Lodges at Cannon Beach. 132 E Surfcrest Ave.; (503) 440-6310; lodgesatcbhotel .com. The lodges are beautiful fully furnished Cannon Beach townhomes with state-of-the-art kitchens, great rooms, and open floor plans. Units with 2 or 3 bedrooms accommodate up to 6 adults; furnishings are warm, cozy, and comfortable. $$$.

The Ocean Lodge. 2864 S Pacific St.; (503) 436-2241; theoceanlodge.com. One of the loveliest and most hospitable inns on the whole coast. With hints of a 1940s beach resort, the Ocean Lodge is great place for simple family fun and nostalgic pleasure. Amenities like a library of games and books on-site and a cookie jar aim to please all generations. $$–$$$.

Sea Sprite. 280 Nebesna; (866) 828-1050; seasprite.com. Three great locations—Sea Sprite at Haystack Rock, Sea Sprite on the Estuary, and Sea Sprite Retreat—with one great sense of beachside charm. Sea Sprite prides themselves on creating lodgings with unique personalities. Each place is special with lovely little suites and great views. $$–$$$.

The Stephanie Inn. 2740 S Pacific St.; (800) 633-3466; stephanie-inn.com. The Stephanie Inn is widely known in Oregon for luxury and romance. With views of majestic Haystack Rock, the Pacific Ocean, and the lovely Oregon Coast Range, the oceanfront Stephanie Inn combines the charm and casual elegance of a New England country inn with the sophistication of a boutique resort hotel. The four-star Stephanie Inn Dining Room serves a complimentary breakfast buffet each morning, and the chef prepares a four-course dinner nightly, which features the freshest in seasonal Northwest ingredients. $$–$$$.

manzanita

Manzanita is Cannon Beach's sister—another artsy town with an impeccable beach and oodles of wood-shaked buildings selling beach-friendly items to happy coastal visitors. But Manzanita is just a little bit smaller and a little bit mellower, and, as a result, you, day tripper, might just feel a little bit more relaxed and comfortable. Manzanita is the sort of place that causes visitors to sink into the atmosphere so deeply they don't want to leave.

Nearly everything shop- and service-wise in Manzanita is located on Laneda Avenue, the town's main business street. It leads directly to the sea and a wide, flat beach just begging for a stroll. You'll see examples of the town's namesake plant on Laneda, too—look for clumps of small, shiny green leaves.

getting there

Manzanita is 13.7 miles south of Cannon Beach on US 101.

where to go

Nehalem State Park. Three miles south of Cannon Beach on US 101; oregonstateparks .org/park_201. Known for 900 acres of forest trails and awesome vistas, Nehalem State Park offers camping, horseback riding, beachcombing, crabbing, and fishing. RV and tent campgrounds, yurts, a horse camp with corrals, airstrip with fly-in camping, and a hiker-biker camp give plenty of overnight options. Take a short walk over the dunes to the beach and watch the sun set over the ocean, in the shadow of Neah-Kah-Nie Mountain.

Oregon Beach Rides. Between Nehalem and Manzanita on US 101; (971)-237-6653; oregonbeachrides.com. Did you know that horse hooves squeak when they hit the sand? Come and find out with a horseback ride on the beach. One-hour, 2-hour, half-day, and full-day rides are offered right on the beach. Cost ranges from $75 to $250.

Oswald West State Park. Five miles north of Manzanita; oregonstateparks.org/park_195. A favorite destination for wildlife viewing, tide pooling, and surfing. The beach is a quarter-mile walk from US 101 and is nestled in a cove that provides you with a feeling of total privacy. Several different trails lead to the beach and the Cape Falcon overlook or to the Oregon Coast Trail. Surrounded by the mountains, the beach at Oswald West offers great views and lovely picnic sites.

where to shop

Cloud and Leaf. 148 Laneda Ave,; (503) 368-2665; cloudandleaf.wordpress.com. This little book store is everything a book store should be, with nooks, crannies, and books galore. You'll also find plenty of Oregon authors' works here, should that be your thing.

Great Northern Garlic Company. 868 Laneda Ave.; (503) 368-7700. Fear garlic? Don't fear the Great Northern Garlic Company. There's much more here than the famed cloves. Good selection of wine, beer, cheese, snacks, gifts, local art, Northwest wine, locally made bread, cheese, and lots more.

Manzanita Bikes and Boards. 170 Laneda Ave.; (503) 368-3337; manzanitabikesand boards.com. Cycle rentals, bike rentals, surf rentals, a retail store with boogie boards, skim boards, bike-related items, beach toys, kites, footwear and headwear, sunglasses, and watches. Whew! Rental season Mar through Oct.

Manzanita Grocery and Deli. 193 Laneda Ave.; (503) 368-5362; manzanitadeli.com. This is one of those fun groceries where you can buy staple food items, fine wine, or a great deli sandwich and rent a movie all in one stop. A 10 percent senior discount is offered every Tues. Open 7 days a week.

Nehalem Bay Winery. 34965 OR 53, Nehalem; (503) 368-9463; nehalembaywinery.com. There aren't a whole lot of wineries on the Oregon Coast—most are inland in the valley. Vintner Ray Shackelford has been making wines here at the ocean for four decades. Try his traditional pinot noir or innovative Valley Peach varietals.

Unfurl. 447 Laneda Ave., Unit 3; (503) 368-8316. Natural and eco-clothing for the hippie and the yuppie alike. Men's and women's clothing, shoes, accessories, and the like, all very fashion-forward. You'll find lots of eco-fiber clothing and planet-friendly accessories for baby and child. Open 7 days a week.

where to eat

Bread and Ocean. 154 Laneda Ave.; (503) 368-5823; breadandocean.com. A fantastic bakery, take-out, and weekend dinner restaurant that serves fresh-baked pastries, hot-from-the-oven bread, homemade soups, and creative fresh dinners. Open Wed through Sun for breakfast and lunch. $–$$$.

Left Coast Siesta. 288 Laneda Ave.; (503) 368-7997; leftcoastsiesta.com. This take on fresh Mexican food deserves a hard look—especially when you consider this little burrito shop celebrated 20 years of service in 2014. The big or wet burritos come loaded with organic fillings (try the sunflower seeds) and are available in five different tortilla flavors. Inside and outside seating is available at this casual, affordable place with eclectic decor. Don't miss the hot sauce bar. $.

San Dune Pub. 127 Laneda Ave.; (503) 368-5080; sandunepub.com. A local's favorite recently voted one of the best bars outside of Portland, this pub and restaurant offers sandwiches and seafood alongside a wide selection of domestic and imported beers. Warm your bones next to their big stone fireplace and have your favorite drink from the full-service bar. On the weekends, dance to live music. In the summer, enjoy the patio with bistro tables and market umbrellas. Open 7 days a week. $–$$.

Vino. 387 D Laneda Ave.; (503) 368-8466. Break away from the usual beach fare at this wonderful little place, great for a pleasant evening savoring something small to eat while sipping fabulous Northwest wines. It's a bit hidden—don't let the nondescript exterior fool you. Specials like the chicken pot pie will warm your bones; live music some nights. $$.

where to stay

The Inn at Manzanita. 67 Laneda Ave.; (503) 368-6754; innatmanzanita.com. A tranquil spot for a romantic weekend, this inn is ensconced in coastal pine and spruce in an open coastal garden. Thirteen rooms each have Jacuzzi tubs, fuzzy robes, fireplaces, wet bars, down comforters, and private decks. $$.

Spindrift Inn. 114 Laneda Ave.; (503) 368-1001; spindrift-inn.com. Built in 1946, Spindrift Inn still retains quaint charm and cozy appeal with beachy, comfortable decor. Affordable rooms open onto a private inner flower garden, where you can relax away from the bustle outside. Quilted bedspreads and kitchenettes make this place cozy and convenient. $–$$.

northwest

day trip 01

northwest

holiday by the sea:
seaside

seaside

Seaside has been the Northwest's beach playground for over 160 years. Even back when settlers had barely arrived in the Willamette Valley and hardly recovered from their journey on the Oregon Trail, some were drawn the final 100 miles over the Coast Range to experience the breathtaking beauty of the Oregon coast. Even the fact that there were no roads didn't daunt these early tourists—vacationers came by water down the Columbia to Astoria and then traveled by stagecoach to the beach. The first guest house opened in Seaside in 1850, and a tourist town was born.

Back then, not surprisingly, Seaside beach vacations were a luxury primarily available to the prosperous. Around the turn of the century, the wealthy and fashionable alone made the trip to Seaside, and when they did, they stayed in elegant comfort. The trek was generally made from Portland via train; the mode of transportation became known as the "Daddy Train," as fathers would use it to join their families on weekends throughout the summer.

Eventually, roads went in, more people adventured to the ocean, and services began to pop up for the common family. Today, Seaside continues to be one of the most visited places on the Oregon Coast, and is also considered one of the most accessible. Everything is within walking distance and most places are wheelchair accessible, making it easy for all to explore. Visitors can still choose pricey accommodations, but there are plenty of more affordable options available, too. Seaside is the rare Oregon Coast city with amenities more

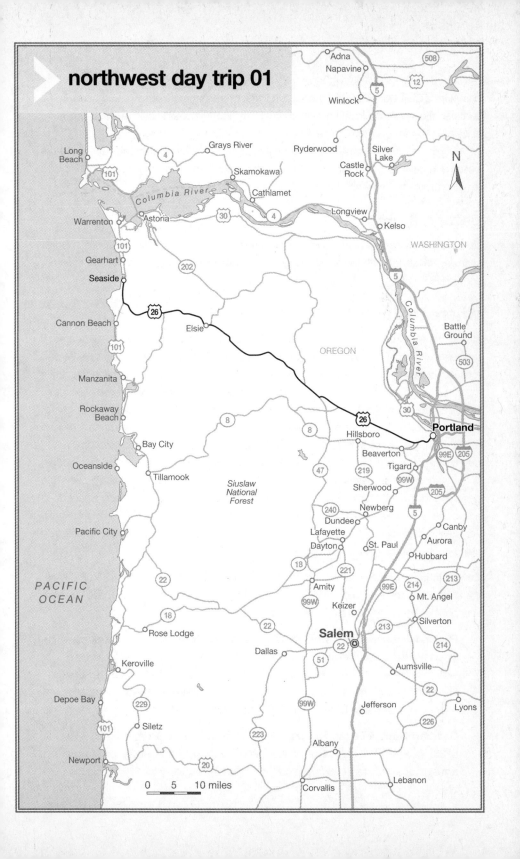

common to East Coast beach towns, including a promenade, carousel, and arcade. In the summer, the streets are packed with families carrying bags of saltwater taffy and ice cream cones, waiting for their turn at the go-carts.

Of course, the amenities that brought visitors here in the first place are still there—the beach and the ocean. For those who require no more than fresh air and sand in their toes for entertainment, Seaside is still a great place to visit.

getting there

Take US 26 W west out of Portland. Travel 74 miles to merge with US 101 N/Oregon Coast Highway, traveling north toward Seaside/Astoria. Seaside is 4 miles north of this intersection on US 101 N.

where to go

Camp 18 Museum and Restaurant. 42362 US 26, Elsie; (800) 874-1810; camp18 restaurant.com. On the highway between Portland and the coast is this huge facility—part museum, part restaurant. This massive wood building includes an 85-foot ridgepole that's the largest such piece in the US and weighs approximately 25 tons, cool wood carvings, 2 fireplaces built with approximately 50 tons of rock found locally, and a fireplace mantle of solid black walnut. The logging museum exists inside and out and includes a huge collection of old logging equipment, including multiple steam donkeys, a large bandsaw from a saw-mill, a self-propelled Ohio steam crane, and Caterpillar-style tracked vehicles that worked in the woods. If this doesn't do it for you, hit the restaurant, which features log-cabin-like decor including a burl table entirely carved from one hunk of wood. The menu would fill up any logger with rib-sticking dishes like ribs, pork chops, sirloin steak, and fish and chips. For breakfast, try one of Camp 18's famous cinnamon rolls. They're so big you're definitely going to need some help. $$–$$$.

Entertainment Centers. When it rains, many Seaside tourists head indoors. In that case, there are a few options—eat, shop, or hit one of the entertainment centers. These three are very popular destinations, rain or shine:

Funland Entertainment Center. 201 Broadway; (503) 738-7361; funlandsea side.com. Just about every video and arcade game you can hope for is here, and then some. On weekends, and throughout the summer, try your hand at Fascination—a game that dates back to the 1920s. Seaside's Fascination parlor is just one of about a dozen remaining in the country. Opens at 9 a.m. daily.

Gearhart Bowl & Fultano's Pizza. 3518 Highway 101 N, Gearhart; (503) 738-5333; gearhartbowl.com. Now under new ownership, this facility underwent a major one-year renovation project and has become a quick hit with locals.

Features 12 lanes, arcade games, projection television screens, pizza, and a full-service lounge.

Interstate Amusement Co. 110 Broadway; (503) 738-5540; shopseaside.com. Bumper cars, tilt-a-whirl, and miniature golf. The snack bar serves "pronto pup" hot dogs, slushies, soft serve ice cream cones, chips, and other snacks. This laid-back complex advertises its hours as "open whenever there is a crowd."

Saddle Mountain. Off US 26 W, 8 miles northeast of Necanicum Junction. Saddle Mountain is the highest point in northwest Oregon and one of the most popular hikes in the state of Oregon. That's because it's easy to get to, traverses flower-filled meadows unparalleled in this part of the state, and boasts a view on top that stretches from the ocean to the mouth of the Columbia River to the Cascades. A 5.2-mile round-trip hike to the top through rough terrain and steep grades makes for challenging climbing, but you'll be so busy marveling at the natural beauty you won't mind. As you climb to the rocky summit, gaze upon mature forest and fields of wildflowers. The view from the apex is a floral show that only exists at that elevation. The temperature is very different at the summit than in the parking lot, so come prepared with a jacket.

Seaside Aquarium. 200 N Prom; (503) 738-6211; seasideaquarium.com. Founded in 1937, the Seaside Aquarium is one of the oldest on the West Coast. This old building on the waterfront is full of fun discoveries, including underwater areas that provide a glimpse of a fascinating world of unusual and rare life forms. An underwater viewing tank and a touch tank with sea anemones, sandpaper textured starfish, and prickly sea urchins are beautiful and full of life. Don't miss the family of seals—which, in some years, includes baby seal pups in the spring. Open daily at 9 a.m. (winter and summer hours may vary at closing time).

Seaside Museum, Historical Society, and Butterfield Cottage. 570 Necanicum Dr.; (503) 738-7065; seasidemuseum.org. This cool old museum includes exhibits on the history of Native Americans in the Seaside area, logging, and local hotels and tourism. The Seaside Museum is the only beach cottage museum in Oregon, existing in and interpreting the Butterfield Cottage to the era circa 1912. Built in 1880 as a beach cottage for a wealthy Portlander, the Butterfield Cottage sits on beautiful grounds. The adjacent gift shop sells all sorts of fun gifts and souvenirs like historic photos. Open Mon through Sat year-round, but call for specific hours.

Seaside Promenade and Turnaround. Seaside's Broadway Avenue leads west directly to the Seaside Turnaround, the epicenter of Seaside with a magnificent view of the Pacific Ocean and a statue of Meriwether Lewis and William Clark that commemorates the explorers' historic expedition. Intersecting the turnaround is the popular Promenade, or Prom, a 1.5-mile paved walkway that leads walkers and runners past grand Seaside homes on one side and gorgeous dunes and beach views on the other. Everybody loves the Prom, which is lined with benches for relaxing.

run, play, party

The Hood to Coast Relay, considered to be the world's largest annual relay, begins on the slopes of Mt. Hood and finishes on the beach at Seaside. The event brings 12,000 runners, their support teams, race staff, and volunteers to this small city each year—numbers that can total 50,000. In effect, a second city is temporarily created to accommodate the masses. Dozens of tents are erected on the beach, a footbridge is installed over US 101, and local businesses stock way up on beer and hot dogs. Depending on your point of view, race weekend—the last full weekend before Labor Day—might be a great time to visit Seaside or a great time to avoid Seaside. One thing is for sure, with 50,000 extra people in town, this is where the party is. See hoodtocoast.com.

Wheel Fun Rentals. 407 S Holladay Dr.; (503) 738-8447; wheelfunrentals.com. At Wheel Fun, you can rent just about anything. Set yourself loose on the streets of Seaside in an electric fun car, including mini-Hummers, mopeds, and a 1923 Ford Roadster. Pedal-powered options include single, double, and triple surries, kids' bikes, tandems, coupes, choppers, and cruiser bicycles. You can even rent kayaks, boogie boards, surfboards, baby joggers, and sandcastle kits. Whatever your beach vacation can't live without, these folks have. Rental prices are $10 to $85 per hour. Summer hours: open daily 9 a.m. to sunset. Winter hours: open Mon through Fri 9 a.m. to 5 p.m. and weekends weather permitting.

where to shop

Beach Books. 616 Broadway; (503) 738-3500; beachbooks37.com. While many independent booksellers have closed up shop, this nine-year-old hideaway expanded operations in early 2013. Now, located in the heart of the Gilbert District near a coffee shop, sushi bar, and two pubs, Beach Books features many regional authors. Complete with a house cat and lots of natural light, the location's upstairs often features book signings, art galleries, and readings. Open 7 days a week, with extended hours on the weekends.

Seaside Carousel Mall. 300 Broadway; (503) 738-6728; seasidecarouselmall.com. Everyone loves a carousel. Twenty unique shops surround a full-size classic carousel in this cheery, colorful mall. Shops offer dining, snacks, coffee, specialty gifts, art, imports, framing, kites, games, clothing, jewelry, toys, candies, ice cream, old-time photos and portraits, and much more. The carousel horses are replicas of original hand-carved vintage carousel horses from the early 1900s. Open 7 days a week, though hours change seasonally.

where to eat

Maggie's on the Prom Restaurant. 581 South Prom; (503) 738-6403; theseasideinn .com. Located on the main floor of the Seaside Oceanfront Inn (and under new ownership since 2013), Maggie's is a favorite for locals and tourists alike. Guests enjoy stunning views of the Pacific Ocean and Tillamook Head. The restaurant decor is Northwest contemporary with a river rock fireplace, solid wood tables and chairs, box-beamed 10-foot ceilings, wrapped windows, and custom millwork. Outdoor dining is available. The seasonal menus offer fresh seafood, salads, sandwiches, chowder and soups, pasta dishes, specialty poultry and meat dishes, vegetarian and gluten-free dishes, and desserts. Maggie's has a large bar. Reservations are recommended. Open for breakfast, lunch, and dinner daily. $$–$$$.

Norma's Seafood & Steak. 20 N Columbia St.; (503) 738-4331; normasoceandiner.com. Norma's has been a Seaside standard since 1976. This restaurant's amazing food has been called "best beach fare," "unpretentious," and "best road food" by national magazines. Simply prepared and excellent seafood, steaks, and pasta dishes are served for lunch and dinner daily in a nice, comfortable, recently remodeled room. Dinners include your choice of a cup of Norma's world-famous clam chowder or dinner salad with shrimp. $$–$$$.

Osprey Cafe. 2281 Beach Dr.; (503) 739-7054; facebook.com/ospreycafe. One of the newest additions to Seaside's dining scene, Osprey serves breakfast all day and a lunch menu from 11:30 until close. Located just off of Avenue U (at the south end of the Prom), the menu includes items with a Latin American flair. Try arroz con pollo and lomo saltado or a flavorful omelet. Open 7:30 a.m. to 3:30 p.m. Closed Tues and Wed. $–$$.

Seaside Brewing Company. 851 Broadway; (503) 717-5451; seasidebrewery.com. Seaside Brewing Company opened in June 2012 nearly 100 years after the building it occupies was established as Seaside City Hall and the old city jail. A year after opening, operations expanded from a nano-brewery to a full-fledged barrel system—and it's been uphill ever since. Featuring standard pub food and a minimum of four SBC brews (including the lovely Lockup IPA), the selection of beer also includes many other Oregon suds. Family friendly, and yet maybe the only place in Oregon where you can hear old-timers boast they were thrown in jail for drinking too much in the same room they are currently drinking in. Open for lunch and dinner 7 days a week. $–$$.

Zinger's Homemade Ice Cream. 210 Broadway; (503) 738-3939; zingersicecream.com. The only ice-cream place in town that makes its own homemade ice cream with ultra-premium 16 percent butterfat that is fresh, smooth, sweet, and creamy. More than 50 flavors are made, and rotated, so that visitors can try everything over the course of a season. Try butter brickle, egg nog, blue moon, black walnut . . . and many, many more. Zinger's is only open seasonally. Call for hours. No debit or credit cards. $.

where to stay

Beachside Inn. 300 5th Ave.; (503) 738-5363; beachsideinnseaside.com. Beachside Inn offers a clean and cozy beach bungalow atmosphere with 12 rooms just 4 blocks to downtown and less than a block from the beach. This lodging is clean, quaint, and a little quieter than some places. Complimentary lobby snacks and a few restaurants nearby make your stay even more convenient. $–$$.

Gilbert Inn. 341 Beach Dr.; (800) 410-9770; gilbertinn.com. The Gilbert Inn is a romantic Queen Anne Victorian home built in 1892. Rooms are fancy and floral. Only 300 feet from the Prom and 1 block south of Broadway, the location is as convenient as it is luxurious and beautiful. No children, smokers, or pets. $–$$$.

Inn at the Prom. 341 S Prom; (503) 738-4142; haystacklodgings.com. Oceanfront rooms on the promenade with views of the Pacific Ocean and Tillamook Head make this recently renovated lodging a great place to relax and enjoy your Seaside stay. Fireplaces and Jacuzzi tubs will mellow you out; fall asleep to the sound of the waves. $–$$.

River Inn at Seaside. 531 Ave. A; (503) 717-5744; riverinnatseaside.com. The River Inn at Seaside is the newest property in town and offers 48 rooms ideal for families or couples. Artwork throughout the four-level property was locally curated with each of the floors dedicated to a different artist. Breakfast is included and a kids' play area out back complements the family-friendly town. $–$$.

day trip 02

northwest

in the footsteps of lewis & clark:
astoria

astoria

Astoria has spent the last decade basking in the past. The years 2005 and 2006 marked the bicentennial of the long, wet, and cold winter that Lewis and Clark spent at Astoria's Fort Clatsop; and 2011 marked the city's bicentennial. Those milestones were cause for much fanfare, as was 2015's 30th anniversary celebration of the film *The Goonies*, which was filmed in and around Astoria and is a much-loved 1980s classic. All of this historical hoopla has contributed to rising visitorship to the small coastal Oregon city at the mouth of the great Columbia River.

The attention is well deserved. Astoria is the oldest American settlement west of the Rockies, and has more historical markers than anywhere else in Oregon. At the same time, it's a forward-thinking and surprisingly hip little city. Many Portland expatriates have settled here, bringing with them high standards and a sense of cool that, coupled with Astoria's incredible natural beauty, makes this city a charming, atmospheric weekend getaway with many wonderful surprises.

The town boasts impressive old architecture including hundreds of Victorian homes perched on Astoria's steep hillsides and a revitalized 1920s-era downtown. The main part of town sits on a hilly peninsula, and the 360-degree views of the ocean and river, and temperate rain forest that surround Astoria are incredibly beautiful.

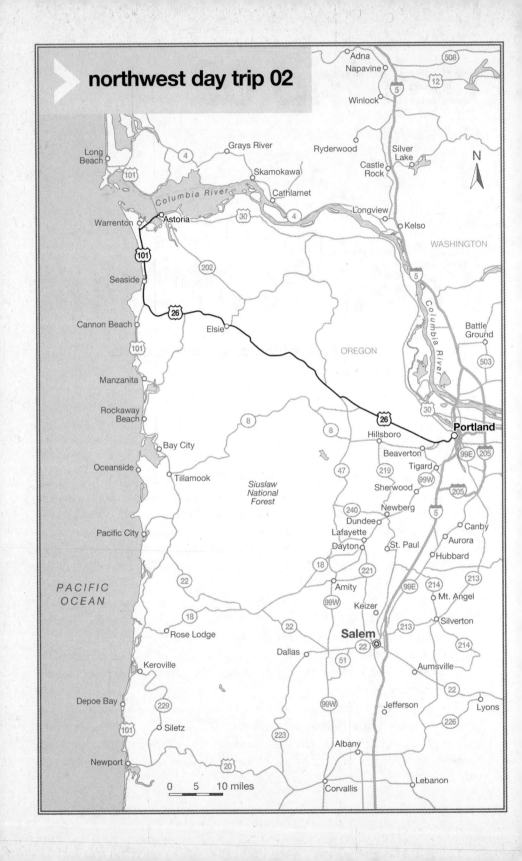

northwest day trip 02

Astoria was named after the American investor John Jacob Astor. His American Fur Company founded Fort Astoria, which would become the first permanent US settlement on the Pacific coast, in 1810. Eventually, Portland, Seattle, and San Francisco surpassed Astoria as the West Coast's main port cities, and Astoria was left to thrive quietly on the pursuits of fishing and logging. Today, tourism is a primary industry. In the last decade, Astoria has caught the attention of cruise ships, which can disembark 2,000 passengers at a time.

getting there

Take US 26 W/OR 26 west out of Portland for 73 miles. Merge onto OR 101/US 101 N toward Seaside/Astoria. Continue north for 19 miles until you reach Astoria. An alternate route, and one that the locals find to be more scenic, is to take US 30 along the Columbia. This way, it's a 95-mile drive, all on US 30. The US 30 route can be made quicker by taking I-5 north to Longview before cutting over west to US 30. The route you choose will likely depend on the time of year, weather, and where you are starting from.

where to go

Astoria Column. At the top of Coxcomb Drive off 15th Street; (503) 325-2963; astoriacolumn .org. For the best view in town, drive up to the top of Astoria's Coxcomb Drive and then climb another 165 steps on foot to the top of the Astoria Column. The column is an Astoria icon, built in 1926 as the dream child of Ralph Budd, president of the Midwest-based Great Northern Railroad, with support from Vincent Astor, great grandson of businessman John Jacob Astor, whose Pacific Fur Company settled Astoria. Stunning views of the Columbia River to the north, the Cascade Range to the east, and the Pacific Ocean to the west wow those willing to test their lungs with the climb up the winding staircase. This is a great place to go when you first arrive in Astoria to begin to get the lay of the land. Even if you don't choose to climb the column, the views from the parking lot are outstanding. Parking comes with a suggested $1 per car donation; the park is open dawn to dusk.

Astoria Riverfront Trolley. 1 Basin St.; (503) 325-6311; old300.org. Adding to downtown Astoria's charm is this restored 1913 trolley, which makes a 2.6-mile run along the Columbia River. The conductor does his part by narrating to passengers tales of Astoria's history and attractions. You can catch a ride on the trolley from just about anywhere on the riverfront between Basin and 39th Streets. Round-trip ride is $1; an all-day pass is $2. The round trip takes about an hour. Hours change seasonally; check website.

Clatsop County Historical Society. 714 Exchange St.; (503) 325-2203; cumtux.org. The society has three museums. Call for hours and details.

   The Flavel House. Corner of 8th and Duane Streets. Captain George Flavel was a prominent sea captain and one of the wealthier residents of early Astoria. This quaint late Queen Anne Victorian home was built for him in 1885 and features park-like grounds, original Eastlake-style woodwork interiors, and exotic hard-wood fireplaces with imported tile surrounds.

Heritage Museum. Corner of 16th and Exchange Streets. A historical exhibit includes Chinook and Clatsop Indian baskets and a partially constructed Astoria saloon. Pick up a booklet here to help guide you on a walking tour of Astoria's famous historical homes. "The Astor Party and the Founding of Astoria" is an exhibit to commemorate Astoria's bicentennial.

The Uppertown Firefighters Museum. Corner of 30th Street and Marine Drive. Astoria's downtown was twice destroyed by fire, in 1883 and 1922, and more recently Fort Clatsop burned to the ground. With Astoria's history of fire, it's no surprise they have a museum dedicated to firefighters. This museum in an old red-brick fire station houses an extensive collection of firefighting equipment and memorabilia from Clatsop County dating back to 1877, including a horse-drawn ladder wagon and a 1912 American LaFrance fire truck.

Columbia River Maritime Museum. 1792 Marine Dr.; (503) 325-2323; crmm.org. Brave souls have been tackling the ocean by boat for hundreds of years. Here you can explore marine transportation from the age of dugout canoes to sailboats to the present. A film introduces the history of life and commerce on the Columbia River. A very cool exhibit titled "Crossing the Bar: Perilous Passage" takes an exciting look at the legendary Columbia River entrance, where the forces of the mighty Columbia and the Pacific Ocean meet, creating waves that can exceed 40 feet during bad winter storms. It's one of the most dangerous waterways on the planet, and watching the pros who navigate it every day at work is pretty amazing. See videos captured while working with the US Coast Guard and the Columbia River Bar Pilots during fierce winter storms. Open daily 9:30 a.m. to 5 p.m.

Fort Clatsop National Memorial. 92343 Fort Clatsop Rd.; (503) 861-2471; nps.gov/lewi. Lewis and Clark spent a winter here, hoping that a ship would pass by to return them to their homes on the East Coast. When that didn't happen, in the spring of 1906, they returned the way they'd come—but not before getting a solid taste of a Pacific Northwest winter spent in a fort they built. What will strike you right away, with your own memories of bad weather and close quarters crowding in, is how small the fort is. The facility includes the reconstructed fort, a visitor center and museum, historical exhibits, a canoe landing, picnic area, trails through the wetlands, and a rain forest of young Sitka spruce and western hemlock. During the summer months, experience living history demonstrations depicting fort activities. Open daily: summer 9 a.m. to 6 p.m.; winter 9 a.m. to 5 p.m.

Fort Stevens State Park. 100 Peter Iredale Rd., Hammond; (503) 861-3170; oregonstateparks.org/park_179. Fort Stevens was the primary military defense installation at the mouth of the Columbia River, serving from the Civil War through World War II. Today the site is a great place to access and walk the beach, as well as catch a glimpse of the wreck of the

Peter Iredale, an oceangoing ship that was destroyed near the mouth of the Columbia River in the early part of the century. The wreck can still be seen at low tide and makes for a striking scene. Fort Stevens State Park is great for all sorts of recreation, including camping, boating, swimming, picnicking, hiking, and biking. Every Labor Day weekend, there's a Civil War reenactment on the site. $3 daily fee; camping also available.

Oregon Film Museum. 732 Duane St.; (503) 325-2203; oregonfilmmuseum.org. Astoria's beauty and architecture have attracted many to the area, including filmmakers. To celebrate the 25th anniversary of the Steven Spielberg film *The Goonies*, the Oregon Film Museum was born in 2010. Housed in the historic Clatsop County Jail, which was featured in the opening scene of *The Goonies,* the museum is dedicated to preserving the art and legacy of Oregon films and filmmaking. Other movies filmed in Astoria include *Overboard, Short Circuit, The Black Stallion, Kindergarten Cop, Free Willy, Free Willy 2: The Adventure Home, Teenage Mutant Ninja Turtles III, Benji the Hunted, The Ring, The Ring Two, Into the Wild, The Guardian,* and *Cthulhu.* If you happen to be in town on June 7 of any year, you're in for a special treat: Annually on that day, fans flock to Astoria for the annual Goonies Day celebration, a weekend of treasure hunting, group truffle shuffles, trivia scavenger hunts, and more. The film's 30th anniversary June 7 event included cast and crew reunions, film screenings, fan gatherings, filming location tours, and much more. Open daily; hours vary seasonally.

Walk the Waterfront. 1 11th St. The Astoria Waterfront provides many opportunities to stretch your legs with a walk and take in the sweep and scope of the Columbia River. Visit Maritime Memorial Park, the 6th Street Viewing Platform, the 14th Street Pier, and the 17th Street Dock. Most of the walking paths are paved.

where to shop

The Astoria Co-op. 1355 Exchange St., Suite #1; (503) 325-0027; astoria.coop/wp. This is the place to pick up picnic supplies for an outing to Fort Stevens or the beach. Great variety of to-go salads, sandwiches, soup, cookies, and more. Pick up one of their lovely organic cotton reusable totes to take along, too.

Commercial Street Antiques and Collectibles. 969 Commercial St.; (503) 325-4388. This is the destination for great finds from the past and lovely old objects to take home and beautify your living space. There are lots of small items here, from housewares to records.

Josephson's Smokehouse. 106 Marine Dr.; (800) 772-FISH; josephsons.com. For nearly 90 years, Josephson's has sold the finest local smoked, canned, and jerked seafood. At their historic smokehouse, an unequaled variety of seafood is smoked daily, sold at retail fresh from the smokers, packed for individual mail order to customers and restaurants, and shipped worldwide.

best seller

American writer Washington Irving mythologized John Jacob Astor and his 3-year reign as head of the Pacific Fur Company in Astoria *(1835). Though much of what Irving wrote was romanticized and overly dramatic—he referred to fur traders as "Sinbads of the wilderness"—the book was a success, and the region was forever planted in the American psyche.*

Phog Bounders Antique Mall. 892 Marine Dr.; (503) 338-0101; phogbounders.com. Here you'll find everything from low-end collectables to high-end and rare antiques in more than 3,000 square feet of small retail spaces. They buy your antiques and collectibles here, too. Open daily.

Vintage Hardware. 101 15th St.; (503) 325-1313; 101publichouse.com/astoria/vintage-hardware. The owners met at a flea market, and the rest is history. Originally opened on the ground floor of the historic Astor Hotel, the owners outgrew that location and moved to a riverfront location in 2014. The new location keeps the charm of the original building but allows for even more great relics to be displayed. A Sunday "Vintage Flea Market" runs the first Sunday of July, August, September, and October.

where to eat

Astoria Coffeehouse and Bistro. 243 11th St.; (503) 325-1787; astoriacoffeehouse.com. This place looks unassuming, but you will no doubt love your experience here, whether it's for a cup of coffee or an utterly fantastic dinner. Astoria Coffeehouse makes everything from scratch—even the ketchup, and serves Stumptown Roasters coffee, fresh gourmet pastries, homemade soups, salads, entrees, and a wide variety of hot and cold beverages, plus cocktails, beer, and wine. The decor is funky and cool; don't miss the collection of globes ringing the room. Centrally located right downtown—look for the neon coffee cup on 11th Street. Open 7 days a week for breakfast, lunch, and dinner. $$.

Baked Alaska. 1 12th St.; (503) 325-7414; bakedak.com. Voted "best happy hour" by the locals, this fine dining and public house serves delicious food inspired by the region and the season. Wild, natural, and sustainable fare dominates the menu. Try the applejack halibut or thundermuck tuna. Bonus: Baked Alaska overlooks the Columbia River and offers lovely views. $$$.

Blue Scorcher Bakery Cafe. 1493 Duane St.; (503) 338-7473; bluescorcher.com. Operating as a worker collective with the motto "joyful work, delicious food, and strong community," Blue Scorcher creates artisan breads, pastries, and handcrafted seasonal foods using local and organic ingredients. A children's area features a play kitchen and makes this restaurant a natural gathering place for families. Located in the historic Fort George building with views of the Columbia River. (P.S. A "scorcher" is a line of bicycles that appeared in the late 1880s, renowned for their speed. Who knew?) Open 7 days a week from 8 a.m. to 5 p.m. $.

Bowpicker. Located across from the Columbia River Maritime Museum, at the corner of 17th and Duane Streets, in a converted gillnet boat; bowpicker.com. Though you'll never leave land, just eating here will make you feel like you've had an adventure on the high seas. Bowpicker is locally famous for their beer-battered albacore tuna and steak fries—the best fish and chips in town. Open Wed through Sun in summer season, Fri through Sun in winter season, weather permitting (just as on the high seas, high winds can shut this boat/restaurant down). $.

Bridgewater Bistro. 20 Basin St., Suite A; (503) 325-6777; bridgewaterbistro.com. This well-lit, high-ceilinged, attractive, and modern wood and metal space in a renovated boatyard provides river and bridge views from every table. The menu is composed of creatively prepared seafood, meats, soups, and vegetarian entrees. Choose tables in the family-friendly casual bistro setting or on the fine dining mezzanine. Open 7 days a week for lunch and dinner; brunch on Sun. $$–$$$.

Buoy Beer Company. 1 8th St.; (503) 325-4540; buoybeer.com. Established in 2013 with a grand opening in 2014, Buoy Beer is the third brewery to open doors in Astoria. Whether you are a beer drinker or not, Buoy's river location is worth a visit for the view alone. A floor window in the main dining room gives a view of resting sea lions and is a great distraction for the kids. Try the habanero oyster deviled eggs or chicken Romesco while large vessels passing by keep you company. Open daily at 11 a.m. $–$$.

Clemente's. 1198 Commercial St.; (503) 325-1067; clementesrestaurant.com. Healthful, local, organic, seasonal, wild, and consistently excellent foods are served here in a beautifully designed but casual space. The menu changes with the season; the place has won many accolades. Specialties include poke and gluten-free fish and chips. Open for dinner Tues through Sun. $$.

Columbian Cafe. 1114 Marine Dr.; (503) 325-2233; columbianvoodoo.com. Three businesses in one: A funky renovated lunch counter called the Columbian Cafe serves only the very best fresh local foods including seafood and lots of spicy vegetarian options, open for breakfast, lunch, and dinner Wed through Sun. The Voodoo Room next door opens at 5 p.m. daily for pizza and music. And finally there's the Columbian Theater, which shows one picture at a time and offers beer and pizza to go with it. $–$$.

Fort George Brewery and Public House. 1483 Duane St.; (503) 325-PINT; fortgeorge brewery.com. Pub food and seafood are served in this popular, hip brewpub built in an incredible old building that was once a service station. Try the sausage sampler with spicy mustard or the albacore tuna melt. Enjoy live music on some weekends, and outdoor dining seasonally. The beers are plentiful, varied, reliably delicious and often on tap around the Pacific Northwest, if you don't catch them here. Fort George, by the way, was one of the original names for Astoria when it was a fur trading post, named for King George. Open 7 days a week for lunch and dinner. $$.

Pig 'N Pancake. 146 W Bond; (503) 325-3144; pignpancake.com. There are six Pig 'N Pancake restaurants in Oregon, five of them on the coast. They serve 35 breakfast options including pancakes, crepes, omelets, and the like all day, prepared fresh in a fun, family-friendly atmosphere. Open daily for breakfast, lunch, and dinner. $.

Ship Inn. 1 2nd St.; (503) 325-0033; shipinn-astoria.com. You might just feel like one of Astoria's long-ago mariners here. Cornish pasties, great fish and chips, and calamari are served in a true English pub atmosphere. Don't miss the fabulous views of the Columbia River, and, of course, there are lots of great beers on tap. $$.

Silver Salmon. 1105 Commercial; (503) 338-6640; silversalmongrille.com. The historic Fisher Building that houses this restaurant was built in 1924, but it's got nothing on the bar that sits inside. The Silver Salmon's ornately carved antique bar is 120 years old, is constructed of Scottish cherry wood, and was shipped around Cape Horn in the 1880s. This romantic, historic restaurant in downtown offers great food, drinks, and desserts. Open for lunch and dinner 7 days a week. $$–$$$.

T. Paul's Urban Cafe and Supper Club. 1119 Commercial St.; (503) 338-5133; tpaulssupperclub.com. Fresh eclectic cuisine including wonderful salads, sweet potato fries, and clam chowder is served at this eclectically decorated restaurant—there's lots of color, light, and fun in here. The prices are good, and live blues, jazz, or folk plays on Fri and Sat nights. $–$$.

Wet Dog Cafe and Brew Pub and Astoria Brewing Company. 144 11th St.; (503) 325-6975; wetdogcafe.com. Microbrews, burgers, and the like delivered to guests on Astoria's waterfront. Wet Dog offers a full menu and 20 Northwest craft beers on tap, including many different handcrafted ales brewed on-site. Open 7 days a week for lunch and dinner. $–$$.

where to stay

Cannery Pier Hotel. 10 Basin St.; (888) 325-4996; cannerypierhotel.com. Built on the site of the former Union Fish Cannery 600 feet into the Columbia River, this hotel is the ultimate in comfort and luxury, Astoria style. Guests, who have up-close and unparalleled views of a real working river, are provided with a list of the ships they should expect to see pass by their windows during their stay, as well as a description of their cargo. Views of the amazing Astoria-Megler Bridge and Cape Disappointment are also impressive. Each room has a private balcony and fireplace; halls are decorated with wonderful historical photographs of

a fire in the night

In October 2005, just weeks before the Lewis and Clark Bicentennial celebration was to commence, Fort Clatsop was ruined by fire. A stray ember from a fireplace was thought to be the cause. The fort was a replica of the original and had been built in 1955, but nevertheless, the loss was devastating to supporters of the National Memorial. The timing was particularly tough, but such a significant setback also served as a powerful motivator to the community. Fourteen months later, with the help of 700 workers and volunteers, Fort Clatsop had been rebuilt.

Astoria. Free wine and hors d'oeuvres in the evening; continental breakfast in the morning. A free chauffeur-driven limo service uses classic old cars to shuttle you to and from your evening destination, making you feel a bit like royalty. The real star is that big old beautiful river out the window; you'll have a hard time tearing your eyes off of it. Expensive, but worth every penny. $$$+.

Clementine's Bed and Breakfast. 847 Exchange St.; (503) 325-2005; clementines-bb .com. This beautiful 2-story classic 1888 Victorian house offers fresh flowers, featherbeds, down pillows, and duvet comforters in each of its 5 rooms. The grounds are done up with gorgeous English gardens, and some rooms have private decks with spectacular views. $$-$$$.

Grandview Bed and Breakfast. 1574 Grand Ave.; (503) 325-5555; grandviewbedand breakfast.com. This lovely and romantic Victorian house on the Historic Homes Walking Tour features wonderful Columbia River views. Three 2-bedrooms and three 1-bedroom lodgings with private baths have lace and floral decor. $-$$.

Hotel Elliott. 357 12th St.; (503) 325-2222; hotelelliott.com. Built in 1924, Hotel Elliott underwent a dramatic 3-year transformation in the early 2000s to expand rooms, glamorize everything, but preserve the classic ambience. This beautifully restored old hotel has a fabulous rooftop terrace, cellar wine bar, and proximity to downtown restaurants. The rooms are designed for relaxed comfort. $$-$$$.

Rose River Inn Bed and Breakfast. 1510 Franklin Ave.; (503) 325-7175; roseriverinn .com. Just 3 blocks from downtown and 4 from the riverfront, this Craftsman-style home built in 1912 is on the local register of historic places. Five private guest rooms have names like Inspiration and Sunflare, and are filled with antiques; in the morning, enjoy a full breakfast. $-$$.

day trip 03

northwest

clams, kites & cranberries:
the long beach peninsula, wa

the long beach peninsula

The 28-mile Long Beach Peninsula juts out of Washington State's southwest corner, just across the bridge from Astoria. Long, narrow, and picturesque, the Peninsula is bounded on the west by the Pacific Ocean, the south by the Columbia River, and the east by Willapa Bay.

On the Pacific Ocean side, a sandy beach stretches continuously for 28 miles. This strip of beach is great for kite-flying, walking, clam digging, sandcastle building, and more, but not so great for swimming. The water is cold and dangerous—in fact, because of the confluence of the Columbia River and the Pacific Ocean, it's some of the most dangerous water on the West Coast.

Many small communities dot Long Beac Peninsula, each a bit different. Downtown Long Beach offers the most festive atmosphere, with kite, candy, ice cream, and T-shirt shops, and a wonderful kite festival in August. Oysterville is known for its historic homes; Ilwaco for the Port of Ilwaco, the comings and goings of a working marina, and a summertime Saturday Market. Only Ilwaco and Long Beach are incorporated, and the residents of the peninsula think of themselves as one community, called the Long Beach Peninsula. The principal industry of the Long Beach Peninsula has become tourism, though fishing, crabbing, oyster farming, and cranberry farming are also important components of the local economy.

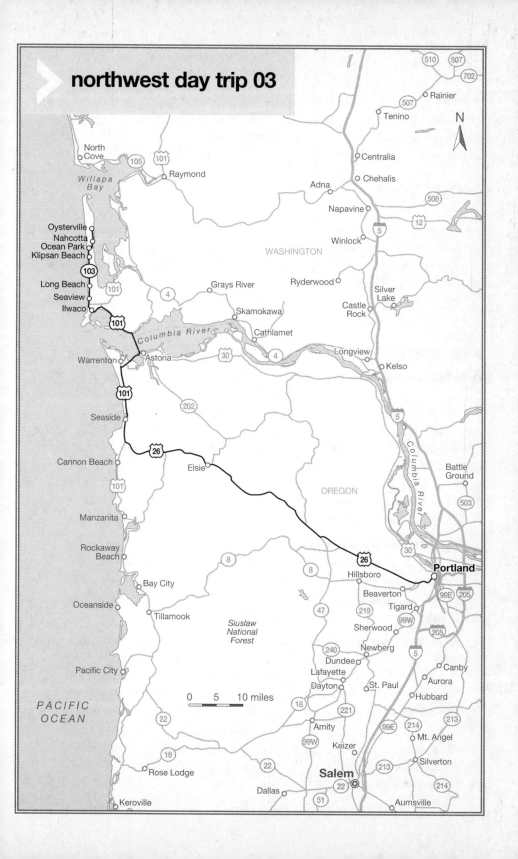

northwest day trip 03

From spring break through mid-October, the peninsula is hopping with visitors, festivals, and activity. The rest of the year, it's awfully quiet. Winter can still be a great time to visit, especially if you are interested in clam digging or want to get a glimpse of some of the epic winter storms that strike the Cape Disappointment headlands from the Pacific.

getting there

Take US 26 W/OR 26 W out of Portland and continue 74 miles to the coast. At the US 101 junction, go north for 36 miles, crossing the Astoria Bridge into Washington State. US 101 will turn into WA 103/Pacific Ave. S, which traverses the entire Long Beach Peninsula.

Note: In the winter, when US 26 can be icy, consider taking US 30 north and west out of Portland, to intersect with US 101 at Astoria. It is not as pretty a drive, but heading to Longview, WA, on I-5, then crossing over to US 30 is another good option and quicker than US 30 out of the city.

where to go

Cape Disappointment State Park. South end of peninsula, south of Ilwaco off WA 100. Cape Disappointment State Park is the most visited park in the Washington State Parks system. Here you can walk a flat sandy beach, explore bunkers of an old military fort, wander through coastal forests, have a picnic, camp, take in spectacular vistas and visit a beach called Dead Man's Cove. The park has an old-growth forest, lakes, freshwater and saltwater marshes, streams, ocean tidelands, lots of watchable wildlife, and a working Coast Guard station. "Cape D" encompasses 1,882 acres and is fronted by both the Pacific Ocean and Baker Bay. The park is open year round for camping and day use, 6:30 a.m. to dusk.

Within its boundaries are these highlights:

Cape Disappointment Lighthouse. On the southeast tip of the peninsula, off WA 100. There are two lighthouses on the south end of the peninsula—the Cape Disappointment and the North Head. Only the North Head is open to the public. Enjoy Cape Disappointment Lighthouse from the outside, knowing that it's the oldest operating lighthouse on the West Coast.

North Head Lighthouse. North Head Lighthouse Road, off WA 100 in Ilwaco; (360) 642-3078. The 65-foot North Head Lighthouse was completed in 1898. Tours include history and gorgeous panoramic views of the peninsula and Pacific Ocean. Incidentally, North Head is the windiest lighthouse area on the West Coast and the second windiest in the nation. Winds of 120 miles per hour have been recorded at the site. The lighthouse grounds are open year-round, dawn until dusk at no charge on foot; those driving will need a Washington State Parks Discover Pass to park in all parts of Cape Disappointment State Park. Call for tour hours, which change seasonally.

Waikiki Beach. On the southern end of the Peninsula off WA 100. Waikiki Beach is considered the only swim-safe beach on the peninsula. Still, whether or not you actually want to venture into the water will depend on your fortitude and/or the air temperature—the water here isn't exactly as warm as the other Waikiki, in Hawaii.

Lewis and Clark Interpretive Center. Cape Disappointment State Park, off WA 100 on the south end of the peninsula; (360) 642-3029. Perched on a cliff 200 feet above the mouth of the Columbia River, the Lewis and Clark Interpretive Center tells the story of the journey of the Corps of Discovery, focusing particularly on their Pacific Coast stay. Terrific, thorough, and vivid exhibits bring home the arduous journey Lewis, Clark, and their crew made, ending with the stories of what happened to each member after their return home. One of the best interpretations of the incredible feats of the Corps of Discovery I've seen. During winter and spring, volunteers help visitors spot migrating gray whales; year-round, views of the Columbia Bar are truly spectacular from this vantage point on the tip of the cape. Open year-round from 10 a.m. to 5 p.m. daily.

Columbia Pacific Heritage Museum. 115 SE Lake St., Ilwaco; (360) 642-3446; columbiapacificheritagemuseum.org. Explore the history of the region where the Columbia River meets the Pacific Ocean. Artifacts, images, and stories interpret the Chinook Indians, European explorers, 19th-century pioneers, fishermen, cranberry growers, loggers, and summer people who have made the Long Beach Peninsula what it is today. Open 10 a.m. to 4 p.m. Tues through Sat, noon to 4 p.m. Sun, closed Mon. Free admission for children ages 12 and under.

Discovery Trail. North end access is off 26th Street NW in Long Beach; south end access is off the corner of Elizabeth Avenue and Waterfront Way in Ilwaco. The Discovery Trail was created to commemorate the Lewis and Clark Expedition and parallels Capt. William Clark's hike to the Pacific Ocean in November 1805. Stretching 8.3 miles between Long Beach and Ilwaco, the trail is closed to motor vehicles and horses and offers peaceful, scenic passage to pedestrians and cyclists. Interpretive markers and several bronze statues can be found on the route. The trail is relatively easy and flat from the northern terminus to Beard's Hollow. The trail gets more challenging at that point, rising in elevation as much as 300 feet between Beard's Hollow and the southern terminus at the Port of Ilwaco. A spur trail to North Head Lighthouse has recently been added.

Green Angel Gardens Farm Store. 6807 Sandridge Rd., Long Beach; (360) 642-4018; greenangelgardening.com. Stocked with organic greens grown on site, local fresh eggs, and a variety of certified organic produce obtained from regional growers. The Green Angel Farm promotes education and is family-friendly, encouraging kids and adults to come and learn how quality food is grown. Open daily 10 a.m. to 4 p.m.

a powerful & yawning sea

The waters off the Long Beach Peninsula are considered some of the most treacherous in the world. Known as the Graveyard of the Pacific, the stretch of water where the Pacific Ocean meets the Columbia River has claimed more than 2,000 ships since the late 1700s. The US Coast Guard set up a Lifeboat School here—perfect training ground for wild and woolly ocean rescues.

Knappton Cove Heritage Center. Right on WA 401 northeast of the Astoria-Megler Bridge; (503) 738-5206; knapptoncoveheritagecenter.org. Everything that happened at New York's famous Ellis Island happened at other US ports during the waves of immigration in the 1800s and early 1900s, only on a smaller scale. In Astoria, boats from overseas anchored and were boarded by an inspector. If fumigation for infestation and disease was deemed necessary, the boats were sent here, across the Columbia River to the US Columbia River Quarantine Station, the only point for federal quarantine on the West Coast north of San Francisco. Today it's a National Historic Site, set on preserving the history of this unique location and the role of the US Public Health Service. Open Sat 1 to 4 p.m. in summer, or by appointment.

Long Beach Boardwalk. Access at Bolstad Avenue and Sid Snyder Drive in Long Beach. *The Today Show* named the Long Beach Boardwalk one of the top five in the nation, calling it the "most unique." That's because, unlike many US boardwalks, the half-mile boardwalk in Long Beach isn't lined with hot dog stands and sunglasses vendors, but instead surrounded by grassy dunes. Interpretive exhibits dot the route, and spectacular views of the ocean, beach, and North Head Lighthouse make this a must-walk.

Pacific Coast Cranberry Research Foundation Museum and Gift Shop. 2907 Pioneer Rd., Long Beach; (360) 642-5553; cranberrymuseum.com. Cranberry farming in the southwest corner of Washington State has a more than 100-year history and remains an important part of the local economy. This 1,200-square-foot facility next to a 10-acre demonstration cranberry farm interprets the history and cultivation of this garnet-colored berry, and offers a self-guided walking tour of cranberry bogs year-round. September is the most spectacular month, when the berries are ripening. Open daily 10 a.m. to 5 p.m., Apr through Dec.

Painted Lady Lavender Farm. 1664 US 101, Ilwaco; (360) 642-3531. This charming 2-acre farm grows lavender and also includes a chicken coop, rabbits, and a guest cabin. Open daily until dusk. Call or stop in for guided tours of the plantings of lavender and other organic herbs.

World Kite Museum and Hall of Fame. 303 Sid Snyder Dr., Long Beach; (360) 642-4020; worldkitemuseum.com. The kite is 2,500 years old. This museum showcases 1,500 kites from around the world and preserves the kite's past, to record its present developments and to honor the people dedicated to kites. Open 11 a.m. to 5 p.m. daily in the summer, Fri through Tues, Oct through Apr.

where to eat

Bailey's Bakery & Cafe. 26910 Sandridge Rd., Nahcotta; (360) 665-4449; baileysbakery cafe.com. Bailey's is famous for their "Thunder Buns," an amazing cinnamon roll described as "the most outrageous on the planet" that sells out early each day. If you miss out on those, there are lots of other treats to tempt you, including bread, scones, sausage rolls, and fresh soups. Open Thurs through Mon 8 a.m. to 3 p.m., Sun 9 a.m. to 3 p.m. $.

The Depot Restaurant. 1208 38th Place, Seaview; (360) 642-7880; depotrestaurantdining .com. Discover great food and ambience at this restaurant in a 120-year-old depot building at the end of the old "Clamshell Railroad." Entrees include "landfood" and "seafood." The Depot's chowder is to die for, with leeks and steamer clams. They offer a regional and international wine list with 6 microbrews on tap. $$$.

42nd Street Cafe. 4201 Pacific Way, Seaview; (360) 642-2323; 2ndstcafe.com. Showcasing the many cuisines of the West Coast in a casual environment, 42nd Street Cafe is a local's favorite. Seafood is a focus, with special dining events around clam digging season, mushroom season, and the like. Service is great, and 42nd Street sells their condiments to go. Breakfast and lunch 8 a.m. to 2 p.m.; American bistro dinners begin at 4:30 p.m. $–$$.

Lost Roo. 1700 S. Pacific Highway; (360) 642-4329; lostroo.com. This big, welcoming establishment offers drinks and fare for the whole family. A restaurant, outdoor patio, and full

the clamshell railroad

The Ilwaco Railway and Navigation Company operated a narrow-gauge railroad that ran for more than 40 years from the bar of the Columbia River up the Long Beach Peninsula. Steamers could only reach the Ilwaco wharf, where the railroad began, to unload their take after the tide was in mid-flood. Therefore the railroad's schedule was based on the tide charts. A schedule for April 1905 shows times of departure from Astoria for the steamer Nahcotta *as varying from as early as 5 a.m. to as late as 8:30 a.m. The railroad had a number of nicknames, including the "Clamshell Railroad."*

bar with plenty of televisions please everyone. A big menu with a (slightly) Australian theme includes burgers, seafood, and "sammies." Open 7 days a week 11:30 a.m. to close. $–$$.

Nanci and Jimella's Klipsan Market Cafe. 21712 Pacific Way, Klipsan Beach; (360) 665-4847. The Market Cafe offers casual cafe dining with delicious seafood entrees, appetizers, desserts, and breads complemented by excellent wines. This location is also a seafood market and community store mecca of fine fresh fish, cheeses, local produce, fresh herbs, wines, and smoked and cured meats, plus exclusive takeout specialties beginning with clam chowder and a tasty array of gourmet sandwiches. A recently added bar is called Lucca and Sofia's. $$–$$$.

Serious Pizza. 243 Robert Grey Drive, Ilwaco; (360) 642-3060; capedisappointmentstore .com. The place doesn't look like much, and is only open seasonally, but the wood-fired artisan pizza is worth the wait here. Calling in ahead is a good plan. $–$$.

where to stay

Adrift Hotel. 409 Sid Snyder Dr., Long Beach; (800) 561-2456; adrifthotel.com. This 80-room hotel is new, modern, and super classy. There is a spa on-site, and they lend out cruiser bikes so guests can explore the Discovery Trail, which is just outside the front doors. Their restaurant, Pickled Fish, serves specialty cocktails, a farm-and-sea-to-table menu, and live entertainment nightly. $$–$$$.

Boreas Bed & Breakfast Inn. 607 Ocean Beach Blvd. N, Long Beach; (360) 642-8069; boreasinn.com. This oceanfront boutique inn only has 5 rooms, making it peaceful and

happy as a clam

Last year, I took my children clam digging for the first time on the Long Beach Peninsula. Recreational digging of the Pacific razor clam has taken off in recent years here, bringing families out during the fall and spring seasons to dig for dinner. It's quick and easy to learn, and very fun for all ages, especially if the catching is good. Watching my girls master the art of the clam gun, work hard at unearthing a clam from the wet sand, and celebrate with a happy dance on the beautiful beach next to the Pacific Ocean was a blast. Bring the kids and your clam gun or shovel and see how much fun this sport can be. Specific times and dates are set for legal harvest, and diggers need a fishing license. See funbeach .com/play/outside/catch-it/clamming.

private. A 3-course award-winning brunch is served daily. Boreas is nestled in the dunes and within walking distance of the Discovery Trail and Long Beach Boardwalk. $$–$$$.

The Breakers. Hwy 103 at 26th St.; (360) 642-4414; breakerslongbeach.com. Four buildings house 122 rooms and suites, making this place a great destination for family lodging. There is an indoor pool and large outdoor hot tub on the property, as well as a children's play area. Beach access is easy; this is one end of the Discovery Trail, and the site of Clark's Tree, marking the spot where Captain William Clark finally reached the Pacific. $$.

China Beach Retreat. 222 Robert Gray Dr., Ilwaco; (360) 642-5660; chinabeachretreat .com. China Beach is the perfect place to unwind. Decorated with an eclectic selection of European and Asian antiques and original artwork, frequently visited by deer, waterfowl, and bald eagles, China Beach Retreat has a view of the mouth of the Columbia River and Baker Bay and offers private spa tubs and gourmet breakfast. With just 3 guest rooms, you may never see another person—aside from the one you bring with you, that is. For even more seclusion, try the Audubon Cottage, a two-story unit that sleeps 2 with an outdoor jetted tub, on the same property. $$$.

Klipsan Beach Cottages. 22617 Pacific Way; Ocean Park; (360) 665-4888; klipsan beachcottages.com. Classic traditional beach cottages, kept up impeccably, the cottages at Klipsan Beach sit on a ridge facing the Pacific Ocean and are surrounded by beautifully landscaped grounds. Well-appointed kitchens, fireplaces, and the ocean nearby—what more do you need? $–$$.

Shelburne Inn. 4415 Pacific Way, Seaview; (360) 642-2442; theshelburneinn.com. Established in 1896, the Shelburne Inn has been spoiling its guests for over 100 years. Four-star dining, a stunning breakfast, and a pub serving fine wines and microbrews distinguish this world-renowned country inn retreat. $$.

appendix a:
regional information

north

day trip 01

Vancouver USA Regional Tourism Office
101 East 8th St., Suite 240, Vancouver
(877) 600-0800
visitvancouverusa.com

day trip 02

South Columbia County Chamber
of Commerce
2194 Columbia Blvd., St. Helens
(503) 397-0685
sccchamber.org

northeast

day trip 01

Cowlitz County Tourism Bureau
105 Minor Rd., Kelso
(360) 577-3137
visitmtsthelens.com

east

day trip 01

Hood River Chamber of Commerce
720 E Port Marina Dr., Hood River
(541) 386-2000
hoodriver.org

Skamania County Chamber of Commerce
& Visitor Information Center
167 NW 2nd St., Stevenson
(800) 989-9178
skamania.org

day trip 02

Hood River Chamber of Commerce
720 E Port Marina Dr., Hood River
(541) 386-2000
hoodriver.org

day trip 03

The Dalles Area Chamber of Commerce
404 W 2nd St., The Dalles
(541) 296-2231, (800) 255-3385
thedalleschamber.com

southeast

day trip 01

Oregon's Mt. Hood Territory
Clackamas County Tourism
& Cultural Affairs
150 Beavercreek Rd., Suite 305,
Oregon City
(503) 742-5910
mthoodterritory.com

day trip 02

Maupin Area Chamber of Commerce
P.O. Box 220, US 197, Maupin
(541) 395-2599
maupinoregon.com

day trip 03

Confederated Tribes of Warm Springs
1233 Veterans St., Warm Springs
(541) 553-1161
warmsprings.com

Crooked River Ranch-Terrebonne Chamber
of Commerce
P.O. Box 1502, Crooked River Ranch
(541) 923-2679
crrchamber.com

Central Oregon Visitors Association
661 SW Powerhouse Dr., Suite 1301,
Bend
(800) 800-8334
visitcentraloregon.com

day trip 04

Central Oregon Visitors Association
661 SW Powerhouse Dr., Suite 1301,
Bend
(800) 800-8334
visitcentraloregon.com

Visit Bend
750 NW Lava Rd. 160, Bend
(541) 382-8048
visitbend.com

south

day trip 01

Oregon's Mt. Hood Territory
Clackamas County Tourism
& Cultural Affairs
150 Beavercreek Rd., Suite 305,
Oregon City
(503) 742-5910
mthoodterritory.com

day trip 02

Travel Salem
181 High St. NE, Salem
(503) 581-4325, (800) 874-7012
travelsalem.com

day trip 03

Travel Salem
181 High St. NE, Salem
(503) 581-4325, (800) 874-7012
travelsalem.com

day trip 04

Travel Salem
181 High St. NE, Salem
(503) 581-4325, (800) 874-7012
travelsalem.com

Silverton Chamber of Commerce
426 S Water St., Silverton
(503) 873-5615
silvertonchamber.org

day trip 05

Mill City Chamber of Commerce
North Santiam Chamber of Commerce/
Visitors Information Center
P.O. Box 222, Mill City
(503) 897-3183
nschamber.org

day trip 06

Eugene, Cascades and Coast
754 Olive St., Eugene
(541) 743-8760
eugenecascadescoast.org

southwest

day trip 01

Chehalem Valley Chamber of Commerce
115 N. College St., Newberg
(503) 883-7770
chehalemvalley.org

Travel Yamhill Valley
P.O. Box 774, McMinnville
(503) 883-7770
travelyamhillvalley.org

day trip 02

Travel Yamhill Valley
P.O. Box 774, McMinnville
(503) 883-7770
travelyamhillvalley.org

McMinnville Area Chamber of Commerce
417 NW Adams St., McMinnville
(503) 472-6196
mcminnville.org

day trip 03

Albany Visitors Association
110 3rd Ave. SE, Albany
(541) 928-0911
albanyvisitors.com

day trip 04

Corvallis Tourism
553 NW Harrison Blvd., Corvallis
(541) 757-1544
visitcorvallis.com

Corvallis Benton Chamber Coalition
420 Northwest 2nd St., Corvallis
(541) 757-1505
cbchambercoalition.com

day trip 05

Newport Chamber of Commerce
555 SW Coast Hwy., Newport
(541) 265-8801
newportchamber.org

west

day trip 01

Washington County Visitors Association
11000 SW Stratus St., Suite 170,
Beaverton
(503) 644-5555
visitwashingtoncountyoregon.com

day trip 02

Tillamook Area Chamber of Commerce
3705 US 101 N, Tillamook
(503) 842-7525
tillamookchamber.org

Nestucca Valley Chamber of Commerce
P.O. Box 75, Cloverdale
(503) 392-4340
pcnvchamber.org

day trip 03

Cannon Beach Chamber of Commerce
207 N Spruce St., Cannon Beach
(503) 436-2623
cannonbeach.org

northwest

day trip 01

Seaside Visitor's Bureau
Seaside Chamber of Commerce
7 North Roosevelt Dr., Seaside
(888) 306-2326
seasideor.com

day trip 02

Astoria-Warrenton Area Chamber
of Commerce
111 West Marine Dr., Astoria
(503) 325-6311
oldoregon.com
travelastoria.com

day trip 03

Long Beach Peninsula Visitors Bureau
P.O. Box 562, Long Beach
(360) 642-2400, (800) 451-2542
funbeach.com

appendix b:
festivals & celebrations

The open road, no agenda, and free-form type exploration of a day trip can be fabulous, but sometimes it's just more fun to go somewhere you know there's going to be action. Festivals offer the opportunity to park the car in one spot and soak up music, food, and entertainment all at once. Luckily for you, the regions surrounding Portland love a good festival, and on just about any given weekend you can find a great party happening somewhere within a one- to three-hour drive of the city. These pages list festivals celebrating classic cars, seafood, wine, Leonardo da Vinci, independent film, cranberries, kites, and more. No matter your interests, you're sure to find an appealing festival here. For more events, see traveloregon.com and oregonfestivals.org.

january

Oregon Truffle Festival. (503) 296-5929; oregontrufflefestival.com. Created to celebrate magnificent, world-famous Oregon truffle mushrooms as they reach the peak of ripeness, this is the first festival in North America dedicated to sharing the experience of chefs, foragers, and fans of Oregon's wild truffles. Three days of workshops indoors and outdoors, packages, and the Grand Truffle Dinner sell out quickly each year.

february

Newport Seafood and Wine Festival. (541) 265-8801; newportchamber.org. Held the last full weekend in February in Newport, this popular festival celebrates two of the things Oregonians love best—seafood and wine. Held outdoors south of town; tastings start at $1 each; and free shuttle buses run from downtown.

march

Tulip Festival. (503) 634-2243; woodenshoe.com/tulip-fest. Held at the Wooden Shoe Tulip Farm outside of Woodburn, this festival lasts as long as the tulips are blooming—late March through May 1, typically. Enjoy more than 40 acres of tulips and daffodils on this farm, where you can also buy cut flowers, order bulbs for fall planting, and visit the children's acre and the gift shop.

The McMinnville Wine and Food Classic. (503) 472-4033; macwfc.org. Held in March at the Evergreen Aviation and Space Museum in the heart of Oregon Wine Country is this 3-day festival. This event showcases terrific food, beautiful arts and crafts, guest chef demonstrations, live musical entertainment, and wine tasting from some of the best wineries and vineyards in Oregon.

april

Astoria Warrenton Crab, Seafood, and Wine Festival. (503) 325-6311; oldoregon .com. Enjoy a great spread of Northwest cuisine, arts and crafts, a selection of Oregon and Washington's finest wines, a beer garden, and more at this annual Astoria event. Try the traditional crab dinner all weekend long and hear live music.

Annual Celilo Wy-am Salmon Feast and Pow Wow. powwowtime.com. Once a year, Celilo Village throws a party and invites everyone in. Food, traditional Native American dance contests, and a royalty contest make these events lots of good fun. Located at the traditional Celilo Longhouse.

Hood River Valley Blossom Festival. (541) 386-2000; hoodriver.org. This festival has been going strong for more than 50 years, and celebrates the time each year when fruit trees bloom. Hood River Valley is the largest pear-growing region in Oregon, and is also home to an abundance of cherry and apple orchards. When they all bloom, it's a beautiful sight. Events typically include a Blossom Fest Craft Show, Blossom Fest Quilt Show, a farm "pansy party," a grange blossom dinner, and a fire department all-you-can-eat breakfast. Visitors can also get a real "taste" of the gorge at several wine- and beer-tasting events.

Northwest Cherry Festival. (541) 296-2231; thedalleschamber.org. Held the fourth week in April in The Dalles, this whopper of a festival includes a lip sync contest, bicycle ride, parade, open air market, entertainment, car show, and coronation—all in celebration of the most famous local fruit.

may

Gorge Artists Open Studio Tour. (541) 478-0171; gorgeartists.org. Artists of the Colum-bia Gorge open their studios to the public annually at this event, held the first weekend in May. Participating artists will invite the public into their work spaces to view how and where they work, and to ask the artist questions. Tourists enhance their knowledge of art and culture in the Columbia Gorge, and view and purchase artwork not available in galleries.

McMinnville UFO Fest. (503) 472-8427; ufofest.com. For two days in May, it's all about aliens in McMinnville. McMenamins Hotel Oregon hosts this event, begun as a way to honor the famous 1950 Trent sighting in which two local citizens witnessed and photographed a UFO. With activities ranging from the serious (UFO experts speak) to the silly (costume contest), this event has become the second largest of its kind in the US.

Mother's Day Wildflower and Birding Weekend. (503) 873-8681; oregonstateparks .org. Flowers, birds, plant walks, and photography are celebrated at Silver Falls State Park during Mother's Day weekend each year. Join other families at the park's South Lodge all day both weekend days to enjoy nature with mom.

River Fest. (541) 395-2222; maupinriverfest.com. Visit Maupin on the Lower Deschutes River for a day of terrific live music, great food, fun, and family-friendly activities. This festival celebrating the river has a 5k/10k walk/run, popular regional bands, a variety of food and beverage vendors, and the artwork of art vendors. Take a mini raft trip on the Deschutes, and cast some fly rods at a casting pond.

Wine Walk. (503) 717-1914; seasidedowntown.com. In Seaside in May, local wineries are invited into local shops to pour samples of their best wines. Each Wine Walk brings hundreds of people to the downtown area for an afternoon and evening of great wines, great food, and, of course, great fun! Buy a commemorative wine glass and join in the fun. There's a second wine walk in November.

june

The Bach Festival. (541) 346-5667; oregonbachfestival.com. Headquartered in Eugene, this festival has grown to include Ashland, Bend, and Portland, and to encompass 11 days in June and July. Masterworks, guest stars, and up-and-coming musical artists are the heart of the Oregon Bach Festival, which pays homage to the music of the great Johann Sebastian Bach.

Muscle N Chrome. (503) 717-1914; seasidedowntown.org. Those who love cars come together in Seaside each year to celebrate all things automobile. A poker run, beach party, and vendor area are part of this 2-day festival of the collector vehicle.

Northwest Garlic Festival. (360) 665-4448; opwa.com. Ocean Park on the Long Beach Peninsula knows there's a lot to love about garlic. Celebrate the passion for this exalted bulb with the faithful throngs who make their annual pilgrimage to the Northwest Garlic Festival, which is held each June in the seaside community of Ocean Park. Garlic games, garlic crafts, and—naturally—garlic food and condiments are on hand at this 2-day event, as well as live music. Festival motto: It's chic to reek.

july

Balloons Over Bend. (541) 323-0964; balloonsoverbend.com. Hot air balloons fly over Bend for 3 days in July, launched from a park on the Deschutes River in the Old Mill District. Tether rides, balloon launches, breakfasts, and a night glow round out this celebration of color and beauty. There is also a marketplace with face painting, live music, and more.

Bridge of the Gods Kiteboarding Festival. (800) 989-9178; botgkitefest.com. Kiteboarders from across the nation converge on the Columbia River Gorge near Stevenson to compete in the nation's longest running amateur kiteboarding contest. The steep riverbanks make the Port of Skamania's East Point Kite Beach a natural grandstand for viewing the event.

Carlton's Walk in the Park. (503) 852-6572; carltonswalkinthepark.com. This 2-day event combines a fabulous selection of artists, musicians, and the region's top restaurants and wineries in an outdoor event in Carlton's Wennerberg Park. The North Yamhill River is a beautiful spot to taste great wine, beer, and food, as well as see great entertainment. Profits benefit local charities.

Columbia Gorge Bluegrass Festival and Fiddle Contest. (509) 427-3980; columbia gorgebluegrass.net. Held on the fourth weekend of July, this festival attracts outstanding national talent as well as premier regional bands. Held on the picturesque Skamania County Fairgrounds, the festival offers 4 days of fun, music, dances, workshops, and jammin'.

Da Vinci Days Festival. (541) 757-6363; davincidays.org. This cerebral festival is held in Corvallis on the Oregon State University campus geographically; metaphorically it's located at the crossroads of art, science, and technology. There's music, entertainment, creative contests, exhibits, races of all kinds, a parade, food and beverages, and hands-on activities for kids and adults. Here's where you can geocache, stargaze, and computer program to your heart's content.

Dory Days Festival. (971) 998-6385; pacificcity.org. There's no other marine fishery exactly like the one at Pacific City anywhere in the world. The modern dory fleet of today has evolved from the boats that went to sea from Cape Kiwanda more than 100 years ago. This 3-day event celebrates that rich history with a parade, marine fair, and fish fry at Cape Kiwanda, and an artisan fair in the downtown area.

Fort Dalles Days Pro Rodeo. (541) 296-2231; thefortdallesrodeo.com. A parade, pageant, and a banquet are part of this 3-day event in The Dalles, as is a full-blown rodeo, of course. Come out and see real bullfighting and a royal rodeo court at this old-fashioned event. There is live music nightly, too.

The International Pinot Noir Celebration. (800) 775-4762; ipnc.org. For 3 lovely days in McMinnville, the pinot noir grape is exalted even more than usual. For nearly 25 years, the IPNC has been uniting international pinot noir producers, journalists, pinot noir devotees, Northwest chefs, and foodies for a weekend of tasting, dining, learning, and celebrating together on the Linfield College Campus. Participants may also take a tour of Oregon wine country.

The Oregon Country Fair. Information: (541) 343-4298; oregoncountryfair.org. This 3-day event of nonstop costumed revelry has been an Oregon tradition for more than 40 years. Held each year in Veneta, west of Eugene, the Oregon Country Fair showcases world-class entertainment, handmade crafts, delectable foods, educational displays, and magical surprises at every turn of the path. The fair is an unforgettable adventure.

Red White and Blue Riverfront Festival. (541) 754-6624; visitcorvallis.com. This Corvallis event takes place over 2 days around July 4 and features lots of musical entertainment to get you up and dancing. A fireworks show is also included in the celebration, which is held on the riverfront.

Sisters Quilt Show. (541) 549-0989; sistersoutdoorquiltshow.org. Held the second Saturday in July in Sisters, this quilt show has become a must-see destination for thousands of visitors who descend on this small town this one day each year. Over 1,300 quilts from around the world are hung around this old-fashioned Western city, providing rich texture and color. Special exhibits and contests make the day even more fun.

St. Paul Rodeo. (800) 237-5920; stpaulrodeo.com. Held over the Fourth of July weekend in St. Paul, this rodeo has been going for more than 75 years and is ranked as one of the top in the nation with prize monies approaching $500,000 and nearly 1,000 competitors. This celebration underscores the grit and fortitude of those folks we know as cowboys and cowgirls.

august

Astoria Regatta Festival. (800) 875-6807; astoriaregatta.org. Five days of fun all about the greatest river in the west, the mighty Columbia. Sailboat races on the Columbia, live music and nightly concerts, a children's parade, fireworks over the Columbia, a salmon barbecue, a car show, and a grand parade bring out the folks in celebration.

Aurora Colony Day Outdoor Antiques Faire. (503) 939-0312; auroracolony.com. Aurora is one of the top 10 destinations for antiquing in the entire country. Downtown Aurora hosts this annual event. As does the city, the whole event has a deep flavor for the past.

Bend Brew Fest. (541) 322-9383; bendbrewfest.com. Bend knows beer, and would like you to know beer, too. This festival celebrates all things microbrewed. Held over 3 days at the Les Schwab Amphitheater, the Bend Brew Fest features more than 150 distinct craft beers for public tasting. There's great live music, as well as views of the mountains and the river.

Bi-Mart Willamette Country Music Festival. (541) 345-WCMF (9263); willamettecountry musicfestival.com. This fast-growing festival celebrates country music for three days of outdoor tunes, camping, and multiple well-known country artists near Brownsville.

Dufur Threshing Bee. (541) 467-2205; dufurthreshingbee.org. This old-time festival allows public enjoyment of wheat harvesting using old-time machinery and draft horses in the high desert community of Dufur. There is a parade, tractor pull, steak feed, grange breakfast, and classic car show to enjoy here, too.

Eugene Celebration. (541) 681-4108; eugenecelebration.com. This big fat celebration held in late summer each year has grown to include a car show, road race, sustainability village, health and wellness area, kid zone, 2 parades, and film festival, just for starters. In addition, there are all the things a good festival needs to please—food, beverages, entertainment, and shopping.

Mt. Hood Huckleberry Festival and Barlow Trail Days. allmounthood.com. This annual festival on the slopes of Mt. Hood between Sandy and Zigzag celebrates tourism on the mountain and the local berry. Come and enjoy huckleberry pies and tarts, a Native American salmon bake, Native American storytelling, and live music, but maybe especially the huckleberry pancakes that are served in the morning as breakfast.

Northwest Art and Air Festival. (800) 526-2256; nwartandair.org. This celebration of art, flight, and entertainment happens the weekend before Labor Day each year in Albany. Hot air balloons kick off each festival morning, and art booths, demonstrations, a kid's village, and live entertainment keep things going all day. At night, enjoy the night glow.

Vancouver Wine and Jazz Festival. (360) 906-0441; vancouverwinejazz.com. This 3-day festival is the largest of its kind in the Pacific Northwest. Internationally acclaimed jazz and blues musicians gather to entertain crowds of thousands, who also enjoy more than 200 wines, fine arts and crafts, and local cuisine.

Washington State International Kite Festival. (360) 642-4020; kitefestival.com. Voted Best Kite Festival in the World by Kite Trade Association, this weeklong festival on the Long Beach Peninsula includes competitions by professional and amateur kite flyers, choreographed kite flies, mass ascensions, fireworks, lighted night kite flies, vendors, and more. You can be sure the skies are full of color this week.

september

Mt. Angel Oktoberfest. (503) 845-9440; oktoberfest.org. This American version of the "Old World" Oktoberfest takes place in Mount Angel, Oregon's answer to a Bavarian paradise. Oregon's largest folk festival lasts 4 days; has 50 alpine food chalets and a traditional biergarten, weingarten and alpinegarten; hosts more than 30 musical groups; and opens the streets for street dancing on Friday and Saturday nights.

Shrewsbury Renaissance Faire. (541) 929-4897; visitcorvallis.com/events. Come be thee blythe and merry at the Renaissance Faire! Just 15 miles and 500 years away from downtown Corvallis, enchantment awaits young and old alike as jousting knights and noble steeds clash on the tourney while minstrels, troubadours, jongleurs, dancers, and bards fill the lanes with delight. More than 125 artisan stalls and 1,000 costumed players entertain visitors as they browse the village for unique handmade goods and one-of-a-kind treasures.

Sisters Folk Festival. (541) 549-4979; sistersfolkfestival.org. The Sisters Folk Festival is a 3-day celebration of American roots music, from blues to bluegrass, held every year the weekend after Labor Day in beautiful Sisters. This little fest has a big reputation and attracts truly great performers each year.

The Vancouver Sausage Fest. (360) 696-2586; stjoevanschool.org. Hosted by St. Joseph Catholic School, this event offers food booths, a carnival, vendors, exhibits, and a beer and wine garden, accompanying lots and lots of sausages and happy people. Held every year the weekend after Labor Day, this Vancouver event draws attendance upwards of 100,000 over 3 days.

Wild Seafood Weekend. (541) 574-5555; visittheoregoncoast.com. The historic fishing town of Newport celebrates seafood at this massive celebration, which features a fish market, a cook-off, a harbor cruise, and a brunch made from seafood straight off of the boat. The festivities occur on the historic Newport Bayfront, where there's always something happening.

october

BendFilm Festival. (866) 261-7096; bendfilm.org. This 4-day celebration of independent film showcases more than 80 films from across the country and brings filmmakers, fans, and experts together in Bend for conversation, lectures, and a whole lot of film watching. It's a life-enriching experience that educates and entertains.

Cranberrian Fair. (360) 642-3446; columbiapacificheritagemuseum.org. This annual fall celebration of local harvest including all things cranberry takes place on the Long Beach Peninsula. During the local cranberry harvest, visitors enjoy vendors, live music, cranberry foods and traditions, and craft demonstrations, and ride the Cranberry Trolley to bog tours.

Hood River Harvest Fest. (541) 386-2000; hoodriver.org. Harvest Fest is held annually on the Hood River waterfront overlooking the Columbia River. Visitors shop for arts and crafts, including glass, wood sculpture, ceramics, photography, and fiber art; listen to music all day and find more entertainment in the evening; visit the kids' zone with a bounce house, face painters, bands, and balloon twisters; and partake of the food court with lots of local and traditional favorites.

Oregon Coast Jazz Party. (541) 265-2787; coastarts.org. Jazz and jazz lovers come together in Newport on the beautiful Oregon Coast each fall. Workshops and education accompany lots and lots of great jazz at this 3-day event.

november

Albany's Veterans Day Parade. albanyveteransdayparade.org. Albany's annual Veterans Day Parade is the biggest Veterans Day Parade west of the Mississippi, with hundreds of entries and more than 40,000 spectators lining the streets of downtown Albany. It's also long-standing, running for more than 60 years. Every year, floats include military color guards, distinguished veterans, classic cars, scout troops, and a motorcycle honor guard leading the way.

Stormy Weather Arts Festival. (503) 436-2623; cannonbeach.org. This Cannon Beach tradition offers a deluge of artistic and musical talent. Live music plays in shops, galleries, and restaurants all over town. There is an auction and demonstrations by local artists, too, during this 3-day festival.

Wine Country Thanksgiving. (503) 646-2985; willamettewines.com. More than 150 wineries from Portland to Eugene open their doors to visitors at this classic event. Barrel taste, sample new releases and older vintages, buy gift packages, enjoy music, and taste specialty foods. Request a list of activities and touring map at the website.

december

Christmas Along the Barlow Trail. (503) 622-4798; mthoodterritory.com. The holiday season arrives at the village Rhododendron along the Oregon Trail with pioneer music, Native American flute music, storytelling featuring Christmas Tales From Old Oregon, Santa Claus, and much more. Come up to the slopes of Mt. Hood for this annual celebration.

Christmas Ships Parade. christmasships.org. A family tradition, this event presents a lighted holiday parade on the rivers around Portland. The Christmas Ships pageant includes two fleets that travel around, landing at many destinations including St. Helens, Milwaukie, Scappoose, Lake Oswego, and Hayden Island.

Oregon Coast Aquarium's Sea of Lights. (541) 867-FISH; aquarium.org. This holiday season tradition draws guests to the aquarium to see it adorned with holiday decorations, a large Christmas tree, and thousands of colorful lights. Enjoy face painting, holiday music, and a visit with Santa. Visitors come from all over the region to spend time together at the beach and enjoy the magic of the season.

Seaside Parade of Lights. (503) 738-6391; seasidechamber.com. This parade comes complete with Santa and takes place in downtown Seaside. Come and see the tree lighting, sing some carols afterward, and partake in some cookies and a gift fair at the Convention Center.

index